names companies and policies and provides figures that enable the consumer to shop for the best value. The book is arranged so the reader can quickly find the answers to the questions he may have.

In addition to such crucial issues as company reliability and prices, Professor Belth also discusses the fine print in typical policies, the choice of an agent, special sources, the management of life insurance after it has been purchased, interest, savings, and tax considerations. In the final chapter he turns to an explicit critique of the industry and provides a powerful argument in favor of price disclosure or what might more aptly be called "truth in life insurance."

Life Insurance: A Consumer's Handbook is a unique work based on years of study by a well known scholar-critic who has the rare ability to present a complicated subject in nontechnical language. Unlike the material put out by or on behalf of the industry, it comes to grips with the crucial issues in specific ways, and unlike the ill-informed and frequently hysterical attacks of other critics, it is based on a thorough understanding of the industry and its marketing practices. A must acquisition for libraries and family heads who want to understand life insurance.

Joseph M. Belth is professor of insurance in the School of Business at Indiana University.

Life Insurance: A Consumer's Handbook

LIFEINSURANCELIFEINSURANCELIFEINSURANCE

Life Insurance
A Consumer's Handbook

Joseph M. Belth

Indiana University Press
Bloomington London

LIFEINSURANCELIFEINSURANCELIFEINSURANCE

Published in Canada by Fitzhenry & Whiteside Limited,
Don Mills, Ontario
Library of Congress catalog card number: 72-76943
ISBN:0-253-14800-6
Manufactured in the United States of America

SECOND PRINTING 1973

To Ann, Michael, and Jeffrey

Contents

List of Tables, xiii
List of Figures, xv
Preface, xvii

1 Introduction   3
The Mythology of Life Insurance, 4
How To Use the Book, 5
Summary of the Book, 5

2 How Much?   8
Financial Requirements, 10
    Final Expenses, 10
    Debts, 10
    Income Needs, 10
    Total Requirements, 12
Financial Resources, 12
    Life Insurance, 12
    Social Security, 13
    Other Assets, 15
    Total Resources, 16
Other Considerations, 16

3 What Kind?   19
Two Major Policy Forms, 20
    Straight Life, 20
        Duration, 20
        Face amount, 21
        Premiums, 21

Savings element, 21
Protection element, 22
Dividends, 23
Summary, 25
Five-Year Renewable Term, 25
Three Important Riders, 28
Waiver of Premium, 28
Accidental Death, 30
Guaranteed Insurability, 31
Nature of the Savings Element, 32
Fixed Dollars, 33
Rate of Return, 33
The Income Tax Situation, 37
Liquidity, 40
Safety, 42
Forced Savings, 43
Protection from Creditors, 44
Life Annuity Rates, 44
Summary, 45
How to Make Your Choice, 46
The Savings Decision, 46
The Premiums Decision, 48

4   From Whom?   53
The Identity Problem, 54
Financial Strength, 55
Best's, 56
Dunne's, 59
The Saga of Century Life, 59
Price, 61
Participating Straight Life, 62
Nonparticipating Straight Life, 66
Five-Year Renewable Term, 69
General Comments About the Tables, 72
Nature of the "values," 72
Conversion of twenty-year values, 73
Data not in the tables, 75
Currency of the data, 75
Nonsmoker discounts, 76
Fractional premiums, 76
Waiver-of-premium adjustments, 77

Age-last-birthday adjustments, 77
Price measurement methods, 77
Stocks versus mutuals, 78
Pro rata refund of premiums, 79
Terminal dividends, 79
Rounding, 80

5 Other Sources and Forms

81

Non-Agency Organizations, 82
   Savings Bank Life Insurance, 82
   Teachers Insurance and Annuity Association, 84
   Ministers Life and Casualty Union, 85
Government Agencies, 85
   Social Security, 85
   Veterans Administration, 85
   Wisconsin State Life Fund, 87
Group Life Insurance, 88
   Employer Group Life, 88
   Credit Life, 89
   Association Group Life, 90
Other Sources of Individual Life Insurance, 91
   Industrial Life Insurance, 92
   Fraternal Benefit Societies, 92
Other Forms of Individual Life Insurance, 93
   Limited-Payment Life, 93
   Endowments, 95
   Retirement Income, 96
   Level Term, 97
   Decreasing Term, 99
   Increasing Term, 101
   Specialty Policies, 102
   Family Policies, 103
   Joint Life, 104
   Split Life, 104
   Variable Life, 106

6 The Agent

107

Why There Are Agents, 107
What the Agent Does, 109
What the Agent Costs, 111
   Value of Commissions, 111

Difference in Retention, 111
How To Select an Agent, 112

7   The Fine Print   115
Contract Provisions Generally, 115
Insuring Agreement, 116
Brief Description of Policy, 116
Death Benefit, 116
The Beneficiary, 117
Settlement Options, 119
Ownership Rights and Assignment, 122
Grace Period, 123
Incontestability, 124
Suicide, 125
Reinstatement, 125
Misstatement of Age, 125
Alteration of Policy, 126
Dividend Options, 127
Straight Life Contract Provisions, 129
The Loan Clause, 129
Automatic Premium Loans, 132
Nonforfeiture Options, 133
Settlement Options, 137
Change of Plan, 137
Renewable Term Contract Provisions, 138
Renewability, 138
Premiums, 139
Grace Period, 140
Convertibility, 140
Incontestability and Suicide, 141
The Waiver-of-Premium Clause, 143
Summary, 144

8   As and After You Buy   146
Applying for Life Insurance, 146
The Application, 147
First Premium, 148
Quantity Discounts, 149
Insurability Problems, 150
Paying the Premiums, 152

Fractional Premiums, 152
Financed Insurance, 154
After the Purchase, 158
Periodic Review, 158
Beneficiary Changes, 158
Storage of Policies, 159
The Replacement Problem, 159
The Death Claim, 162
Complaint Procedure, 162

9 Some Illustrative Cases 163
The Adams Case, 164
The Baker Family, 165
The Clark Family, 167
The Donaldson Family, 168
The Elliott Family, 170
The Fischer Family, 172
The Gilbert Family, 173
The Harris Family, 175

10 Conclusion 178
Ignorance, 178
Complexity, 180
Apathy, 181
The Results, 182
What Is Being Done? 184

Appendixes

A Computation of Present Values, 191
B Alphabetical Listing of Companies With Most
Strongly Worded Recommendation in 1971
Edition of *Best's Life Insurance Reports*, 194
C Policy Abbreviations Used in Tables of Values, 199
D Additional Tables of Price Information, 201

E   Values for Policies Issued by Non-Agency
    Organizations, 228
F   Addresses of Insurance Commissioners, 230
G   Computation of Price-of-Protection and
    Rate-of-Return Figures for One Policy Year, 234
H   Computation of Values, 236
    Notes, 239
    Index, 241
    The Author, 249

LIFEINSURANCELIFEINSURANCELIFEINSURANCE

Tables

3–1   page 24
       Twenty Years of Data for $25,000 Participating Straight Life Policy
       Issued in 1970 to Men Aged 35 by Connecticut Mutual
3–2   page 26
       Twenty Years of Data for $25,000 Participating Five-Year
       Renewable Term Policy Issued in 1970 to Men Aged 35 by
       Connecticut Mutual
4–1   pages 64–65
       Values for $25,000 Participating Straight Life Policies Issued in
       1970 to Men Aged 35
4–2   page 67
       Values for $25,000 Nonparticipating Straight Life Policies Issued in
       1970 to Men Aged 35
4–3   pages 70–71
       Values for $25,000 Five-Year Renewable Term Policies Issued in
       1970 to Men Aged 35
8–1   page 153
       Factors Commonly Applied to Annual Premiums and the
       Associated Annual Percentage Rates
9–1   page 166
       Summary of Data on Illustrative Cases
A–1   page 192
       Present Value of $1,000 Per Year
D–1   pages 202–203
       Values for $10,000 Participating Straight Life Policies Issued in
       1950 to Men Aged 35
D–2   pages 204–205
       Values for $5,000 Participating Straight Life Policies Issued in 1940
       to Men Aged 35
D–3   pages 206–207
       Values for $5,000 Participating Straight Life Policies Issued in 1930
       to Men Aged 35

D-4   pages 208–209
        Values for $25,000 Participating Straight Life Policies Issued in
        1970 to Men Aged 25
D-5   pages 210–211
        Values for $25,000 Participating Straight Life Policies Issued in
        1970 to Men Aged 45
D-6   pages 212–213
        Values for $10,000 Participating Straight Life Policies Issued in
        1970 to Men Aged 35
D-7   pages 214–215
        Values for $100,000 Participating Straight Life Policies Issued in
        1970 to Men Aged 35
D-8   page 216
        Values for $25,000 Nonparticipating Straight Life Policies Issued
        in 1970 to Men Aged 25
D-9   page 217
        Values for $25,000 Nonparticipating Straight Life Policies Issued
        in 1970 to Men Aged 45
D-10   page 218
        Values for $10,000 Nonparticipating Straight Life Policies Issued
        in 1970 to Men Aged 35
D-11   page 219
        Values for $100,000 Nonparticipating Straight Life Policies Issued
        in 1970 to Men Aged 35
D-12   pages 220–221
        Values for $25,000 Five-Year Renewable Term Policies Issued in
        1970 to Men Aged 25
D-13   pages 222–223
        Values for $25,000 Five-Year Renewable Term Policies Issued in
        1970 to Men Aged 45
D-14   pages 224–225
        Values for $10,000 Five-Year Renewable Term Policies Issued in
        1970 to Men Aged 35
D-15   pages 226–227
        Values for $100,000 Five-Year Renewable Term Policies Issued in
        1970 to Men Aged 35
H-1   page 238
        Interest Rates Used in Calculations
H-2   page 238
        Mortality Rates Used in Calculations
H-3   page 238
        Lapse Rates Used in Calculations

Figures

3–1 page 23
Rough Diagram of a $25,000 Straight Life Policy Issued at Age 35
3–2 page 27
Comparison of Premiums for Straight Life and Five-Year
Renewable Term Policies Issued in 1970 to Men Aged 35 by
Connecticut Mutual
3–3 page 50
Components of Premium Dollar
5–1 page 94
Rough Diagram of a $25,000 Twenty-Payment Life Policy Issued at
Age 35
5–2 page 95
Rough Diagram of a $25,000 Twenty-Year Endowment Issued at
Age 35
5–3 page 97
Rough Diagram of a $25,000 Retirement Income at 65 Policy
Issued at Age 35

Preface

The decision to write this book was based on a conviction that it is needed. Although there are many books available on life insurance, none of them provides the kind of specific information that the consumer needs in order to buy and own life insurance efficiently. Some of these books are prepared by the life insurance industry, or on behalf of the industry, or in a manner acceptable to the industry. Most such books are technically sound, as far as they go, but they do not provide specific guidance for the consumer.

Then there are the books written by the critics of the life insurance industry. Most of these books appear to be aimed primarily at reforming the industry, rather than helping the consumer find his way in the life insurance market as it now exists. Furthermore, the authors of most of these books display an abysmal lack of knowledge about the fundamentals of life insurance.

This book, then, is aimed down the middle. While it may not please either the life insurance industry or the more noisy critics of the industry, I hope the book will help the consumer stretch his life insurance dollar to the maximum.

I am grateful to the many persons who assisted in the preparation of this book. Professor John D. Long, my colleague at Indiana University, was a constant source of encouragement, both as sounding board and critic. Numerous graduate and undergraduate students assisted in various ways with the book and furnished a testing ground for the ideas presented. Many of the calculations were performed through the facilities of Indiana University's Research Computing Center. Mrs. Nan Ward and Mrs. Linda Cuzan did the typing. And the staff of the Indiana University Press handled the many details connected with publication.

The following persons, who have no special background in life insurance, read the draft from the viewpoint of consumers and offered suggestions: Robert M. Craig, science teacher, John Marshall High School, Indianapolis; George N. Lewis, M.D., Bloomington; Leo A. Robinson, psychometrist, Albion (Indiana) Elementary School; and Frank G. Wenzel, restaurant proprietor, Bloomington. The following persons also read the draft and offered suggestions: Milton Amsel of the Institute of Life Insurance; two prominent insurance educators—William T. Beadles of Illinois Wesleyan University and Robert I. Mehr of the University of Illinois at Urbana-Champaign; two prominent actuaries—Dale R. Gustafson of the American Life Convention and E. J. Moorhead of the Integon Life Insurance Corporation; and Allan Kent, editor and publisher of *Life Insurance Selling* magazine. I am indebted to all of these readers, and I am especially grateful to Professor Mehr for his superb comments.

I owe a considerable debt to Indiana University's School of Business. The School has contributed significantly to this and other projects by preserving an atmosphere conducive to the teaching, research, and public service efforts of its faculty members.

But I owe the greatest debt of all to my wife, Marjorie. She cheerfully handles more than her share of the responsibilities in our home. By so doing, she contributes immeasurably to my writing efforts.

All of these persons and organizations must be absolved from responsibility for the statements of fact and expressions of opinion set forth in this book. The author alone assumes full responsibility for the views expressed in the book and for any errors that may remain.

Life Insurance: A Consumer's Handbook

Chapter 1

Introduction

The purpose of this book is to help you buy and own life insurance efficiently.

- How much life insurance should you buy?
- What kind should you buy?
- What company should you buy from?

These are the three big questions that this book attempts to answer. It also discusses various sources of life insurance other than commercial life insurance companies, the role of life insurance agents, the fine print in the contract, and things to keep in mind as you buy and after you buy.

The mythology of life insurance

This book is needed because the public has not been receiving accurate and useful information about life insurance. Instead, the public has been exposed primarily to two sets of mythology—one promulgated by or on behalf of the life insurance industry, and the other by various critics of the industry. Among the myths promulgated by the industry are the following:

- All life insurance companies charge about the same price. (The fact is that there are very large price differences among companies for essentially the same kind of insurance.)

- Life insurance companies are subject to strict regulation by the states, so it doesn't matter what company you patronize. (Actually, regulation is much weaker in some states than in others, and the requirements frequently constitute a minimal if not inadequate form of protection for the public.)

- Life insurance companies, particularly the mutual companies, are operated for the benefit of policyholders and their families. (Actually, the life insurance companies, including the mutual companies, are in business to make money, and the profit motive weighs heavily in every decision, just as in other businesses.)

Among the myths promulgated by the critics of the life insurance industry are the following:

- The life insurance companies are overcharging the public through the use of outdated mortality tables that overstate death rates. (The facts are that up-to-date mortality tables are used in many of the companies' calculations, and, moreover, the choice of a mortality table, in and of itself, has little to do with how well the policyholder fares financially in his dealings with a life insurance company.)

- The kind of life insurance that includes a savings accumulation is more expensive than pure life insurance protection, and is an inferior way to save money. (Actually, the price of life insurance protection in savings-type life insurance, *when carefully pur-*

chased, compares favorably to the price of pure life insurance protection, and the savings portion is a satisfactory accumulation device.)

- Life insurance agents are scoundrels who are exploiting the public. (Actually, much of what the agents say and do is learned from their companies, and many agents do not realize that some of what they learn is slanted, misleading, or false.)

How to use the book

Ideally, the book should be read from cover to cover. Realistically, the book has been organized like a reference book, so that you can select the desired topics.

The book necessarily contains some technical words and phrases. These terms are explained the first time they appear. They are also included in the index, so that you can locate discussions of them quickly when you encounter them later in the book. There are numerous cross references in the text, and an outline of each chapter is included in the table of contents.

Throughout the book, the life insurance buyer and policyholder are referred to by words with a male connotation (he, husband, and so forth), while the person who is to receive the funds at the policyholder's death is referred to by words with a female connotation (she, wife, and so forth). This language is not intended as an affront to women; rather, it is used for simplicity and because men are the breadwinners in most families, men buy most of the life insurance, and women are the beneficiaries of most of the life insurance.

Summary of the book

Chapter 2 deals with the first of the three big questions with which this book is concerned—how much life insurance you should buy. Emphasis is placed on the personal nature of such a determination. The first step is an estimation of the financial requirements of your family following your death. The second step is an estimation of the financial resources available after your death. The amount of life insurance you should buy, then, is the difference between your financial requirements and the financial resources available.

Chapter 3 deals with the second of the three big questions—what kind of policy or policies you should buy. This question should be attacked only after you have determined how much life insurance you need. The first section of the chapter describes two major forms of life insurance that can meet the needs of virtually all buyers. The second section describes three important riders that may be attached to many of the basic policy forms. The third section describes the nature of the savings portion of the kind of life insurance that includes a savings accumulation, so that you can decide whether to put any savings into it, and if so, how much. The fourth section explains how you should make your choice between the two major forms of life insurance referred to earlier.

Chapter 4 deals with the third of the three big questions—what company you should buy from. This question should be attacked only after you have determined how much life insurance you need and what kind of policy or policies to buy. The first section of the chapter explains the company identification problem, which arises because there are so many companies and so many sound-alike names. The second section contains suggestions on how to be reasonably certain that the company with which you deal is financially strong. The third section contains price information on forty-five major companies and explains how to identify relatively low-priced life insurance protection.

Chapter 5 contains a description of various sources and forms of life insurance other than those discussed in earlier chapters. The first section of the chapter deals with savings bank life insurance and certain other organizations that operate without agents and deliver low-priced coverage. The second section describes government sources of life insurance, the third section discusses several forms of group life insurance coverage, and the fourth section refers to industrial life insurance and fraternal benefit societies. The final section describes several forms of life insurance other than those described in Chapter 3.

Chapter 6 contains a discussion of why there are agents, what agents are supposed to do, what it costs to deal with an agent, and how you should go about selecting an agent. This is an important chapter because most of the life insurance in the United States is sold through agents, and you may deal with one.

Chapter 7 contains an analysis of the fine print in life insurance contracts. The first section of the chapter covers policy provisions common to both of the major types of policies, the second section covers provisions peculiar to the kind of life insurance that includes a savings accumulation, and the third section covers provisions peculiar to policies that provide pure life insurance protection. Although the chapter contains considerable detail, emphasis is placed on the important points that the buyer should understand in order to protect himself and his beneficiary against potential future problems.

Chapter 8 includes a number of miscellaneous subjects that a person should consider as he buys life insurance and following the purchase. The first section of the chapter covers several points that are relevant at the time of application. The second section deals with the payment of premiums, including an analysis of the cost of paying other than annually, and a detailed discussion of financed insurance. The third section contains a number of suggestions to be followed after the purchase of life insurance.

Chapter 9 contains a description of eight hypothetical family situations and how decisions about life insurance were arrived at in each instance. The cases are designed to illustrate many of the suggestions contained in earlier chapters.

Chapter 10 is the author's conclusion. The first three sections describe the ignorance, complexity, and apathy that permeate the life insurance market. The fourth section shows how the combined effect of these three characteristics produces fertile ground for the exploitation of consumers. The final section explains what is being done in an attempt to improve the life insurance market.

Appendix A explains some of the arithmetic needed in estimating your financial requirements and your financial resources. Appendix B lists those life insurance companies that received the most strongly worded recommendations by a major publisher that analyzes companies from the standpoint of financial strength. Appendix C lists abbreviations of the policy names in the various tables of price information.

Appendix D contains price information that supplements the material in Chapter 4. Appendix E contains price information that supplements the material in Chapter 5. Appendix F shows the addresses of the various state insurance commissioners. Appendix G shows certain formulas referred to in the text. Appendix H contains technical material primarily for use by life insurance company actuaries who wish to calculate price information for their companies parallel to that which appears in the book.

Chapter 2

How much?

The determination of your life insurance needs is an individual matter. No hard and fast rules can be laid down to apply to everyone, because no two people view their own circumstances in the same way.

You might ask, "How much life insurance is owned by the average man in my age and income bracket?" Even if the data were available to answer the question, it wouldn't mean much. Many people own little or no life insurance, many others own substantial amounts that are far short of their needs, and some own substantial amounts that bear a reasonable relationship to their needs. The average breadwinner probably is underinsured.

A life insurance agent might suggest that you should have life insurance equal to at least five times (or perhaps seven times) your annual earnings. Or he might suggest that your life insurance premiums should be about 5 percent (or 7 percent) of your earnings. Such rules of thumb are useless.

Consider, for example, two hypothetical families that are in exactly the same position in terms of family status, income, assets, and liabilities. The two families differ in only one respect. One feels that in the event of the husband's death a substantial income would be needed for ten years. The other feels that a substantial income would be needed for only one year, and then a reduced income would be needed for an additional four years. For the first family, total life insurance needs are about four times their annual earnings. For the second family, total life insurance needs are equal to about one year's earnings. These are the Baker and Clark cases described in Chapter 9. And in one instance—the Gilbert case—total life insurance needs were more than ten times their annual earnings.

Here are some of the tough, personal questions you and your wife must ask yourselves:

- Will your widow be able to find a job and will she be able to work?
- Will your widow remarry?
- Will your widow move in with relatives?
- Will your widow dispose of your present home?

You may want to answer all such questions in the negative. Or you may want to answer one or more in the positive. Or you may want to work out your life insurance needs under various assumptions and make your decision after comparing the results. The method described in this chapter is flexible enough to permit any of these approaches.

The procedure described in this chapter is based on the assumption that your death occurs immediately. There is a discussion of the financial requirements your family would then have, and a discussion of the financial resources that would be available to them. Life insurance fits into the picture as a device for making up any difference between their requirements and their resources. Once you master the procedure, and assuming you do not in fact die immediately, you can repeat the steps every two or three years to check the adequacy of your life insurance.

Financial requirements

Your family will have certain financial requirements to meet after your death. These may be grouped for convenience into three categories: final expenses, debts, and income needs.

Final expenses

Your family will have to pay funeral expenses and the cost of settling your estate. They also may have to pay state and federal death taxes. These expenses will have to be met within a fairly short time after your death.

A rule of thumb may be useful here. These final expenses may be about 10 percent of your estate, provided you are a person of modest means. (The percentage would be larger for wealthy families.) For the purposes of applying this rule, your "estate" may be estimated by adding up the value of all the property you own, either solely or jointly. In this total it is suggested that you include, among other items, the net value of your home (current market value minus outstanding indebtedness) and the total death benefits of the life insurance you already own.

Debts

Your family may have to pay off various short-term obligations, such as charge accounts, installment loans, and short-term notes. The balances of such items should be added and the total considered among the financial requirements of the family immediately after your death.

Long-term obligations, such as the mortgage on your home, may be viewed in either of two ways. You may want to treat the mortgage in the same manner as other debts and consider the unpaid balance as an immediate financial requirement of your family. Or you may want to treat the mortgage as a part of the cost of housing your family and consider it in establishing their income needs, which are discussed below.

Income needs

The most important aspect of your financial requirements, in terms of its impact on the final result, is the income your family will need. Presumably the figures you select here will be based in part on your current earnings and on various other considerations to be discussed in the following paragraphs.

To determine the income requirements of your family, you must consider many things. First, careful thought should be given to the question of whether your wife would work. If she would, presumably the income requirements of your family would be smaller than if it is assumed she would not work.

Second, the remarriage question should be considered. If it is assumed your wife would remarry, presumably the income requirements of your family would be for a shorter period of time than if it is assumed she would not remarry.

Third, you should be consistent with the way you handled your mortgage in the previous section on debts. If you decided to treat it as a debt that should be paid off at your death, the income requirements of your family presumably would be smaller than if you decided to treat future mortgage payments as part of the cost of housing your family.

Fourth, an interest rate must be selected in order to calculate the present value of the required income. Suppose your family would need $8,000 per year for fifteen years after your death. The simple total would be $120,000. However, if interest could be earned, an amount less than $120,000 would be needed at death. For example, if it is assumed the funds earn 5 percent interest, the amount needed at death to provide $8,000 per year for fifteen years would be $87,192. The calculation of this figure is explained in Appendix A (Example 1).

The choice of the interest rate is important. It has a powerful effect on the results, particularly when the income requirements stretch over a long period of time. It is suggested that a conservative rate be chosen—one that your wife could reasonably expect to earn with a high degree of safety. Many savings accounts today earn 5 percent. Although there is no assurance that this rate will continue indefinitely, it is used in most of the illustrations in this book. If you wish to be somewhat more conservative, a 4 percent rate might be appropriate.

Fifth, you should consider inflation. If your family would receive $8,000 per year for fifteen years, and if inflation continues, then their income would be declining in real terms. To offset inflation, it is necessary to provide for an income that increases in dollar terms. You can get an approximation of the effect of inflation by using, in the present value calculation, an interest rate that is reduced by the rate of inflation you wish to assume. For example, if you use a 5 percent interest assumption, but also want to assume an inflation rate of 3 percent, you can approximate the effect of inflation on your financial requirements by performing the present value calculations using 2 percent interest (5 percent minus 3 percent). Referring to Appendix A, it would take $104,848 to provide $8,000 per year for fifteen years at 2 percent interest. This figure is about $18,000 larger than the earlier figure of $87,192 calculated at 5 percent. This difference of $18,000 is the approximate impact of a 3 percent inflation rate assumption on your financial requirements.

When you have decided how much income your family would need and how long they would need it, and when you have decided on the interest rate to be used in the calculations, the next step is to determine the present value of the income requirements. In other words, you have to find out how much would be needed right now (assuming you die right now) to provide the required income. The calculations can be made by referring to Appendix A.

Total requirements

After you have estimated your final expenses, debts, and income requirements, the three figures are added to arrive at the total financial requirements in the event of your death. The next step is to estimate the financial resources that are available to meet those requirements.

Financial resources

Your family will have certain resources with which to meet their financial requirements after your death. These may be grouped for convenience into three categories: life insurance, Social Security, and other assets.

Life insurance

Add the total death benefits of your present life insurance policies. Don't forget to add in the death benefits under any government life insurance you may own, any group life insurance you may have with your employer, or any group life insurance you may have as a member of an association.

Some or all of your policies may provide for additional death benefits in the event of accidental death. Frequently such benefits are called "double indemnity." Much publicity often accompanies accidental deaths, but these are still in the minority. For example, accidental deaths comprise about 38 percent of the deaths at age 25, 22 percent of the deaths at age 35, and 9 percent of the deaths at age 45.[1] Thus, most deaths are caused by illnesses, and in such cases accidental death benefits are not available to the survivors. To be on the conservative side, therefore, you should disregard accidental death benefits in your listing of resources.

Social Security

Perhaps the best known segments of the federal Social Security program are the retirement benefits and the relatively recent Medicare benefits. Also provided by the program, however, are substantial monthly income survivors' benefits, particularly for families with young children.

Suppose you are 35 years old and have worked under Social Security since you were 21. You have always earned in excess of the Social Security tax base, which has been as follows since 1957:

1957–1958	$4,200 per year
1959–1965	$4,800 per year
1966–1967	$6,600 per year
1968–1971	$7,800 per year

Your wife is also 35, and you have two children whose ages are 8 and 5.

If you die now, Social Security would provide a monthly income to your widow. This income is a combination of a mother's benefit and a children's benefit. The mother's benefit is payable as long as she has children under 18 in her care; this benefit ceases if she dies or remarries, and is reduced, possibly to zero, depending on the amount of her annual earnings. The children's benefit is payable until they reach age 18, or, if they remain in school, until they reach 22.

In your case, the total survivors' benefits payable to your widow would be about $5,000 per year until the first child becomes ineligible, and then about $4,000 per year until the second child becomes ineligible. If the mother's benefit should terminate because your widow dies, remarries, or earns a substantial income, the children's benefit would be about $4,000 per year until the first child becomes ineligible, and then about $2,000 per year until the second child becomes ineligible.

The present value of your Social Security survivors' benefits may be calculated by reference to Appendix A, in the same way that the present value of your income requirements was calculated earlier. To be consistent with the calculation of the present value of your income requirements, it is appropriate to use the same interest rate and the same inflation rate. You are then assuming that Congress will revise the benefit structure of Social Security periodically to keep up with inflation, and this is not an unreasonable expectancy.

When you calculate the present value of your Social Security survivors' benefits, you should consider only the benefits payable over the period of time for which income requirements were indicated earlier. For example, if you included ten years of income in the calculation of your financial requirements, you should include Social Security survivors' benefits only for ten years, even though the benefits might be payable longer than that.

Social Security also provides a monthly income for a widow who is aged 60 or over. In your case, for example, given the situation described above, your widow's income would be about $2,000 per year beginning at her age 60.

Social Security also provides a small cash benefit at death. It may be disregarded in your listing of resources, however, because it has so little effect on the results. Given the situation described above, this benefit would be $255, the present maximum.

This discussion of Social Security is oversimplified. Also, the figures pertain only in the illustrated situation. Social Security survivors' benefits have substantial value and therefore are an important part of the resources available to your family. It is recommended that you call or visit your local Social Security office. They will furnish you with a post card to be mailed to the Baltimore data center. The response you receive will be a detailed statement of your Social Security account, and from it your local office can give you specific information about the various survivors' benefits as they apply to your situation at the present time. Then you can determine the present value of those benefits. You must keep up with changes in Social Security benefit levels, because these changes occur frequently. You should contact your local Social Security office each time you review your life insurance program.

Other assets

Add the current values of the other assets that would be available to your family at your death. Included here would be marketable stocks and bonds, marketable real estate other than your home, the death benefit under any pension plan in which you are a participant, savings bonds, savings accounts, savings and loan accounts, and checking accounts. To be on the conservative side, you might wish to include stocks, long-term bonds, and real estate at somewhat less than current market values.

Many other items might or might not be included here, depending on your view of them. You might wish to include the current value of your home, but you should be consistent with the approach you took earlier in estimating your family's income requirements. If you figured the income requirements at a low level because you already own your home, you should not include the home as an asset here. But if you figured on a comfortable provision for the cost of housing, it would be appropriate to include the value of your home.

The same can be said of your cars. If your income requirements included a realistic transportation figure, you might wish to include your cars as assets. Because cars depreciate rapidly, however, you might prefer to disregard them.

You might or might not wish to include here such items as stamp collections, coin collections, valuable antiques, art objects, horses, and so forth. The basic test for inclusion should be marketability of the item in question.

You or your wife might have a potential inheritance. You will have to judge whether such an item should be included among the resources available to your family in the event of your death, and if so, the value that should be placed on it for planning purposes.

You might have a substantial interest in a business in which you are a principal. If so, and if you feel that the business would help your family meet its financial requirements after your death, you might wish to include its value here. In many instances, however, a business is of little value after the death of a principal. In any case, the disposition or conservation of a business interest is a complex matter that should be dealt with in close consultation with the team of professional advisors referred to later in this chapter.

Total resources

After you have estimated the total death benefits of your life insurance, the present value of your Social Security survivors' benefits, and the value of your other assets, the figures are added to arrive at the total resources available to your family. The total is then compared to the financial requirements of your family, and the shortage of resources, if any, is the amount of additional life insurance you need.

If you have never gone through this kind of exercise before, you may be startled by the large amount of additional life insurance you need. This is a frequent occurrence, because most people are accustomed to thinking about life insurance in small amounts. For example, $10,000 sounds like a lot of money, but even at 5 percent interest it would provide only $1,000 per year for less than fourteen years.

The important thing to remember is that the purpose of life insurance is to meet the financial objectives you have established. If your objectives are large, a large amount of life insurance will be needed. If you feel that the additional amount of life insurance indicated is more than you wish to buy or can afford, one possibility is to go back and revise your objectives downward. Another possibility is to leave your objectives unchanged at least for the moment. After you have read this book, you will have a better idea of what it costs to own life insurance and you can then reconsider your objectives.

To illustrate the procedure described in this and subsequent chapters, several hypothetical cases are presented in Chapter 9. It is suggested, however, that you refrain from consulting Chapter 9 until you have read the other chapters that precede it.

Other considerations

The discussion in this chapter applies most directly to persons with dependents. If you have no dependents, your primary concern is to see that the financial resources available at your death are sufficient to cover final expenses and debts, unless you would also like to make bequests to relatives, friends, or charities. Beyond these considerations, the primary reason for a person without dependents to buy a substantial amount of life insurance is to get it while he is able to furnish evidence of insurability. In that way he will be sure to have it later when he may need it.

It is often said that a person should buy insurance when he is young because it's cheaper that way. This argument is fallacious. Other things equal, the premiums are smaller when you are younger, but when you are younger there are more years until your death. Presumably life insurance companies attempt to determine their premiums so as to allocate their expenses and profits equitably among their policyholders. This being the case, the companies should be indifferent as to the age of their new policyholders, and policyholders should be indifferent with regard to their age at the time of purchase. In short, it doesn't make much difference when you buy, *provided you can qualify at a later date.*

An important question arises with respect to life insurance on your wife. If she is the sole breadwinner, the procedure in this chapter would apply directly. If she produces a substantial part of the family income, the procedure in this chapter would have to be modified, but a substantial amount of life insurance might be indicated. Even if she produces no income directly, her duties as a housewife and mother may call for a substantial amount of life insurance.

Men have a tendency to underestimate the financial consequences of the death of a wife. There are the final expenses, and there are the income tax consequences of a loss of the joint return privilege. In addition, there are the potentially large expenses associated with hiring someone to take care of the house and children so that the widower can continue to earn a living. In other words, insurance on the wife can be important, although in most cases it should be considered of lower priority than adequate life insurance on the husband. The procedure described in this chapter can be applied to determine an appropriate amount of life insurance for the wife.

Another question relates to life insurance on the children. About all that needs to be considered here are final expenses and the idea that the child will be sure to have the insurance when he needs it later. In contrast to insurance on the father and mother, insurance on the children should be considered of low priority.

The discussion in this chapter applies most directly to persons who have not accumulated a substantial amount of wealth and whose incomes are derived primarily from personal efforts. For such persons, life insurance performs primarily a property creation function in the sense that existing assets must be greatly enlarged in order to provide for the family after the death of the breadwinner.

The special problems of persons of substantial wealth are beyond the scope of this chapter. For these persons, life insurance may perform primarily a property conservation function in the sense that life insurance can be used to protect the existing assets from death taxes and from the shrinkage that arises at death. For persons in this category, there is no substitute for a team of professional advisors —including an attorney experienced in estate planning, a certified public accountant, an experienced trust officer, and a highly qualified life insurance agent.

Chapter 3

What kind?

The number of different life insurance contracts on the market is very large. Most companies have dozens of basic policies and a number of riders that may be added to almost any one of the basic policies. The possible combinations, therefore, approach infinity. The primary effect of this proliferation is to confuse and frustrate the buyer.

Fortunately, there is a way out for the consumer. The life insurance needs of virtually any buyer can be met satisfactorily with just two policy forms—straight life and five-year renewable term—or some combination of the two. The first section of this chapter, therefore, is designed to familiarize you with these two policy forms. Several other policy forms are described in Chapter 5.

The second section of the chapter contains a description of three important riders that may be attached to many of the basic policy forms. You should consider these riders when you buy life insurance.

The third section of the chapter describes the savings element of cash-value life insurance policies. This is a crucial section, because an understanding of the savings element is needed for a sound decision on how much of your life insurance should be straight life and how much should be five-year renewable term.

The final section of the chapter explains how to decide upon the appropriate amounts of straight life and five-year renewable term. Once this decision is made, the next step is the selection of a company, which is the subject of Chapter 4.

Two major policy forms

This section of the chapter describes two major forms of life insurance coverage—straight life and five-year renewable term. The life insurance needs of virtually any buyer can be met satisfactorily with these two forms.

At the outset, a comment on terminology is needed. The "policyholder" is the person who owns a policy. The "insured" is the person on whose life the policy is issued. In most situations, these two are the same person, although there are situations in which the policy is owned by someone other than the insured. In the discussion that follows, it is assumed that the policyholder and the insured are the same person.

Straight life

The straight life policy, which is sometimes called "ordinary life" or "whole life," is a widely offered and widely purchased form of coverage. To understand the straight life policy—or any life insurance policy, for that matter—you must have detailed information on the following six aspects of the contract: duration, face amount, premiums, savings element, protection element, and dividends.

Duration.—A modern straight life policy generally provides protection from the issue date of the policy until the policyholder reaches age 100. (Straight life policies issued prior to 1948 generally provided protection until age 96.) If the policyholder survives until the termination of the coverage at age 100, and if he keeps up the premium payments that long, he would receive a payment equal to what would have been paid to his beneficiary if the policyholder had died at that point. In the case of a straight life policy issued at age 35, therefore, the potential duration of the contract is sixty-five years.

Face amount.—The face amount is the basic contractual amount payable at the death of the policyholder. The face amount of a straight life policy generally is level (unchanging) for the entire duration of the contract.

Premiums.—The annual premium is the amount that is paid by the policyholder each year. Premiums may be paid more frequently than once a year, but carrying charges are then imposed by the insurance company. This point is discussed in Chapter 8.

The premiums for a straight life policy usually are level and payable for the entire duration of the contract. The word "payable" in this context means that the premiums *may* be paid, and if they are, the insurance company must accept them. But the premiums do not *have* to be paid. In the first place, the policyholder may decide to discontinue premium payments. He would then have certain options, which are discussed later.

In the second place, premiums are no longer payable after the policyholder dies. Although this may seem obvious, it is mentioned here because of the anecdote about a life insurance company's receipt of the following letter:

Gentlemen:
We just received a notice from you that the annual premium on my husband's life insurance policy is due. Unfortunately, we cannot afford to pay it, and must therefore cancel the policy. You see, my husband died seven years ago, and we are having an increasingly difficult time making ends meet.
Sincerely,
Jennie Mae Jenkins

Savings element.—When a policyholder discontinues premium payments on a straight life policy, he is entitled to receive the "cash value" of the contract. The amount of the cash value is specified in the policy. In a straight life contract, the cash value grows steadily larger as the policy gets older. In a $25,000 straight life policy issued at age 35, for example, the cash value might be $1,662 after five years, $3,999 after ten years, $8,552 after twenty years, $13,208 after thirty years, and $25,000 after sixty-five years. The cash value is equal to the face amount after sixty-five years, because, as mentioned earlier, if the policyholder survives to age 100 and keeps up the premiums that long, he would receive a payment equal to what his beneficiary would have been paid if the policyholder had died at that point.

Cash values are found in most long-term, level-premium policies. The reasons for the presence of cash values and the alternatives available to the policyholder who discontinues premium payments are explained in Chapter 7 in the discussion of nonforfeiture options.

The level-premium arrangement, with its associated cash values, makes established life insurance companies major financial institutions. At the same time, the level-premium arrangement transforms what otherwise would be purely an insurance transaction into a combination or package transaction involving both life insurance protection and a savings element. The characteristics of this savings element are discussed in the third section of this chapter.

Protection element.—Since the face amount is payable at the policyholder's death, and since the cash value is available to the policyholder during his lifetime, the amount of life insurance protection at any point in time is the difference between the face amount and the cash value at that point. For example, consider the $25,000 straight life policy referred to above. Suppose the policy is now twenty years old, so that its cash value, as mentioned earlier, is $8,552. This figure is the amount available to the policyholder while he is alive, and for that reason is the amount he would show as an asset on his personal balance sheet. If he dies at this point, his beneficiary would receive the face amount of $25,000, which exceeds the cash value by $16,448. Because this latter figure is the amount the beneficiary would receive over and above the amount that was available to the policyholder while he was alive, it should be viewed as the amount of life insurance protection in effect at that point.

The notion that the amount of life insurance protection is the difference between the face amount and the cash value is based on the premise that the cash value is an asset of the policyholder. The logic of this premise will become evident in the third section of this chapter, in which the nature of the savings element in cash-value life insurance policies is described in detail.

In a straight life policy, since the cash value grows steadily larger as the policy gets older, the amount of life insurance protection grows steadily smaller. In the case of the $25,000 straight life policy referred to earlier, for example, the amount of life insurance protection would be $23,338 at the end of five years, $21,001 at the end of ten years, $16,448 at the end of twenty years, $11,792 at the end of thirty years, and zero at the end of sixty-five years.

The relationships among the face amount, the savings element, and the protection element of a straight life policy issued at age 35 are illustrated in Figure 3–1. Note that the face amount is level for the entire 65-year duration of the contract, that the savings element steadily increases, and that the protection element steadily decreases.

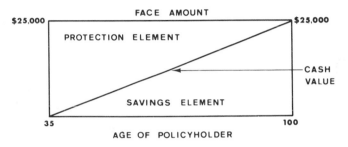

Figure 3–1
Rough diagram of a $25,000 straight life policy issued at age 35

Dividends.—Most policies sold today are "participating," which means that the company contemplates the payment of periodic (usually annual) dividends to the policyholder. The word "dividend" in this context is a misnomer, because it is quite different from the typical cash dividend paid to the owner of a share of stock. Most knowledgeable observers view the life insurance policy dividend either as a kind of benefit payment provided for in the premium or as a refund of an overcharge in the premium.

The life insurance policy dividend is not taxable income to the policyholder, since the Internal Revenue Code views such a dividend as a refund. However, when dividends are left with an insurance company to accumulate, the interest on such accumulation is taxable income to the policyholder in the same manner as interest on a savings account.

It is sometimes argued that the word "refund" would be an excellent substitute for "dividend." But the word "dividend" has been used for so long and is so deeply imbedded in life insurance terminology that a change is unlikely.

To be in a position to judge the price of a policy, you must have information on the year-by-year dividends. In the case of a newly issued policy, such figures are referred to as "illustrated dividends" or as a "dividend illustration." These phrases mean that the dividends shown are the ones that will be paid by the company if no future changes are made in the factors that enter into the calculation of the dividends. Dividends are not guaranteed, but rather are subject to change—upward or downward—by the company. Moreover, companies do not "estimate" dividends; instead, they merely "illustrate" what the dividends would be if no changes were made.

In the case of a policy issued years ago, the dividends actually paid by the company may be listed. Such figures are referred to as "historical dividends" or as a "dividend history."

Table 3–1
Twenty years of data for $25,000 participating straight life policy issued in 1970 to men aged 35 by Connecticut Mutual
(Figures rounded to nearest dollar)

(1)	(2)	(3)	(4)	(5)	(6)
					Protection Element
Policy Year	Annual Premium	Illustrated Dividends	Face Amount	Savings Element (Cash Values)	(Col. 4 minus Col. 5)
1	$534	$ 57	$25,000	$ 14	$24,986
2	534	69	25,000	341	24,659
3	534	81	25,000	774	24,226
4	534	94	25,000	1,214	23,786
5	534	106	25,000	1,662	23,338
6	534	118	25,000	2,117	22,883
7	534	131	25,000	2,578	22,422
8	534	145	25,000	3,045	21,955
9	534	158	25,000	3,519	21,481
10	534	171	25,000	3,999	21,001
11	534	184	25,000	4,435	20,565
12	534	198	25,000	4,877	20,123
13	534	212	25,000	5,323	19,677
14	534	226	25,000	5,775	19,225
15	534	240	25,000	6,230	18,770
16	534	247	25,000	6,689	18,311
17	534	256	25,000	7,151	17,849
18	534	264	25,000	7,616	17,384
19	534	273	25,000	8,083	16,917
20	534	281	25,000	8,552	16,448

Summary.—Figures for the first twenty years of a $25,000 participating straight life policy issued in 1970 to 35-year-old men by the Connecticut Mutual Life Insurance Company (Hartford, Connecticut) are shown in Table 3–1. To understand a policy, you must have the kind of information shown in that table. Note the level premiums, the increasing illustrated dividends, the level face amount, the increasing savings element, and the decreasing protection element.

Five-year renewable term

Another important form of life insurance is the five-year renewable term policy. The duration of the contract is five years. The premium and the face amount usually are level for the five years. There usually are no cash values in a contract of this type, so the protection element is level and equal to the face amount.

Other examples of term policies with a level face amount are one-year renewable term and ten-year renewable term. The reason for the emphasis on five-year renewable term in this book is that nearly all major companies offer such coverage. Relatively few companies offer renewable term coverages of other durations.

In five-year renewable term policies, the word "renewable" means that the contract may be continued for one or more additional five-year periods, after expiration of the original five-year period, without the policyholder's having to qualify for the insurance again. In insurance jargon, the policy may be "renewed" for one or more additional five-year periods "without evidence of insurability." In other words, the policyholder has the option to continue the coverage with no questions asked—even if his health has deteriorated, or even if he has entered a hazardous occupation, or even if he has otherwise become ineligible for life insurance.

Each time a five-year renewable term policy is renewed for an additional five-year period the premium goes up. Furthermore, each increase in premium usually is larger than the previous increase. The reason for the schedule of increasing premiums is that mortality rates increase with advancing age, as discussed in Chapter 7. The only leveling of premiums in a five-year renewable term policy is within each five-year period.

Five-year renewable term policies usually may be continued to an age such as 65 or 70. When such a policy can no longer be continued, it expires without any cash value. A discussion of the renewability feature is contained in Chapter 7.

Table 3–2 shows figures for the first twenty years of a $25,000 participating five-year renewable term policy issued in 1970 to 35-year-old men by Connecticut Mutual, assuming that it is renewed for at least three additional five-year periods. Note the increasing premiums, the level face amount, the absence of a savings element, and the level protection element.

Table 3–2
Twenty years of data for $25,000 participating five-year renewable term policy issued in 1970 to men aged 35 by Connecticut Mutual
(Figures rounded to nearest dollar)

(1) Policy Year	(2) Annual Premium	(3) Illustrated Dividends	(4) Face Amount	(5) Savings Element (Cash Values)	(6) Protection Element (Col. 4 minus Col. 5)
1	$133	$10	$25,000	$0	$25,000
2	133	13	25,000	0	25,000
3	133	15	25,000	0	25,000
4	133	17	25,000	0	25,000
5	133	20	25,000	0	25,000
6	173	16	25,000	0	25,000
7	173	20	25,000	0	25,000
8	173	23	25,000	0	25,000
9	173	26	25,000	0	25,000
10	173	29	25,000	0	25,000
11	239	21	25,000	0	25,000
12	239	26	25,000	0	25,000
13	239	31	25,000	0	25,000
14	239	35	25,000	0	25,000
15	239	40	25,000	0	25,000
16	347	29	25,000	0	25,000
17	347	36	25,000	0	25,000
18	347	42	25,000	0	25,000
19	347	49	25,000	0	25,000
20	347	56	25,000	0	25,000

A five-year renewable term policy usually is "convertible" also. This means that it may be exchanged, without evidence of insurability, for a straight life policy or some other cash-value kind of policy. Usually five-year renewable term policies are convertible until an age such as 60 or 65. A discussion of the convertibility feature appears in Chapter 7.

It is important that you understand the major similarities and

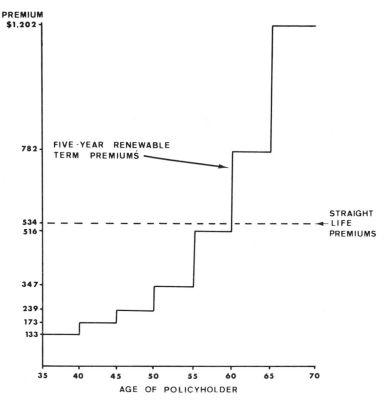

PREMIUM
$1,202

782

534
516

347

239
173
133

FIVE-YEAR RENEWABLE
TERM PREMIUMS

STRAIGHT
LIFE
PREMIUMS

35   40   45   50   55   60   65   70
AGE OF POLICYHOLDER

Figure 3–2
Comparison of premiums for straight life and five-year renewable term policies issued in 1970 to men aged 35 by Connecticut Mutual

differences between straight life policies and five-year renewable term policies. With regard to duration, straight life policies run to age 100; five-year renewable term policies run for five years, with renewal and conversion privileges that make it possible for the coverage to be continued to age 100. With regard to face amount, both types of policies provide level face amounts for the entire duration of the contract.

With regard to premiums, straight life policies have level premiums for the entire duration of the contract; five-year renewable term policies have premiums that increase with the beginning of each additional five-year period. The initial premium for a five-year renewable term policy is much smaller than the premium for a straight life policy. Eventually, however, the five-year renewable term premium increases to a level that is well above the straight life premium. To illustrate, the premiums for the straight life and five-year renewable term policies referred to earlier are shown in Figure 3–2.

With regard to the savings element, straight life policies have a steadily increasing savings element; five-year renewable term policies have no savings element. With regard to the protection element, straight life policies have a steadily decreasing protection element; five-year renewable term policies have a level protection element.

It was mentioned at the beginning of the chapter that the needs of virtually all life insurance buyers can be met satisfactorily with straight life, five-year renewable term, or some combination of the two. The way in which to make the decision in your own situation is discussed in the final section of this chapter.

Three important riders

This section of the chapter describes three important riders—the waiver-of-premium rider, the accidental death rider, and the guaranteed insurability rider. These may be attached to many basic policy forms, and should be considered when you buy life insurance.

Waiver of premium

A waiver-of-premium rider usually provides that premiums are waived after the policyholder has been totally disabled for six months. However, when a policyholder qualifies for waiver of premium, the usual provision makes the waiver retroactive to the beginning of the disability; thus any premiums paid by the policyholder during the first six months of his disability would be refunded to him.

Such a rider is a form of disability income insurance; in the event of a total disability, the benefits of the rider take the form of waived premiums on the life insurance policy. During the continuance of the disability, the premiums are waived and the various benefits provided in the contract (including the face amount, cash values, and dividends) continue just as though the premiums were being paid by the policyholder. When he recovers, he merely resumes premium payments and has no liability for repayment of the waived premiums. The definition of "totally disabled" varies among companies, but a common definition provides that the policyholder is totally disabled if he is unable, because of an illness or injury, to perform any of the duties of his occupation or any other occupation for which he is reasonably suited as a result of his education, training, and experience.

Most companies impose a specific charge for the waiver-of-premium rider. Although the cost may appear small relative to the straight life premium, the range of prices among companies for the waiver-of-premium rider is substantial.

To illustrate, the author tabulated the waiver-of-premium rider costs for $25,000 participating straight life policies issued in 1970 to men aged 35 by thirty-three major companies. In each instance, the annual cost of the rider was expressed as a percentage of the annual premium including the cost of the rider, because the entire premium including the cost of the rider would be waived in the event of a disability. For example, if the annual premium rate per $1,000 of face amount without the rider were $23.40, and if the corresponding rate for the rider were 60 cents, the cost of the rider would be expressed as 2.50 percent (60 cents divided by $24). Among the thirty-three policies in the tabulation, the cost of the waiver-of-premium rider ranged from 1.74 percent to 3.02 percent, with a mean of 2.62 percent.

A few companies include the waiver-of-premium rider in their contracts "without specific extra charge." This practice makes comparisons more difficult. The companies that follow this practice, and for which data were assembled in Chapter 4, furnished at the author's request the amount of the charge for the waiver-of-premium rider. The author then deducted the amount of the charge from the premium before making the various computations.

If you are buying a term policy and contemplating the addition of a waiver-of-premium rider, the comparison problem is extremely difficult. The waiver-of-premium riders that are available for term policies differ widely among companies; a relatively low-priced rider may be a relatively restrictive one as well. The waiver-of-premium rider as it relates to term policies is discussed in Chapter 7.

It is a good idea to add the waiver-of-premium rider when you buy a life insurance policy. It is particularly important in the case of a large policy, because a large premium would be a substantial burden in the event of a serious, long-term disability.

Some companies will attach to a life insurance policy a rider providing for the payment of a monthly income in the event that the insured becomes totally disabled as the result of an illness or injury. Like the waiver-of-premium rider, this is disability insurance, but the benefit here is a monthly income in addition to waived premiums.

A disability income rider should be analyzed as though it were a separate disability income policy. The subject of disability income insurance, which is a part of the subject of health insurance, is an extensive one and is beyond the scope of this book.[1]

Accidental death

Nearly all life insurance companies will attach to a basic life insurance policy a rider that is often called "double indemnity." It provides a death benefit in addition to and usually equal to the benefit provided in the basic policy if the death of the insured results from an accident, and if the accident occurs prior to a specified age such as 65 or 70.

The author tabulated the accidental death annual premium rates per $1,000 for participating straight life policies issued in 1970 to men aged 35 by twenty-eight major companies. The costs ranged from 78 cents to $1.25 per $1,000, with a mean of 94 cents. These are in contrast to a rate of about $2 for accidental death insurance purchased in a separate policy.

The premium looks small, but most deaths do not qualify for accidental death benefits. Automobile accidents are spectacular and often make the newspaper front pages, but they are far outnumbered by the more obscure notices back on the obituary pages. It is difficult to justify accidental death insurance on rational grounds. Why should a man provide more protection for his family if he dies in an automobile accident than if he dies of a heart attack? Indeed, if a differentiation is to be made, it probably would be logical to provide more protection in the event of a non-accidental death, because a long illness preceding such a death might leave the family in a more difficult financial situation than a sudden death from an accident.

If you conscientiously measure your life insurance needs, using the procedure outlined in Chapter 2, and if you buy life insurance accordingly, there would be no need for you to buy additional accidental death coverage. (Nor would it be necessary for you to buy other more limited forms of life insurance, such as the air trip coverage available at airports. Air trip coverage is frowned upon as an invitation to a person who might plant a bomb aboard an airplane, and would be prohibited outright if the Air Line Pilots Association had its way.) Should you decide to buy accidental death insurance, however, be sure to read the definition of accidental death in the contract, paying particular attention to the various exclusions from coverage.

Guaranteed insurability

Many companies will attach to a life insurance policy a rider that permits the insured to purchase additional life insurance at certain specified future dates without evidence of insurability. This type of rider is a relatively recent development, first offered in 1957 by the Bankers Life Company (Des Moines, Iowa).

A guaranteed insurability rider specifies the dates on which the insured may purchase additional life insurance with no questions asked. For example, the dates might be the policy aniversaries nearest the policyholder's twenty-fifth, twenty-eighth, thirty-first, thirty-fourth, thirty-seventh, and fortieth birthdays. Thus, the older the applicant, the fewer options he has, and the rider usually is not available for applicants beyond age 37.

The amount of additional life insurance that can be purchased on any one option date is equal to the face amount of the basic policy to which the guaranteed insurability rider is attached, subject to a minimum and a maximum. For example, the minimum might be $5,000 and the maximum $20,000. If the basic policy were less than $5,000, the guaranteed insurability rider would not be available; if the basic policy were at least $5,000 and not more than $20,000, the amount available on an option date would be equal to the face amount of the basic policy; and if the basic policy were more than $20,000, the amount available on an option date would be $20,000.

On any one option date, the policyholder may exercise the option in full or in part, or he may pass. Usually the options are not cumulative, however, so that an option once passed is lost forever.

The author tabulated the guaranteed insurability rider costs per $1,000 of option amount for participating straight life policies issued in 1970 to men aged 25 by twenty-six major companies. The costs ranged from $1.19 to $2.55, with a mean of $1.48. The range is substantial, but there are also major differences in the riders. For example, one of the most significant questions is whether the waiver-of-premium rider may be included without evidence of insurability in a policy purchased through the exercise of an option.

The premium for the additional insurance purchased under an option is determined by the age of the policyholder at the option date. Thus, the advantage of the rider is not premium savings, but rather that no evidence of insurability is required. The guaranteed insurability rider should be purchased by young men who have reason to believe they will be adding to their life insurance from time to time.

Nature of the savings element

The key to making a sound decision about the type of life insurance to buy is a good understanding of the nature of the savings element in a straight life policy. The purpose of this section is to describe the major characteristics of the savings element. Then, the final section of the chapter explains how to make the decision.

Although an understanding of the nature of the savings element is important to buyers, no area of life insurance has been subjected to more double talk, half-truths, and falsehoods. There are those in the life insurance industry who would have you believe that cash values constitute the finest savings device ever conceived by the mind of man. Some of these persons manipulate figures to show a rate of return of 15 percent, or 30 percent, or even more, on the savings element of cash-value life insurance. On the other hand, some of the life insurance detractors argue in a superficially convincing manner that the policyholder earns little or nothing on his cash values.

Some of the cash-value proponents seem to suggest that no one in his right mind should buy term insurance. On the other hand, some of the cash-value opponents seem to suggest that no one in his right mind should buy anything other than term insurance. Little wonder, then, that cash values are so misunderstood by the buying public, which is caught squarely in the middle of these conflicting views.

Let me make my position clear at the outset. I am not suggesting that you should buy cash-value life insurance, nor am I suggesting that you should avoid cash-value life insurance. Cash values are simply available, and I feel they can be useful for those who understand their characteristics and wish to utilize them. No one can make the decision for you as to whether you should allocate some or all of your savings to cash values. You have to make that decision yourself on the basis of your own situation and your knowledge of the characteristics of cash values.

This section covers eight aspects of the savings element of cash-value life insurance: its fixed-dollar nature, the rate-of-return question, the income tax situation, liquidity, safety, the alleged "forced savings" characteristic, the availability of the savings element to creditors, and the question of settlement options. A brief summary of the eight topics is included at the end of the section.

Fixed dollars

The savings element of cash-value life insurance is a fixed-dollar savings device. This means that the value of the accumulation is specified in advance in terms of dollars, without regard to what those dollars may buy. Those who sing the praises of cash values like to describe them as guaranteed by the insurance company. Those who criticize cash values like to describe them as subject to erosion by the forces of inflation. Both descriptions are accurate, and they are applicable generally to fixed-dollar savings media.

Other major savings media that closely resemble cash values in this respect are savings accounts, savings and loan accounts, credit union share accounts, and United States government "E" bonds. Long-term debt instruments, such as government bonds, industrial bonds, and mortgages, usually are classified as fixed-dollar devices, but these are subject to interim market value fluctuations as market interest rates fluctuate. In this sense, long-term debt instruments differ fundamentally from life insurance cash values.

Such devices as common stock and real estate are classified as equity-type investments, in the sense that their value is determined by market forces rather than being specified in advance. Most mutual funds deal primarily in common stocks and are therefore classified as equity-type investments themselves. Equity-type investments are completely different from life insurance cash values.

Rate of return

The critics of cash-value life insurance usually assert that the rate of return on the savings element is very low. One recent writer, for example, asserted, without any supporting evidence, that the rate

of return is 2 percent. Others have asserted that the rate runs between 2 percent and 3.5 percent.

The most likely source of these incorrect statements is the fact that
life insurance policy contracts mention, deep in the fine print, the
interest rate or rates on which policy reserves and cash values are
based. Policy reserves are the main liabilities of a life insurance
company and are used in measuring the solvency position of the
company; they are related to the price of a policy only in an indirect
way. Although cash values are one element of the price of a policy,
they are not the sole determinant of the price. To judge the price
of a policy, you must look not only at cash values, but also at premiums and, in the case of participating policies, dividends. In nonparticipating policies, on which the company does not contemplate paying dividends, an interest rate much higher than the one used in
determining cash values frequently is used in premium calculations.
In participating policies, an interest rate much higher than the one
used in determining cash values frequently is used in dividend calculations. In short, *the interest rate or rates mentioned in the policy
contract are not indicative of the rate of return on the savings
element.*

Life insurance industry representatives, on the other hand, sometimes assert that the rate of return on the savings element is very
high. It is possible, for example, to manipulate figures in such a way
that the rate of return appears to be 15 percent, 30 percent, or even
more. Such deceptive practices are complex and tricky, but an analogy may help you understand the general nature of the problem.

Suppose you put $1,000 into a savings account at the beginning
of each year for ten years and that the account is credited annually
with 5 percent interest. You would start the tenth year with $11,578,
and you would add $1,000 to it. At the end of the year, your account
would be credited with interest of $629 (5 percent of $12,578), making your account $13,207 at the end of the tenth year. In other words,
your account would increase in the tenth year by $1,629 (from
$11,578 to $13,207). Suppose someone describing the account told
you that you were earning 62.9 percent on your tenth year deposit
of $1,000! The problem here stems from a misallocation of the inter-
est, in this case all of it being allocated to the tenth year deposit
of $1,000. This same kind of misallocation takes place in many
life insurance sales presentations. But the error is not nearly as

evident, because of the complexity of the life insurance contract.

If the interest rates mentioned in the policy are not indicative of the rate of return on the savings element, and if the glamorous rates sometimes mentioned by enthusiastic life insurance agents are false, what is the correct figure? The question is unanswerable: there is no such thing as *the* rate of return on the savings element of a cash-value life insurance policy.

Suppose you are examining a package called AB. It consists of an element A and an element B. If the price of the package were $100, what would be the price of element A? And what would be the price of element B? There is no such thing as *the* price of A or *the* price of B. You can make a statement about the price of A only by making an assumption about the price of B, and vice versa. For example, let's assume that the price of A is $30. Then we can say that the price of B is $70, but this figure holds only when we assume that the price of A is $30.

In the case of cash-value life insurance, the package consists of a protection element and a savings element. To determine a price for the protection element, given that we know the premium for the entire package, it is necessary to assume a rate of return (or interest rate) on the savings element. On the other hand, to determine a rate of return on the savings element, it is necessary to assume a price for the protection element. In other words, it cannot be said that any one figure is *the* rate of return on the savings element; rather, it can only be said that a particular rate of return applies when a particular price of the protection element is assumed.

Let's take a specific case to illustrate these points. Consider just the eighth year of the $25,000 Connecticut Mutual straight life policy for which data are shown in Table 3–1. To determine the price of the protection element, it is necessary to make an assumption about the rate of return on the savings element. If it were assumed that the rate of return is 5 percent, the price of the protection element in the eighth year would be $3.53 per $1,000 of protection. The details of this calculation are explained in Appendix G. If a lower rate of return were assumed, the price of protection would be lower; if a higher rate of return were assumed, the price of protection would be higher. For example, various assumed rates of return produce the following prices per $1,000 of protection in the eighth year of the illustrative policy:

Assumed Rate of Return	Price per $1,000 of Protection
0%	$—3.55
1%	—2.14
2%	—0.72
3%	0.70
4%	2.12
5%	3.53
6%	4.95

When someone wants to show that the protection element in a cash-value policy is very low-priced, all he has to do is assume that you are receiving a very low rate of return on the savings element. Traditionally, many life insurance agents and companies make presentations that effectively assume a 0 percent rate of return on the savings element, thus producing a very low (frequently negative) price for the protection element.

The opposite procedure is to make an assumption about the price of the protection element and calculate the rate of return on the savings element. In the eighth year of the same Connecticut Mutual policy mentioned above, let's assume that the price of protection is $4 per $1,000 of protection. The rate of return on the savings element would then be about 5.3 percent. The details of this calculation are also explained in Appendix G. If the assumed price of the protection element were reduced, the rate of return on the savings element would be reduced; if the price of the protection element were increased, the rate of return on the savings element would be increased. For example, various assumed prices per $1,000 of protection produce the following rates of return on the savings element in the eighth year of the illustrative policy:

Assumed Price per $1,000 of Protection	Rate of Return
$0	2.5%
1	3.2%
2	3.9%
3	4.6%
4	5.3%
5	6.0%
6	6.7%

When someone wants to show that the savings element provides a high rate of return, all he has to do is assume that the price of the protection element is high. Suppose, for example, that a company charges a high price for its five-year renewable term policies. The agent can use that high price as the price-of-protection assumption in order to calculate the rate of return on the savings element of his company's straight life contract. The result is an apparently high rate of return on the savings element of the straight life contract, but the fact is that the company simply charges a high price for its term insurance.

The evaluation system used in this book is based on certain assumed rates of return on the savings element. For the policies issued in 1970, for example, it was assumed that you will earn a 5 percent rate of return on the savings element. This figure was selected because it is the current interest rate paid on savings accounts in the Bowery Savings Bank, which is the largest mutual savings bank in the United States. Also, remember that the savings element of cash-value life insurance is a kind of fixed-dollar savings device that closely resembles a savings account.

Some evaluations were also performed for policies issued in 1950, 1940, and 1930. In these cases, it was assumed that the rate of return on the savings element was comparable to the interest rates paid in the past by the Bowery Savings Bank. The year-by-year interest rates used in these calculations are shown in Appendix H.

In summary, there is no such thing as *the* rate of return on the savings element of a cash-value life insurance policy, because the contract is an integrated package of protection and savings. In this book, it is assumed that you will earn a rate of return similar to that currently being paid on certain savings accounts, which are somewhat comparable to cash values as a savings device. In appraising cash values as a savings medium; then, you should look upon them as earning the same rate that would be earned on comparable savings devices.

The income tax situation

So far cash values have been likened to other savings media. As fixed-dollar savings, they closely resemble savings accounts, savings and loan accounts, credit union share accounts, and United States government "E" bonds. Since the rate-of-return question is unanswerable, it has been suggested that you view cash values as earning a rate of return equal to that earned on such comparable savings devices. In the income tax arena, however, the savings element of cash-value life insurance is in a class by itself.

By this time it should be evident that interest is an important factor in the price structure of a cash-value life insurance contract. Without the interest factor, an insurance company would have to charge a much higher premium in order to take care of death benefits, pay cash values, pay dividends in the case of participating policies, take care of its expenses, and make a profit. This means that, as you pay premiums, interest is hard at work. Sometimes the interest factor in this context is referred to as the "inside interest" or the "inside interest build-up."

To illustrate the income tax treatment of the inside interest, let's assume you buy a $25,000 nonparticipating straight life contract for which the premium is $500 per year. Further, let's assume you pay premiums for ten years. During the ten years, inside interest is hard at work in your behalf, but you do not have to declare any interest as taxable income during that period.

Now let's assume that you discontinue premium payments at the end of the tenth policy year and that you receive the cash value. The amount you receive will be equal to, greater than, or less than the simple total of the premiums you paid.

First, let's assume that the cash value is $5,000, or exactly equal to the simple total of the ten $500 annual premiums you paid. Under the current income tax rules, you have no taxable income. This means that the income tax on the inside interest was deferred until you surrendered the policy, and then you were allowed to apply the cost of the life insurance protection against the inside interest. In other words, the inside interest for the ten years was exactly equal to the cost of the protection for the ten years. If you had bought five-year renewable term insurance and put the difference in premiums into a savings account, the cost of the protection would not have been deductible, and the interest on the savings account would have been taxable each year as earned. By acquiring the cash-value contract, you are allowed to apply the cost of the protection against the inside interest.

Second, let's assume that the cash value is $5,100, or exactly $100 greater than the simple total of the ten $500 annual premiums you paid. Under the current income tax rules, you now have taxable income of $100. Here again, you have been allowed to apply the cost of the life insurance protection against the inside interest, and you are taxed only to the extent that the inside interest exceeded the cost of the protection.

Third, let's assume that the cash value is $4,900, or exactly $100 less than the simple total of the ten $500 annual premiums you paid. In this instance, the cost of the life insurance protection exceeded the inside interest by $100. You are not allowed a deduction, because the cost of the protection is not deductible, but you have been allowed to apply the cost of the protection against the inside interest so as to eliminate any taxable income.

Finally, let's assume that, instead of surrendering the policy at the end of the tenth year, you die at that point. If you owned the policy at the time of your death, the $25,000 of life insurance funds would be part of your estate for federal estate tax purposes. But there would be no taxable *income* to your beneficiary. This is sometimes mentioned as a tax advantage of life insurance, but it is not. Rather, it means that life insurance is treated at death in the same manner as other property.

For example, suppose you had put the $500 per year for ten years into common stock. Assume for convenience that no cash dividends were paid and that the stock by the end of ten years had miraculously grown to $25,000 in market value. The $25,000 of stock would be part of your estate at the time of your death, but there would be no taxable income or taxable capital gain to your beneficiary. When she subsequently sells the stock, her gain or loss on the transaction would be determined by reference to the $25,000 value of the stock at the time of your death. In other words, the tax treatment of the common stock in this illustration is exactly the same as the tax treatment of the life insurance.

The handling of inside interest from an income tax standpoint constitutes a substantial tax advantage for the savings element of cash-value life insurance, as opposed to other comparable savings media. In the case of savings accounts, savings and loan accounts, or credit union share accounts, the interest earnings are taxable income as earned. In the case of United States government "E" bonds, the interest earnings are taxable income as earned or may be deferred, at the option of the bondholder. But in the case of cash-value life insurance, the income tax on the inside interest is not only deferred, but also may be entirely or substantially eliminated. Thus, when a person buys a cash-value life insurance policy, he is acquiring an important income tax shelter for his savings. The higher the income tax bracket of the policyholder, the more important this tax shelter is. This explains the attractiveness of cash-value life insurance to persons in high income tax brackets.

Liquidity

The cash value of a life insurance contract is a highly liquid savings medium. It is directly comparable in this respect to savings accounts, savings and loan accounts, and credit union share accounts, and is even more liquid than United States government "E" bonds.

There are three ways in which to get at the savings element of a cash-value life insurance contract and make use of the funds. First, the policy can be discontinued so that the policyholder will receive the cash value. This approach, however, means that the protection element of the contract is terminated. For that reason, life insurance cash values would not compare favorably with savings accounts in terms of liquidity if this were the only way in which the policyholder could gain access to the funds.

Second, the policy may be pledged as collateral for a loan. Normally such transactions are carried out with commercial banks, but occasionally the lender might be some other type of financial institution or even an individual. A loan up to the amount of the cash value usually is regarded as fully secured. This arrangement is made possible through the assignment clause of the life insurance contract, which is discussed in Chapter 7.

Third, the policyholder may obtain a loan directly from the life insurance company. Here again the available amount is anything up to the cash value. This arrangement is made possible through the policy loan clause of the life insurance contract, which is also discussed in Chapter 7.

Life insurance cash values are superior to United States government "E" bonds in terms of liquidity. "E" bonds have no loan clause and are "not transferable," which is another way of saying that they cannot be pledged (or "assigned") as collateral for a loan. The only way a bondholder can get at the funds is to cash in the bond. This is costly, because the effective interest rate when the bond is held to maturity substantially exceeds the effective interest rate when the bond is redeemed prior to maturity.

It is sometimes argued that life insurance cash values are not as liquid as a savings account because, if you take a policy loan, you "have to pay interest on your own money," while if you take money from a savings account you do not have to pay interest. This argument is totally without merit, because you *lose* interest when you draw funds from a savings account. It can be shown that the effect on your financial condition of a withdrawal from a savings account is identical to the effect of a policy loan in terms of both cost and liquidity, provided that the interest rate being paid on the savings account is equal to the policy loan interest rate.

Consider the case of John Smith. He has $5,000 in a savings account that is earning 5 percent interest. He also has a $25,000 straight life policy that has a $5,000 cash value and a 5 percent policy loan interest rate. He has decided to buy a $3,000 car.

Suppose John draws the money from his savings account and then replaces the funds at the end of one year (when he receives a bonus from his employer). He would lose $150 in interest on the account; so to be back where he would have been without making the withdrawal, he would have to put an additional $150 in the account.

But suppose John takes a policy loan instead of withdrawing the funds from his savings account. Again, he repays the loan at the end of one year, together with $150 of loan interest. He would now be back where he would have been without the loan, and he would also have the full savings account including the $150 of interest.

To summarize, let's assume that John takes $3,000 in cash to buy the car and puts back $3,150 at the end of one year. Whether he draws the funds from his savings account or takes a policy loan, his savings account would now be $5,250 (the original $5,000 enhanced by one year's interest), and his cash value would be about $5,400 (because the policy would now be one year older and an additional annual premium would have been paid). Either way, therefore, his liquid assets would now be $10,690 and his nonliquid asset would be a one-year-old car.

In the case of a savings account, the funds normally may be obtained quickly by going to the bank. In the case of a policy loan, if you live near an insurance company office that is authorized to issue policy loan checks, you would be able to get the funds just as quickly as from a bank. In the usual case, however, policy loans are delayed by the need to use the mail and in this respect might take about as long as a savings account withdrawal by mail. In short, the policy loan clause makes the savings element of a cash-value life insurance contract comparable to a savings account in terms of liquidity.

Safety

It was mentioned earlier that proponents of cash values describe them as "guaranteed." This expression means that the cash values, and therefore the annual increases in cash value, are backed by the entire resources of the life insurance company. In the case of a large, well-established company, these are significant guarantees.

Even in the case of smaller and younger companies, the guarantee usually can be relied upon. When a company gets into financial difficulties it is usually taken over by a major company. When this happens, the larger company usually carries out the guarantees provided in the contracts of the defunct company. The major companies are willing to do this not only because they need to preserve public confidence in life insurance, but also because a takeover usually is a profitable venture.

Only occasionally does a policyholder or beneficiary receive less than provided for in the contract. An example of this relatively rare type of occurrence was the recent liquidation of the Century Life Insurance Company (Fort Worth, Texas), which is discussed in Chapter 4. In that instance, the effect of the liquidation was a reduction in guaranteed cash values and, in effect, an increase in premiums.

Frequently savings accounts are covered by the Federal Deposit Insurance Corporation, and savings and loan accounts by the Federal Savings and Loan Insurance Corporation. Recently the share accounts of most federal credit unions became covered by the National Credit Union Administration. United States government "E" bonds are backed by the integrity of the federal government and usually are considered as safe as any savings device can be.

Life insurance companies are regulated primarily by the states rather than by the federal government, and in some states there are guaranty funds that can be used to meet the obligations of defunct companies. Such funds do not exist in all states, however, and there is no life insurance company guaranty fund at the federal level.

The financial integrity of the life insurance company, therefore, is very important. If you follow the suggestions in Chapter 4, it is unlikely that you will encounter a situation in which your company fails to meet its obligations under the contract.

Forced savings

People tend to give the payment of life insurance premiums a high priority in their financial affairs. Since the premiums for cash-value life insurance policies provide for both protection and savings, the result is an element of compulsion that is missing from most other savings devices.

The proponents of cash values tend to emphasize the importance of this characteristic of the savings element of life insurance policies. They argue that people tend to keep their life insurance policies in force, but constantly open and close savings accounts. They argue that cash-value life insurance is superior in this respect to other savings media and that a long-term, systematic savings program is more likely to be successful when cash values are the vehicle. In short, they suggest that this characteristic of cash-value life insurance is of great value to the policyholder.

The opponents of cash values, on the other hand, tend to pooh-pooh the notion of forced savings. They argue that many policyholders lapse their policies and that the higher initial premiums associated with cash-value life insurance may actually cause lapses and prevent people from buying adequate amounts of life insurance protection. They argue that the use of the forced savings argument by life insurance agents means that the buyer is being accused of a lack of self-discipline. In short, they suggest that this characteristic of cash-value life insurance is of little or no value to the policyholder.

The answer, as in many controversial areas, probably lies between the extreme arguments. And, in any case, the question is a highly subjective and personal one. No one can tell you whether you will be more successful with a systematic savings program in life insurance cash values or in some other savings medium.

Perhaps your experience to date can shed some light on the question. If you have been successful in accumulating savings in other media, the forced savings aspect of cash-value life insurance may be of little value to you. If you have been unsuccessful to date, however, perhaps the compulsion would be of value. In short, the value *to you* of this characteristic of cash-value life insurance is something you must decide for yourself.

Protection from creditors

Many of the assets a person owns can be attached by a creditor in order to satisfy a debt. The savings element of a cash-value life insurance policy, however, frequently cannot be successfully attached by a creditor.

The value of this characteristic of cash values is highly subjective and perhaps impossible to assess. First, many policyholders who get into financial difficulties borrow against their life insurance policies at some point prior to the imposition of strong pressure by their creditors. Should such policyholders borrow the maximum under the loan clause, there would be no savings element left for the creditors to attach.

Second, the question of the availability of cash values to creditors of the policyholder is a highly complex subject. It is difficult to determine in advance what would happen in any given situation, and no attempt is made here to go into any detail. Suffice to say that the savings element of a cash-value life insurance policy may enjoy an advantage over many other kinds of assets in the event that the policyholder gets into financial difficulties.[2]

Life annuity rates

The funds provided by a life insurance contract may be paid to the recipient in a single sum or in one of a variety of installment arrangements known as "settlement options," which are discussed in Chapter 7. Some of the commonly available settlement options involve life contingencies; that is, the number of installment payments to be made depends at least in part upon the continuation of one or more lives. Stated another way, some of the settlement options are life annuities that provide for periodic payments to the recipient for as long as he lives.

Settlement options, including various kinds of life annuities, are available with regard to the funds payable at death under almost any kind of life insurance policy. In the case of cash-value policies, however, settlement options also are generally available to the policyholder in lieu of a single sum payment at the time he discontinues his policy. This means that the savings accumulation in a cash-value policy may be used by the policyholder to produce a life income for himself, or perhaps for both himself and his wife.

The amount of the periodic income provided under a life annuity is determined by calculations similar to those made for life insurance premiums; that is, interest assumptions, mortality tables, and expense and profit assumptions are made. The results of such calculations frequently are shown in the life insurance contract, so that the policyholder is guaranteed a certain lifetime income for each $1,000 of accumulation in the contract.

The person who accumulates savings through a cash-value policy, therefore, obtains what amounts to an upper limit on the prices of a variety of life annuities that may be utilized by him many years in the future. If life annuity premium rates rise substantially in the future, the policyholder would have a valuable set of guarantees in his contract. If life annuity premium rates should decline, however, he can take his cash value in a lump sum and purchase a life annuity on the open market.

There is at least a possibility of major developments that would extend the longevity of elderly people. The effect of such developments would be substantial increases in life annuity premium rates, and under such circumstances the life annuity settlement options in cash-value life insurance policies would be quite valuable. It is difficult if not impossible to put a specific price tag on the value of the settlement options in a cash-value life insurance contract, but the existence of such options is a point worth considering in any examination of the characteristics of the savings element of cash-value life insurance.

Summary

Here then, in summary, are the major characteristics of the savings element of cash-value life insurance policies:

- It is a fixed-dollar savings device and is similar in this respect to savings accounts, savings and loan accounts, credit union share accounts, and United States government "E" bonds.
- The rate of return on the savings element is not determinable because of the "package" aspect of cash-value life insurance. However, it is suggested that the rate of return be viewed as equal to the rate of return on comparable savings devices. In most of the calculations for this book, the assumed rate of return is 5 percent.

- It enjoys a substantial income tax advantage over other comparable savings devices. The income tax on the so-called inside interest is completely deferred, and then eventually it may be completely or almost completely eliminated.
- It is comparable in liquidity to savings accounts, savings and loan accounts, and credit union share accounts, and it is superior to United States government "E" bonds in this respect.
- It is reasonably safe. If the policyholder selects his company carefully from the standpoint of financial strength, it is unlikely that he will encounter a situation in which his company fails to meet its contractual obligations.
- It provides an element of compulsion that may be helpful in carrying out a systematic savings program over a long period of time.
- It may enjoy an advantage over many other kinds of assets in the event that the policyholder gets into financial difficulties.
- It provides certain settlement options that may become quite valuable if life annuity premium rates increase substantially in the future.

How to make your choice

The next steps are to decide upon the appropriate balance between straight life and five-year renewable term insurance and to decide whether you are able and willing to pay for the amount of life insurance you need. The purpose of this section is to explain how these decisions may be made.

The savings decision

The life insurance needs of virtually any buyer can be met satisfactorily with straight life, five-year renewable term, or some combination of the two. Once you have determined your life insurance needs, along the lines discussed in Chapter 2, you should decide how much of those needs to meet with straight life. Then the remainder may be met with five-year renewable term.

To decide how much straight life to buy, you should ask yourself how much you would like to invest per year in the savings element of cash-value life insurance. The answer depends on several things. First, you should decide upon the total amount you would like to set aside in savings each year. Second, you should decide upon the proportion of that total you would like to place in fixed-dollar savings instruments. Third, you should decide upon the proportion of fixed-dollar savings you would like to place in the savings element of cash-value life insurance.

Suppose you decide to put nothing into the savings element of cash-value life insurance. In that case, you should consider meeting all of your life insurance needs with five-year renewable term. You should exercise caution if you decide to follow this route, however. You may wish to continue at least a portion of your life insurance until your death, even if that does not occur until well beyond the usual retirement age. When you rely completely on five-year renewable term insurance, and when you do not convert at least a portion to straight life, the coverage cannot be continued beyond age 65 or 70. Also, the five-year renewable term premiums are very high as you approach those ages. And when you do not convert for many years, the straight life premiums are very high when you do convert.

Many persons probably should put some amount into the savings element of cash-value life insurance each year. The next step, then, is to translate that annual amount of savings into an appropriate face amount of straight life insurance. Since the savings elements of most straight life policies are similar in size, a few rules of thumb should suffice. Roughly speaking, the average yearly amounts that go into the savings element of a straight life policy per $1,000 of face amount are as follows:

Age at Issue	Average Annual Amount
25	$ 8
35	10
45	13

To illustrate, suppose you are aged 35 and have decided you need $50,000 of life insurance. Also, suppose you have decided to put about $250 per year into the savings element of cash-value life insurance. According to the above rules of thumb, the average yearly amount that goes into the savings element is about $10 for each $1,000 of face amount. Under these circumstances, you should buy $25,000 of straight life in order to put about $250 per year into the savings element. To meet your total life insurance needs you should then buy the remaining $25,000 in the form of five-year renewable term.

The premiums decision

Once you have determined how much straight life and how much five-year renewable term you should buy, you must decide whether you are able and willing to pay for the coverage. A sound decision here requires an understanding of the major components of straight life premiums.

Consider the Connecticut Mutual $25,000 participating straight life contract for which the first twenty years' data are shown in Table 3–1. The annual premium is $534. The "value" of the first twenty years' premiums, expressed as of the policy's issue date, is $5,232. This latter figure takes into account interest and probabilities of payment. (Technically, the expression should be "present expected value" rather than "value." The words "present value" convey that interest has been taken into account. The word "expected" conveys that probabilities of payment have been taken into account. In this book, the word "value" is used for the sake of brevity.)

Earlier it was explained why it is appropriate to assume that the rate of return on the savings element is 5 percent. Consistent with that discussion, the interest rate used in the calculation of the various values discussed here is 5 percent.

When the value of a series of payments is calculated, it is appropriate to take into account not only interest but also probabilities of payment. Any given future premium might not be paid, either because the policyholder has died or because he has discontinued the policy. The probabilities of payment are taken into account, therefore, by the use of a mortality table, which shows probabilities of death, and a lapse table, which shows probabilities of discontinuation of the policy. The tables used in the calculations, and the calculations themselves, are explained in Appendix H.

In our example, the value of the first twenty years' protection is $652. This figure is determined in a manner similar to that described above and represents the raw material value of the protection element, expressed as of the policy's issue date.

The value of the savings element for the first twenty years of the policy is $2,449, and the value of the illustrated dividends for the same period is $1,362. These figures are also expressed as of the policy's issue date and are determined in a manner similar to that described above for premiums.

The difference between what the policyholder pays in and what he gets back is what the insurance company keeps to cover its expenses and make a profit. What the company keeps is referred to in this book as the "company retention," or simply "retention."

In this instance, what the policyholder pays in is the value of the premiums, which is $5,232. What he gets back is the value of the protection element, the value of the savings element, and the value of the illustrated dividends. These three items total $4,463 ($652 plus $2,449 plus $1,362). The company retention, therefore, is $769 ($5,232 minus $4,463).

"Retention" is not synonymous with "price." The "price of the protection" is the sum of two items: the value of the protection element and the value of the company retention. When similar policies are ranked by both price and retention, the ranks are similar, because the protection elements of similar policies have similar values. In this book, the emphasis is placed on retention figures rather than price figures, but the price figures may be determined readily from the various tables and illustrations by combining the values shown for the protection element and the company retention.

In summary, the components of the straight life premiums may be shown in terms of twenty-year values expressed as of the policy issue date. The figures are as follows:

Protection element	$ 652
Savings element	2,449
Illustrated dividends	1,362
Company retention	769
Premiums	$5,232

The same components of the straight life premiums may be shown either as percentages or as cents per dollar of premiums. For example, it may be said that 12.5 cents of each premium dollar are associated with the protection element of the policy, 46.8 cents with the savings element, 26.0 cents with the illustrated dividends, and 14.7 cents with the company retention. These relationships are illustrated in Figure 3–3.

The same components of the straight life premiums may also be

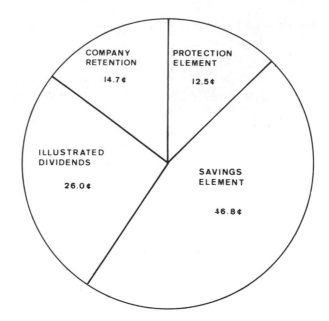

Figure 3–3
Components of premium dollar°

    ° The figures in this chart are based on the first twenty years of a $25,000 par-
ticipating straight life policy issued in 1970 to men aged 35 by Connecticut Mutual.
The interest, mortality, and lapse assumptions used in the calculations are those
described in Appendix H.

expressed on a yearly basis. The yearly figures may be determined
by dividing each of the above twenty-year values by 9.8023. (The
source of this factor is explained in Chapter 4.) The results are as
follows:

Protection element	$ 67
Savings element	250
Illustrated dividends	139
Company retention	78
Premiums	$534

    Several points about these figures should be noted. First, the an-
nual premium is $534. In deciding whether you are willing and able
to buy $25,000 of participating straight life, however, you must look
beyond this figure.
    Second, the yearly figure associated with the savings element is

$250, which means that this is the average annual amount going into the savings element. This is precisely the figure mentioned earlier on the basis of the rule of thumb that $10 is the average annual amount that goes into the savings element of a straight life policy issued at age 35 for each $1,000 of face amount. You have already indicated a desire to put $250 per year into the savings element of cash-value life insurance, and this portion of the premium should be viewed as going into savings rather than as buying protection. When the $250 is subtracted from the premium of $534, the remainder is $284.

Third, the average annual amount associated with the illustrated dividends is $139. (It might bear repeating that this is *not* the simple average of the twenty years' dividends; rather, it is calculated by taking interest and probabilities into account.) Table 3–1 shows that the first-year dividend is $57 and the twentieth-year dividend is $281. These and the other dividend figures are not guaranteed, but are the only dividend figures you have on which to make your decisions. Since it is reasonable to view dividends as refunds, you should subtract the average annual figure in estimating your ability and willingness to buy the $25,000 of participating straight life. When the $139 is subtracted from the previous remainder of $284, the result is $145. (If you are concerned about the first year, you might subtract the first-year dividend of $57 rather than the average of $139.)

Fourth, the figure of $145 is the sum of two items: the $67 raw material cost of the life insurance protection, and the $78 that the company keeps to cover its expenses and make a profit. This yearly figure of $145 is your estimate of what you pay, on the average, for the life insurance protection in the $25,000 participating straight life contract. It is the annual price of the protection.

You also decided to buy $25,000 of five-year renewable term. Table 3–2 shows that the Connecticut Mutual's annual premium for the first five years is $133. Dividends are illustrated, but they are small and may be disregarded for your purposes here. The total annual price of the protection in both policies, therefore, is $278 ($145 plus $133) for the first five years. This is the amount you must be able and willing to spend on life insurance protection if you are to buy the $25,000 of participating straight life and the $25,000 of five-year renewable term.

To summarize, the combined annual premiums for both policies

for the first five years are $667 ($534 plus $133). But your willingness
and ability to buy the coverage should be based on the figure of $278,
because $250 of the $667 should be viewed as going into savings, and
another $139 of the $667 should be viewed as coming back to you
in the form of dividends. If you are willing and able to spend the $278
per year, you should buy the $25,000 participating straight life and
the $25,000 five-year renewable term. If you are unwilling or unable
to spend that amount, you should go back to Chapter 2 and cut back
on your financial objectives.

Chapter 4

From whom?

Nearly 2,000 life insurance companies exist in the United States today. Some of these are major financial institutions, but many are companies operating almost literally on a shoestring. The purpose of this chapter is to help you find your way through this labyrinth. Here are a few suggestions that are discussed in detail in this chapter:

- Because of the proliferation of company names, be sure you know the full name and home office location of any company you are considering.
- Because of the importance of life insurance in your affairs, deal with a company that is financially strong.

- Because of the very large price differences among companies, try to deal with a company that charges relatively low prices.

The identity problem

The similarity of company names is a problem, because there are so many companies and so few names that companies are willing to adopt. Very popular in the life insurance industry are words that suggest financial strength (Guaranty, Protective, Reserve, Security), words that suggest financial sophistication (Bankers, Commercial, Financial, Investors), words that suggest maturity (Colonial, First, Old, Pioneer), words that suggest dependability (Assurance, Great, Reliable, Trust), words that suggest fair treatment (Beneficial, Equitable, Mutual, Progressive), words that suggest friendliness (Citizens, Family, Home, Peoples), words that suggest breadth of operations (Continental, National, International, Universal), words that suggest government (American, Capital, Republic, State), and the names of well known Americans (Washington, Jefferson, Lincoln, Roosevelt).

Confusion can arise quite easily. One day I received a letter from an Indiana agent of the National Life and Accident Insurance Company, whose home office is in Nashville, Tennessee. The letter referred to a study in which I had supposedly mentioned his company. He had not seen the study, but a prospective customer had told him about it. Actually, I had not mentioned his company; rather, his customer had misinterpreted a reference to the National Life Insurance Company, whose home office is in Montpelier, Vermont.

To illustrate further the proliferation of names, consider some of the companies whose names begin with Lincoln. The Lincoln National Life Insurance Company (home office: Fort Wayne, Indiana) is one of the giant companies. If an agent identifies himself to you as representing "The Lincoln," however, he might be representing either the Lincoln National or any one of the following companies:

Lincoln American Life Insurance Company (Memphis, Tennessee)
Lincoln Annuity Life Insurance Company (Louisville, Kentucky)
Lincoln Benefit Life Company (Lincoln, Nebraska)
Lincoln Continental Life Insurance Company (Mattoon, Illinois)
Lincoln Income Life Insurance Company (Louisville, Kentucky)
Lincoln Liberty Life Insurance Company (Lincoln, Nebraska)

Lincoln Life & Casualty Company (Lincoln, Nebraska)

Lincoln Mutual Life and Casualty Insurance Company (Fargo, North Dakota)

Lincoln Mutual Life Insurance Company (Lincoln, Nebraska)

Confusion can also arise if you try to read some meaning into a company's name. For example, consider The United States Life Insurance Company in the City of New York, which is often called the United States Life. This company is not an agency of the United States government, nor is it connected with the United States government. Its life insurance should not be confused with United States Government Life Insurance or with National Service Life Insurance. These are subsidized, low-priced forms of life insurance that were available to servicemen and veterans of World War I and World War II, respectively.

Many other companies have names that may carry false connotations. For example, the Chase National Insurance Company (Springfield, Missouri) is not connected with the Chase Manhattan Bank and does not operate nationally. The company is controlled by the Chase National Investment Company, a Missouri holding company, and operates only in a handful of states in the midwest, south, and southwest.

The Columbus Mutual Life Insurance Company (Columbus, Ohio) is not a mutual company. It is a stock company owned by the State Automobile Mutual Insurance Company of Columbus.

The International Life Insurance Company (Louisville, Kentucky) does not operate internationally, or nationally, for that matter. It operates in fourteen states primarily in the midwest, south, and southwest.

The Mammoth Life and Accident Insurance Company (Louisville, Kentucky) is not a large company. It is a small company, with about $20 million of assets at the end of 1970.

The Old Heritage Life Insurance Company (Lincoln, Illinois) is not an old company. It is a new company organized in 1965.

Financial strength

The office of your state insurance commissioner is one source of information about life insurance companies. By contacting your commissioner's office, you can at least find out whether a particular company has met your state's requirements for a license, although you are unlikely to learn much more than that. The addresses of the various insurance commissioners are listed in Appendix F.

In some states, such as New York, the requirements for a license are quite rigorous. In many states, however, the requirements are meager. At present, the state in which the birth rate of new life insurance companies is most out of control is Arizona, which requires the organizers to put up only $37,500 to form a company. Since your life insurance is a cornerstone of your family's financial affairs, you should require more of a company than simply a license to do business in your state.

Several publishing firms assemble data on life insurance companies. Looking at such data, however, is likely to be a frustrating and unproductive experience unless the reader has detailed knowledge of the intricacies of life insurance company financial statements. About all the lay reader of these statements can expect to glean from them is an idea of the size of the company, which is not necessarily synonymous with financial strength.

Best's

Two publishers "rate" life insurance companies in terms of financial strength. One of these is the Alfred M. Best Company (Post Office Box 600, Morristown, New Jersey 07960), which publishes each year a volume entitled *Best's Life Insurance Reports.* The volume is expensive (the 1971 edition costs $75, including a one-year subscription to the life insurance edition of *Best's Review,* a monthly magazine), but is available in many libraries.

Best's engages in the financial analysis of insurance companies, and its reports contain recommendations of some life insurance companies. The strongest recommendations are couched in the following language:

POLICYHOLDERS' RECOMMENDATION

The results achieved by the company have been most favorable. In our opinion it has most substantial over-all margins for contingencies. Upon the foregoing analysis of its present position we recommend this company.

In Best's 1971 edition, 127 companies received this strongly worded recommendation. The full names and home office locations of these 127 companies are listed in Appendix B.

Best's also gave the same strongly worded recommendation to 127 companies in its 1970 edition. However, between 1970 and 1971, three companies were added to the list and three were dropped from the list. Added to the list were Midwestern United Life Insurance Company (Fort Wayne, Indiana), Sunset Life Insurance Company of America (Olympia, Washington), and Union National Life Insurance Company (Baton Rouge, Louisiana). Dropped from the list, although still recommended but in weaker language, were Bankers Life Insurance Company of Nebraska (Lincoln, Nebraska), State Mutual Life Assurance Company of America (Worcester, Massachusetts), and Union Mutual Life Insurance Company (Portland, Maine).

Best's recommended 301 other companies in its 1970 edition, but in weaker language. (This and the subsequent references to Best's 1970 edition are based on a tabulation carried out prior to the availability of the 1971 edition.) Instead of "most favorable," some companies' results are described as "very favorable" or "favorable." Instead of "most substantial," some companies' over-all margins for contingencies are described as "very substantial," "substantial," or "considerable."

In its 1970 edition, Best's reported on a total of 1,242 companies (out of the nearly 2,000 companies operating in the United States). Besides the previously mentioned 428 companies it recommended, 814 were not recommended. The reports on the latter companies do not mention the lack of a recommendation, but simply omit the recommendation. Each report contains information on the company's history, a description of its management and operation, and some statistics. Each report contains either favorable comments or no comments at all. In short, companies are not criticized directly, but are criticized indirectly with faint praise.

The use of faint praise is not restricted to the wording of the recommendation or the absence of a recommendation. Rather, it cuts through all of the narrative portions of the various company reports. To illustrate, consider the reports of the Connecticut Mutual Life Insurance Company (Hartford, Connecticut) and the Gulf Life Insurance Company (Jacksonville, Florida). The former is one of the companies recommended in the strongest possible language, and the latter is recommended in language slightly less strong. Following a brief description of Connecticut Mutual's mortgage portfolio, Best's says, "The mortgages seem of excellent quality." The corresponding statement concerning Gulf Life's mortgages is "The mortgages seem of good quality." The careful reader who is familiar with Best's "code" would interpret the latter statement to mean "Watch out!"

Two aspects of this procedure of "damning with faint praise" should be mentioned. First, Best's is an insurance trade publisher. Besides its *Best's Life Insurance Reports,* it publishes a monthly magazine and other items for consumption by the life insurance industry. It sells life insurance companies and other organizations a considerable amount of advertising in its magazine. It sells abridged reprints of its reports to the companies it recommends, so that such companies can distribute the reprints to their agents for subsequent distribution to policyholders and prospective policyholders. To avoid jeopardy to its advertising revenue and to enhance its sales of reprints and other items, the publisher must refrain from direct criticism of companies.

Second, there appears to be a feeling within Best's that direct criticism—"calling a spade a spade"—might lead to harassment of the publisher through libel suits by insurance companies who feel they have been criticized unjustly. Furthermore, it is felt that direct criticism of an insurance company in trouble might tend to magnify the difficulty and even destroy the company, which might otherwise survive the difficulty. These feelings may be justified, or they may be rationalizations of the firm's policy. In any case, it is important that you be aware of the fact that Best's reporting policies result in subtle rather than clearly stated information for buyers.

The technical details of the procedure by which Best's decides upon its recommendations and upon the various adjectives and adverbs have not been published and are not made available for scrutiny by outsiders. Nevertheless, the nature of its reports shows that Best's engages in careful financial analysis of companies, and it is a respected publishing firm. It is suggested that you utilize its recommendations, at least until something better becomes available.

Some of the companies not recommended by Best's probably are worthy of your patronage. But the absence of a recommendation should serve as a warning. In the absence of other strong evidence, it is suggested that you limit your choice of companies to those recommended in *Best's Life Insurance Reports.* Better yet, it is suggested that you consider limiting your choice to those 127 companies (listed in Appendix B) that received the most strongly worded form of recommendation.

Dunne's

The other firm that rates life insurance companies is Dunne's (Post Office Box 1738, Louisville, Kentucky), which also publishes an annual volume of reports on life insurance companies. This firm, despite the similarity of names, has no connection with the venerable Dun & Bradstreet.

In its 1970 edition, Dunne's reported on 1,167 companies. Of these, 791 were rated "A+ Excellent" and 376 were not rated. There is no such thing as an "A" rating or a "B" rating, let alone a "C," "D," or "F" rating. There is no such thing as a "Very Good" rating or a "Good" rating, let alone a "Fair" or "Poor" rating.

There were 408 companies that were both recommended by Best's and rated "A+ Excellent" by Dunne's. (Only 20 companies recommended by Best's were not rated by Dunne's.) You can expect many of these companies to place primary emphasis on their Dunne's rating, perhaps because they feel that the "A+ Excellent" label packs more wallop than the relatively wordy recommendation by Best's.

There were 383 companies that were rated "A+ Excellent" by Dunne's but not recommended at all by Best's. You can expect these companies to display their Dunne's rating quite extensively, through advertising and through the distribution of reprints purchased from Dunne's.

It is suggested that you disregard Dunne's ratings, because the ratings have been given to many companies that Best's has not recommended and because all of the companies rated by Dunne's have been given equal ratings. Furthermore, although it is possible that Dunne's engages in careful financial analysis of companies, the nature of its reports does not show evidence of that kind of work.

The saga of Century Life

The importance of financial strength, Best's technique of "damning with faint praise," and the need to exercise caution even in the face of a recommendation in Best's are all graphically illustrated by the story of the Century Life Insurance Company (Fort Worth, Texas). The situation described here is unusual in the life insurance business, but the story shows that it can happen.

Century Life was organized in 1938 and began business in 1939. The company was reported on in Best's beginning in the 1940 edition, but was not recommended by Best's until its 1950 edition. It was recommended each year from 1950 through 1968, although the recommendation was in the weakest possible language—"favorable" results and "considerable" over-all margins for contingencies.

In its 1969 edition, Best's reported on the company but did not recommend it. There were certain peculiarities in the company's financial statements (as of December 31, 1968), but there was no mention of these peculiarities in the narrative portions of Best's report. Although Best's recommendation had been withdrawn, it was impossible for a reader of the 1969 edition alone to know of the withdrawal. In short, there was no specific reference in the 1969 edition to either the withdrawal or whatever it was that caused the withdrawal after nineteen consecutive years of recommendations.

Century Life went out of business in 1969. In an effort to minimize the impact on policyholders, the Texas Insurance Department negotiated an arrangement under which the National Old Line Insurance Company (Little Rock, Arkansas) took over the assets and liabilities of Century Life. Because the assets were insufficient to cover the liabilities, two interest-bearing liens—one temporary and one permanent—were placed against the cash values of Century Life policies. The liens totalled approximately 35 percent of the cash values as of October 1, 1969, so that anyone discontinuing his policy at that time would have received approximately 65 percent of the cash value provided for in his contract. The effect of the liens was a substantial and unexpected price increase for the policyholders of Century Life.

No liens were placed against the death benefits, and the policyholders were given the opportunity to continue their coverage. Things could have been worse. For example, the policyholders could have been paid off at some fraction of their cash values and had their coverage terminated. This would have been particularly unfortunate for policyholders who were no longer insurable because of health problems or other complications. Presumably the Texas Insurance Department did the best it could with a bad situation.

The moral of the story is that you should check out the financial integrity of any company you are considering as carefully as you can. You will be running the least risk if you limit your choice to the companies listed in Appendix B.

Price

It is sometimes said that "you get what you pay for," the implication being that you get a better product or service if you pay a higher price. In life insurance, the phrase perhaps should be reworded to read, "the lower the price you pay, the better off you are likely to be." And there are very large price differences among life insurance companies for essentially the same coverage, despite what you may have heard about life insurance companies all charging pretty much the same price.

It was mentioned in the final section of Chapter 3 that the price of the protection in a policy is the sum of two items—the value of the protection element and the value of the company retention. Even among similar straight life contracts, however, the protection element values differ slightly. For that reason, it is slightly better to base your choice of a policy on the company retention, rather than on the sum of the two items representing the price of the protection.

In the final section of Chapter 3, it was also explained that the components of the straight life premiums may be shown in terms of twenty-year values expressed as of the policy issue date. The purpose of this section is to present that same kind of information for various straight life and five-year renewable term policies issued by a group of major life insurance companies.

The tables in this section and in Appendix D show figures for all those United States companies that had at least $3 billion of "ordinary" life insurance in force at the end of 1969 and were among those most strongly recommended in the 1970 edition of *Best's Life Insurance Reports.* Also included are all those Canadian companies that met the above requirements and operate in the United States. Forty-five companies were included in the study. (The word "ordinary" in this context refers to the kind of life insurance in which policies usually have a face amount of at least $1,000, and in which premiums other than the first usually are paid by mail. It is in contrast to "industrial" life insurance and "group" life insurance, which are discussed in Chapter 5.)

The data needed for the calculations were gathered, to the extent possible, from various sources.[1] The information was recorded on policy data forms and sent to the respective companies, with the request that they verify the figures and insert any missing figures.

All forty-five companies complied with the request. After the data had been assembled and the computations performed, each company was sent the computer output relating to its policies. It was accompanied by detailed instructions so that each company had the opportunity to check the accuracy of the keypunching, and, if desired, the accuracy of the computations.

Participating straight life

Table 4–1 shows data for $25,000 participating straight life policies issued in 1970 to 35-year-old men. The companies are listed in alphabetical order, and the name in each case is somewhat abbreviated. The complete name and home office location of each company are shown in Appendix B. The companies marked with an asterisk in Appendix B are the ones included in the price survey.

In the second column of Table 4–1, the name of the policy is shown by an abbreviation. The meanings of these abbreviations, not only for this table but also for all of the price tables in the book, are listed in Appendix C. For some companies, more than one policy is shown in a given table. Proper identification of the policy is important because companies frequently rank quite differently on one policy than on another. All of the policies shown in Table 4–1 are either straight life or minor modifications of straight life.

The other five columns in Table 4-1 show the values of the premiums, protection element, savings element, illustrated dividends, and company retention. In each instance, the figures are twenty-year values expressed as of the policy issue date, as explained in Chapter 3.

When you select a policy, you should consider primarily those that show relatively low company retention figures. A summary of the retention figures is shown at the end of the table. By looking at the summary, you can determine quickly whether a given policy has a relatively low retention, a relatively high retention, or a retention that falls near the middle.

The figures pertain only to the policies shown. No attempt should be made to generalize about a company from the one or two sets of data in the table. A couple of examples from the table may illustrate the significance of this point.

Consider the two John Hancock policies. The Signature 25 Life 95 contract has relatively large cash values, particularly in the early policy years. This accounts for the larger value of its savings element and for the slightly smaller value of its protection element, relative to the Preferred Whole Life Modified 3 contract. Along with the larger cash values, however, the Signature contract provides for higher premiums and lower dividends than the Modified 3 contract. The result is a company retention for the Signature contract $387 larger than that for the Modified 3 contract—a substantial difference. The Modified 3 contract is in the low-retention half of the array, while the Signature contract is near the high-retention end of the array. The point of the illustration is that generalizations about a company are difficult to make.

By way of contrast, consider the two National Life (Vermont) policies. The Policy for Executives and Professionals contract has somewhat larger cash values than the Ordinary Life contract. However, after the value of the premiums and the value of the dividends are also taken into account, the retentions for the two contracts are the same.

When you use tables such as 4–1, you should disregard small differences in company retention. In that table, for example, a difference of less than $200 could be disregarded because the dividend values are quite substantial to begin with and are not guaranteed. But when the company retention figures differ widely, you should assign such figures considerable weight in your decision.

Note the variation in company retention figures in Table 4–1. They range from $652 to $1,481, with a mean of $1,058. And the companies in the table are the big, well established ones. The differences shown are modest compared to those that would turn up if the analysis were expanded to cover many more companies.

It has been mentioned that the values of the illustrated dividends in Table 4–1 are quite substantial and are not guaranteed. If you are considering the purchase of participating straight life, therefore, you should check to see how the companies have performed relative to one another on the basis of historical dividends. To assist in this endeavor, Tables D–1, D–2, and D–3 (in Appendix D) have been assembled on the basis of historical dividends. These tables show figures similar to those in Table 4–1, except that the policies are those issued in 1950, 1940, and 1930. In each instance, the values cover just the first twenty policy years and are expressed as of the policy issue date, just as they are in Table 4–1, but the dividends used in

Table 4–1
*Values for $25,000 participating straight life policies issued in 1970
to men aged 35*

Company	Policy	Premiums	Protection Element	Savings Element	Illustrated Dividends	Company Retention
Aetna Life	WL	$5,722	$658	$2,522	$1,245	$1,296
Aetna Life	E95	5,891	649	2,621	1,521	1,100
American National	OL	5,555	649	2,537	988	1,381
American United	ESL95	5,661	647	2,561	1,343	1,111
Bankers Life (Iowa)	SpWL	4,416	662	2,361	635	758
Bankers Life (Iowa)	PWL	5,406	643	2,582	1,529	652
Canada Life	PL	5,112	647	2,553	910	1,002
Canada Life	ExPf	5,274	643	2,612	848	1,171
Confederation Life	WL	5,242	657	2,414	1,273	898
Confederation Life	SL85	5,631	632	2,767	1,305	928
Connecticut General	L90	5,254	638	2,691	642	1,283
Connecticut Mutual	WL	5,232	652	2,449	1,362	769
Continental Assurance	WL	5,734	646	2,572	1,417	1,099
Crown Life	SOL	4,411	672	2,198	633	908
Equitable (New York)	AWL	5,592	648	2,556	1,243	1,146
Franklin Life	ESWL	5,457	655	2,463	1,127	1,213
Great-West Life	EPWL	5,479	645	2,557	1,286	991
Guardian Life	POL	5,394	649	2,571	1,137	1,038
Home Life (New York)	WL	5,543	645	2,596	1,396	906
Jefferson Standard	WL	5,401	659	2,405	1,027	1,311
Jefferson Standard	L90	5,587	640	2,633	1,295	1,020
John Hancock	S25L95	5,739	643	2,714	1,043	1,340
John Hancock	PWLM3	5,402	647	2,602	1,200	953
Lincoln National	OL	5,627	649	2,532	1,322	1,123
Manufacturers Life	WL	4,695	673	2,191	845	985
Massachusetts Mutual	CL	5,668	640	2,645	1,530	853
Metropolitan Life	PL90	5,445	653	2,586	1,033	1,174
Mutual Benefit	OL	5,653	640	2,638	1,409	966
Mutual of New York	WL	5,475	650	2,584	1,098	1,143
National Life (Vermont)	OL	5,575	632	2,836	1,094	1,013
National Life (Vermont)	PEP	5,575	630	2,882	1,050	1,013
Nationwide Life	EE	5,428	643	2,597	1,269	919
New England Life	OL	5,624	642	2,639	1,357	985
New York Life	WL	5,597	653	2,475	1,428	1,042
North American (Canada)	WLIP	5,337	648	2,550	1,167	973
Northwestern Mutual	L90	5,666	638	2,687	1,533	808
Occidental (California)	PWL	5,502	644	2,595	1,073	1,190
Penn Mutual	WL	5,646	641	2,619	1,302	1,084
Phoenix Mutual	OL	5,607	637	2,799	1,055	1,115
Provident Mutual	WL	5,504	641	2,631	1,284	948
Provident Mutual	PLM2	4,994	653	2,448	1,046	846
Prudential	EWL	5,492	651	2,611	932	1,299

Table 4–1 — Continued

Company	Policy	Premiums	Protection Element	Savings Element	Illustrated Dividends	Company Retention
Republic National	L90	5,293	654	2,469	715	1,455
State Farm Life	SpOL	5,232	665	2,391	1,115	1,061
State Mutual	WL	5,541	641	2,633	1,427	841
Sun Life (Canada)	WL	5,612	655	2,478	1,577	902
Western & Southern	EP	5,700	646	2,583	990	1,481
Western & Southern	SE	5,707	655	2,517	1,264	1,272

SUMMARY

Company Retention	Number of Policies
$ 600–$ 699	1
700– 799	2
800– 899	5
900– 999	12
1,000– 1,099	9
1,100– 1,199	9
1,200– 1,299	5
1,300– 1,399	3
1,400– 1,499	2
	48

the calculations are those that were paid by the companies. The interest rates and probabilities used in the calculations are explained in Appendix H.

Table D–1 shows retention figures for $10,000 participating straight life policies issued in 1950. Table D–2 shows figures for $5,000 policies issued in 1940, and Table D–3 shows figures for $5,000 policies issued in 1930. (Today a $25,000 policy is considered fairly substantial. In 1950, a $10,000 policy was viewed in a similar fashion. And in 1940 and 1930, a $5,000 policy was considered fairly substantial. This was the reasoning behind the choice of face amounts for Tables D–1, D–2, and D–3.) Again, each table contains a retention summary that allows you to determine quickly where a policy is located.

Some companies show up well on the basis of historical dividends but poorly on the basis of illustrated dividends in 1970. Other companies show up poorly in terms of their track records but better in terms of 1970 illustrations. Ideally, you should choose among companies that show up well on both bases. Although illustrated dividends are not guaranteed and history does not necessarily repeat itself, a careful choice of company based on Tables 4–1, D–1, D–2, and D–3 is likely to be a good one.

Table 4–1 should be helpful if you have decided to buy a participating straight life policy, if you are around age 35, and if you are contemplating the purchase of a policy with a face amount of about $25,000. If you are much younger or much older than 35, you should consult Table D–4, which shows figures for age 25, or Table D–5, which shows figures for age 45. If you are contemplating a policy much smaller or much larger than $25,000, you should consult Table D–6, which shows figures for $10,000 policies, or Table D–7, which shows figures for $100,000 policies.

Nonparticipating straight life

Table 4–2 shows data for $25,000 nonparticipating straight life policies issued in 1970 to 35-year-old men. The table is constructed in the same manner as Table 4–1, except that the dividend column is omitted.

Note the variation in company retention figures in Table 4–2. They range from $779 to $1,502, with a mean of $1,251.

A special comment is in order concerning the Southwestern Life contract. The premiums are lower than most of the others, and the value of the savings element is large for a nonparticipating contract. The result is a company retention well below the nearest other contract in the table. At the time the data were being assembled, a company official informed me that they were no longer issuing the contract with the cash values shown in the 1970 trade publications. He sent me the revised data so that I was able to perform the calculations both ways. The company retention on the basis of the revised contract was $798, only slightly larger than the $779 figure shown in the table.

The results in Table 4–1 are based in part on illustrated dividends, which are not guaranteed; while the results in Table 4–2 are based entirely on contractually guaranteed figures. This brings us to a discussion of participating versus nonparticipating policies.

Generally, participating policies carry higher premiums than otherwise comparable nonparticipating policies, as shown by a comparison of the premium columns of Tables 4–1 and 4–2. Also, at least with respect to the fairly low-retention participating policies, the divi-

Table 4–2
*Values for $25,000 nonparticipating straight life policies
issued in 1970 to men aged 35*

Company	Policy	Premiums	Protection Element	Savings Element	Company Retention
Aetna Life	WL	$4,090	$663	$2,364	$1,063
American National	EWL	4,401	648	2,612	1,141
Business Men's	PWL	4,472	658	2,433	1,382
Connecticut General	OL	4,399	667	2,344	1,388
Continental Assurance	WL	4,328	662	2,352	1,314
Crown Life	LL90	4,149	676	2,129	1,343
Crown Life	EWL	3,806	680	2,070	1,056
Franklin Life	PPWL	4,421	664	2,358	1,399
Great-West Life	ESpWL	4,132	679	2,097	1,356
Jefferson Standard	WL	4,428	659	2,405	1,365
Jefferson Standard	L90	4,176	656	2,459	1,061
Lincoln National	OL	4,529	661	2,365	1,502
Lincoln National	L95	4,132	669	2,248	1,215
Manufacturers Life	WL	4,041	682	2,045	1,314
National Life & Acc.	WL	4,475	655	2,487	1,332
National Life & Acc.	WLP	4,396	655	2,487	1,254
Occidental (California)	C95	4,083	673	2,199	1,211
Provident Life & Acc.	WL	4,377	642	2,659	1,075
Republic National	L95	4,088	678	2,120	1,290
Southwestern Life	ES	4,019	648	2,592	779
Travelers	POL100	4,122	670	2,223	1,229
United Benefit	ExP	4,173	682	2,048	1,443

SUMMARY

Company Retention	Number of Policies
$ 700–$ 799	1
800– 899	0
900– 999	0
1,000– 1,099	4
1,100– 1,199	1
1,200– 1,299	5
1,300– 1,399	9
1,400– 1,499	1
1,500– 1,599	1
	22

dends generally more than offset the higher premiums. For example, the low-retention participating policies in Table 4–1 are below $900, while the low-retention nonparticipating policies in Table 4–2 are below $1,100.

The dividend values, however, are not guaranteed, and they are quite large. An important reason for my decision to show the elements of the retention figures, rather than the retention figures alone, was so that you could see the magnitude of the dividend values. Since most of the dividend values in Table 4–1 are in excess of $1,000, a reduction of only 20 percent would wipe out the entire retention advantage enjoyed by the participating contracts over the nonparticipating contracts. On the other hand, favorable developments might allow dividends to be increased, thus widening the retention advantage of the participating contracts.

In an earlier study, I compared participating policies and nonparticipating policies issued at various times in the past. In some cases, participating policies turned out better, on the average, but in other cases nonparticipating policies turned out better. It seemed to depend on the year of issue, and the study led me to suggest an approach that might be of help to you. If you think interest rates are going to remain fairly stable or increase significantly over the next ten or twenty years, you ought to buy participating insurance. If you think interest rates are going to decline significantly over the next ten or twenty years, however, you ought to buy nonparticipating insurance.[2]

This approach seems logical for two reasons. First, the interest factor is extremely important in cash-value policies. Second, the approach is consistent with the results of that earlier study. The approach does not answer the participating-nonparticipating question, since it requires a forecast of the trend in interest rates—a tough problem even if you own a crystal ball. But it does provide a framework within which to consider the question.

Nonparticipating insurance also protects the policyholder against the effects of increased taxation of insurance companies. Should you feel that insurance companies are likely to be taxed much more heavily in the future than they are now, you should consider buying nonparticipating insurance.

Whether you decide to buy a participating policy or a nonparticipating policy, you should seriously consider only those policies with relatively low retention figures. If you decide to go the participating route, you should also consult Tables D–1, D–2, and D–3, and observe the results based on historical dividends. If you decide to go the nonparticipating route, however, you need not consider historical results because the figures in Table 4–2 are based entirely on contractual guarantees.

Again, the figures in Table 4–2 should be helpful if you have decided to buy a nonparticipating straight life policy, if you are around age 35, and if you are contemplating the purchase of a policy with a face amount of about $25,000. If you are much younger or much older than 35, you should consult Table D–8, which shows figures for age 25, or Table D–9, which shows figures for age 45. If you are contemplating a policy much smaller or much larger than $25,000, you should consult Table D–10, which shows figures for $10,000 policies, or Table D–11, which shows figures for $100,000 policies.

Five-year renewable term

Table 4–3 shows data for $25,000 five-year renewable term policies issued in 1970 to 35-year-old men. The table is constructed in the same manner as are Tables 4–1 and 4–2.

The protection element and savings element columns are omitted from Table 4–3 because they are identical for all the policies. In each instance, the value of the protection element is $806 and the value of the savings element is $0.

Note the variation in company retention figures in Table 4–3. They range from $657 to $1,285, with a mean of $893.

Both participating and nonparticipating policies are shown in Table 4–3. The nonparticipating policies are those with a zero in the dividend column, and the others are participating policies. The dividends here are not nearly as significant as in participating straight life policies.

The company retention figures in Table 4–3 are not directly comparable to the corresponding figures in Tables 4–1 and 4–2. Because of the major differences between straight life policies and five-year renewable term policies, you should avoid any attempt at direct comparison of the figures. Your decisions on policy forms should be based on the approach described in Chapter 3, and not on differences in company retention.

In the case of five-year renewable term policies, the company retention figures reflect not only the expenses and profit of the company, but also the value of the renewal and conversion privileges built into the policies. The liberality of these privileges varies among the companies, and the value of the privileges is substantial. Since these features constitute an important element of noncomparability

Table 4–3
*Values for $25,000 five-year renewable term policies issued in 1970
to men aged 35*

(For all policies in this table, the value of the protection element is $806 and
the value of the savings element is $0.)

Company	Continuable to Age	Convertible to Age	Premiums	Illustrated Dividends	Company Retention
Aetna Life	65	60	$1,902	$ 0	$1,096
American National	65	65	2,091	0	1,285
American United	65	62	1,925	271	848
Bankers Life (Iowa)	70	65	2,032	476	750
Business Men's	65	62	1.909	0	1,103
Canada Life	65	62	1,991	319	866
Confederation Life	70	65	1,613	10	797
Connecticut General	70	70	1,804	0	998
Connecticut Mutual	70	68	1,888	216	866
Continental Assurance	70	65	1,916	0	1,110
Continental Assurance[a]	70	64	1,736	0	930
Crown Life	70	65	1,579	0	773
Equitable (New York)	70	65	1,961	314	841
Franklin Life[b]	—	—	—	—	—
Great-West Life	65	64	1,664	0	858
Guardian Life	70	70	1,965	275	883
Home Life (New York)	65	60	1,958	397	755
Jefferson Standard	65	63	2,040	0	1,234
John Hancock	65	62	2,067	496	765
Lincoln National	65	62	1,750	0	944
Manufacturers Life	70	65	1,654	0	848
Massachusetts Mutual	65	62	2,031	462	763
Metropolitan Life	70	65	2,112	503	803
Mutual Benefit	65	60	1,983	333	844
Mutual of New York	65	65	2,070	452	812
National Life & Acc.	65	63	1,970	0	1,164
National Life (Vermont)	65	62	2,099	555	738
Nationwide Life	70	60	2,163	357	1,000
New England Life	65	65	1,887	320	760
New York Life	70	70	2,033	528	698
North American (Canada)	70	65	1,531	0	725
Northwestern Mutual[b]	—	—	—	—	—
Occidental (California)	70	65	1,699	0	893
Penn Mutual	65	65	1,952	353	792
Phoenix Mutual	65	60	1,806	196	804
Provident Life & Acc.	65	62	2,029	0	1,223
Provident Mutual	65	65	1,886	249	831
Prudential	70	62	2,323	548	969
Republic National	65	62	1,740	0	934
Southwestern Life	70	65	1,765	0	959
State Farm Life	65	65	1,694	231	657

Table 4–3 – Continued

Company	Continuable to Age	Convertible to Age	Premiums	Illustrated Dividends	Company Retention
State Mutual	70	65	1,915	281	828
Sun Life (Canada)	70	65	1,571	0	765
Travelers	70	70	1,810	0	1,004
United Benefit	65	65	1,674	0	868
Western & Southern[c]	—	—	—	—	—

[a] Executerm 4/6 policy. First term is four years; subsequent terms are six years.
[b] Company does not issue a five-year renewable term policy.
[c] Company's policy is not convertible until age 65.

SUMMARY

Company Retention	Number of Policies
$ 600–$ 699	2
700– 799	11
800– 899	15
900– 999	6
1,000– 1,099	3
1,100– 1,199	3
1,200– 1,299	3
	43

among the retention figures, some information on renewability and convertibility is shown in Table 4–3.

The second column shows the last age to which the term policy may be continued without evidence of insurability, assuming that the policy is issued at one of the quinquennial ages (such as 25, 30, 35, 40, and so forth). The third column shows the last age at which the term policy may be converted to another plan of insurance (such as straight life) without evidence of insurability. When you buy a term policy, it is important that you be aware of this information, as well as certain other aspects of the contract. These points are discussed in Chapter 7.

The comments above lead to another aspect of the information in Table 4–3. Since the conversion privilege is an important element in term insurance, you should consider not only the retention figures on term policies but also the retention figures on straight life policies. For example, suppose you anticipate having a preference for participating straight life when and if you convert your term policy. In that case, you should look for more than a low-retention term policy. You should make sure that the company offers participating straight life (several of the companies in Table 4–3 do not, as evidenced by their absence from Table 4–1). Also, you should consider the relative position of the company's policies in Tables 4–1, D–1, D–2, and D–3. The conversion privilege becomes very valuable if something impairs your ability to qualify for life insurance. You should try to maximize the value of the conversion privilege by selecting carefully the company in which you buy term insurance.

Again, the figures in Table 4–3 should be helpful if you have decided to buy a five-year renewable term policy, if you are around age 35, and if you are contemplating the purchase of a policy with a face amount of about $25,000. If you are much younger or much older than 35, you should consult Table D–12, which shows figures for age 25, or Table D–13, which shows figures for age 45. If you are contemplating a policy much smaller or much larger than $25,000, you should consult Table D–14, which shows figures for $10,000 policies, or Table D–15, which shows figures for $100,000 policies.

In summary, when you buy term insurance, you should follow these steps:

- Consider primarily those companies that show relatively low retentions in Table 4–3.
- Examine the renewal and conversion privileges carefully.
- Consider primarily those companies that show relatively low retentions on straight life policies in Tables 4–1, D–1, D–2, and D–3, or in Table 4–2, depending on your preference in the event of conversion.

General comments about the tables

The various tables in this chapter and in Appendix D contain a considerable amount of valuable data. The remainder of the chapter is devoted to additional information about the tables, so that you will be in a better position to utilize the data effectively. It is suggested that you read all of the material, but if you prefer not to read all of it, the subtitles will help you select the areas that most concern you.

Nature of the "values."—Each of the dollar figures in the various tables is the value (present expected value) for the entire contract for the first twenty policy years, expressed as of the policy issue date. In the calculation of these values, both interest and probabilities are taken into account. For example, suppose that two participating policies you are considering—Policies A and B—show retention figures of $800 and $1,200, respectively. If you buy Policy B, and if you assume that the illustrated dividends are paid, it would be comparable to buying Policy A and plunking down an additional $400—cash on the barrelhead—at the time of issue.

It is suggested that you view the difference in retention between any two policies in absolute rather than relative terms—that is, in dollars rather than in percentages. The reason for this suggestion is that a change in the assumptions used in calculating the retention figures often causes a substantial change in the percentage difference but often little change in the absolute difference. To illustrate, let's assume that 5 percent interest was used in calculating the retention figures of $800 and $1,200. The absolute difference between Policies A and B is $400, and Policy B has a retention 50 percent larger than that of Policy A. If the figures were recalculated using 4 percent interest, the retentions might drop to $500 and $900, respectively. The absolute difference still would be $400, but Policy B's retention now would be 80 percent higher than that of Policy A. You are less likely to misinterpret differences in retention if you consider only the absolute or dollar differences.

Also, each of the values in the various tables was calculated from the buyer's point of view; that is, the interest, mortality, and lapse assumptions used in the calculations were selected by the author as reasonable from the buyer's point of view. They bear no necessary relationship to the actual experience of any one company or the assumptions used by any one company in the calculation of its premiums, cash values, and dividends.

Conversion of twenty-year values.—You may prefer to think in terms of yearly figures, rather than values representing the entire twenty-year period. To obtain an approximation of the yearly equivalents of the various values, divide the latter by 10. (The precise levelling factors are given later.) *Under no circumstances should you divide the twenty-year values by 20.*

The reason you should not divide by 20 may be explained by an analogy. Suppose you borrow $20,000 at an interest rate of 5 percent, and plan to repay the loan in twenty equal annual installments, with each payment to be made at the end of the year. If you divide the $20,000 by 20, the resulting annual payments of $1,000 would be too small and would not take account of interest. So you would divide the $20,000 by a smaller number (12.4622) obtained from a table of compound interest factors, and the resulting figure ($1,604.85) would be the appropriate annual payment including interest.

The twenty-year values under discussion here are expressed as of the policy issue date and take account of both interest and probabilities. To determine a yearly equivalent of such a twenty-year value, therefore, you must divide by a number that reflects both interest and probabilities. For the policies issued in 1970 to 35-year-olds (Tables 4–1, 4–2, 4–3, D–6, D–7, D–10, D–11, D–14, and D–15), the appropriate levelling factor is 9.8023. For the policies issued in 1970 to 25-year-olds (Tables D–4, D–8, and D–12), the factor is 9.8958. For the policies issued in 1970 to 45-year-olds (Tables D–5, D–9, and D–13), the factor is 9.4526.

For the tables based on historical dividends, different factors are appropriate because different interest rates were used in the calculation of the values. For the policies issued in 1950 (Table D–1), the appropriate levelling factor is 11.4182. For the policies issued in 1940 (Table D–2), the factor is 12.3327. For the policies issued in 1930 (Table D–3), the factor is 11.5840.

To illustrate, consider a policy with a company retention figure of $800. If you are interested in the yearly equivalent of that figure, divide the $800 by 10 (or, more precisely, by 9.8023 if the policy was issued in 1970 at age 35). The resulting figure of $80 is the approximate yearly retention.

You might prefer to reduce the values to a "per $1,000 of face amount" basis. This may be accomplished by dividing any of the twenty-year values by the number of thousands of dollars of face amount. For example, assume that the $800 retention figure applied to a $25,000 policy. Divide the $800 by 25, and the resulting figure of $32 is the retention per $1,000 of face amount.

Finally, you might prefer to reduce the values to a "per year per $1,000 of face amount" basis. This may be accomplished by reducing the twenty-year values to yearly figures and then dividing the results by the number of thousands of dollars of face amount. For example, we have already described the manner in which the $800 retention may be reduced to a yearly figure of about $80. Divide the $80 by 25, and the resulting figure of $3.20 is the approximate retention per year per $1,000 of face amount.

Data not in the tables.—The tables in this chapter and in Appendix D include data for only forty-five of the nearly 2,000 companies operating in the United States. What would happen to the range of retention figures in a given table if more companies were included? The range would increase substantially.

For example, the retention figures in Table 4–1 range from $652 to $1,481. Recently I had occasion to analyze the Pyramid III contract issued by Alexander Hamilton Life Insurance Company of America (Farmington, Michigan). The contract is a participating straight life policy with certain additional guaranteed payments. The retention for a $25,000 Pyramid III contract issued to men aged 35, with the additional payments taken into consideration, is $2,724— more than $2,000 above the lowest-retention policy and more than $1,200 above the highest-retention policy in Table 4–1.

If a company is not among the forty-five for which price information has been assembled in this book, an agent of the company might attempt to tell you what the corresponding figures would be for his company. *Do not accept such figures as reliable unless they are given to you in writing and over the signature of an officer of the company.* The figures shown in Tables 4–1, 4–2, 4–3, and D–1 through D–15 are based on extensive calculations, the technical details of which are explained fully in Appendix H. The purpose of the explanation there is to allow persons knowledgeable in life insurance arithmetic to duplicate the calculations. Most agents, however, are not equipped to perform such calculations.

Currency of the data.—The data in the tables in this chapter and in Tables D–4 through D–15 were calculated from policy information appearing in the 1970 editions of various trade publications. Even before this book was completed, however, some of the companies had made changes. Therefore, the data shown here should be used only to approximate the relative positions of the various companies' policies.

Since life insurance is a long-term business, the data shown here should provide reliable guidance for a number of years. For example, most of the companies with low-retention policies in the tables in this chapter also showed up favorably in an earlier study based on 1962 policy information.[3]

Should an agent insist that his company has since improved its standing, you might ask him to furnish the more current figures corresponding to those in the tables. Again, be sure to get the figures in writing over the signature of a company officer.

Nonsmoker discounts.—In the midst of the furor in recent years about the hazards of cigarette smoking, a few companies have begun to offer discounts for persons who do not smoke. Such discounts are not reflected in the calculations for this book but are worth taking into consideration. Among the forty-five companies for which price data were assembled in this book, those offering some sort of special arrangement for nonsmokers are American National, Guardian Life, Home Life (New York), Phoenix Mutual, and State Mutual.[4]

If you are a nonsmoker and if you are dealing with a company that offers a discount for nonsmokers, find out the amount of the annual premium reduction per $1,000 of face amount. Multiply that figure by the number of thousands of dollars of face amount you are contemplating, and then multiply the result by 10. (To be more precise, the latter multiplication should be by the levelling factors of 9.8958, 9.8023, or 9.4526 for ages 25, 35, or 45, respectively.) The final product is the amount by which the premium figures and retention figures in the various price tables should be reduced to show the effect of the nonsmoker discount.

To illustrate, suppose you are buying $25,000 of participating straight life at age 35, you qualify for a nonsmoker discount, and the company reduces its annual premium for nonsmokers by 70 cents per $1,000 of face amount. First, multiply the 70 cents by 25 (the number of thousands of dollars of face amount), and then multiply the product by 9.8023 (the appropriate levelling factor). The result is about $172, which is the amount you should subtract from the company's premium and retention figures in Table 4–1.

These comments are based on the assumption that the company pays the same dividends on its nonsmoker policies and its regular policies. When the company pays different dividends, the figures in the tables in this book cannot be adjusted readily. You should handle such a situation in the manner described earlier for data not in the tables.

Fractional premiums.—Annual premiums were used in the calculations in this book. Companies vary widely with respect to their carrying charges for semi-annual, quarterly, and monthly premiums. Should you plan to pay premiums other than annually, consider these carrying charges. This topic is discussed in Chapter 8.

Waiver-of-premium adjustments.—The waiver-of-premium rider was discussed in Chapter 3. The cost of this rider was not included in the premiums used in the calculations for this book.

Some of the companies include the cost of the waiver-of-premium benefit automatically in their premiums. In those cases, the companies were asked to provide the author with figures representing the cost of the waiver-of-premium benefit, and these amounts were deducted from those companies' premiums before the calculations were performed.

Age-last-birthday adjustments.—Most of the companies classify a policyholder by his age at his nearest birthday. Some companies, however, use the age at the last birthday. On the average, assuming a random distribution of applicants by date of birth and date of application, the policyholders at any given age in an age-last-birthday company would be about six months older than the policyholders at the corresponding age in an age-nearest-birthday company.

To compensate for this element of noncomparability, the author gathered policy information for ages 34 and 35 in the case of age-last-birthday companies. Then an average was calculated for each pair of figures, and the resulting set of policy information was used in the calculations. Similar adjustments were made for the age 25 and age 45 data in Appendix D.

Price measurement methods.—You may hear it said that there are many ways to measure the price of life insurance. Actually, there is general agreement that the price is what the policyholder pays in minus what he gets back. The problem is to evaluate what he pays in and what he gets back.

The so-called traditional net cost method, which is widely used by life insurance companies and agents, is the simple total of what the policyholder pays in minus the simple total of what he gets back. The calculation fails to consider either interest or probabilities. The method not only understates the price, but also distorts comparisons even among similar policies.

The "interest adjusted method" is the same as the traditional net cost method except that interest is taken into account. This method, which was recommended by a prestigious industry committee (discussed in Chapter 10), is slowly gaining some acceptance. Numerous companies are furnishing interest adjusted cost figures to their agents. And a major publisher has assembled interest adjusted cost figures for the policies of many companies.[5] Unfortunately, the volume costs $25, and it contains no information on term insurance. Moreover, the data are arranged by company, rather than by policy; this arrangement makes it difficult to see comparative figures quickly.

The interest adjusted method was not used in this book primarily for two reasons. First, the interest adjusted method fails to show the four major components of the premiums. Such information is of critical importance in deciding on the type of policy to buy, as explained in Chapter 3.

Second, the method fails to take account of the probabilities of death and lapse. One result of this omission is that some companies may enjoy an unfair competitive advantage by deferring the payment of large dividends until relatively late in the usual twenty-year period of analysis. The benefit to the companies stems from the fact that the bigger dividends in the later years are paid to fewer policyholders, because some die and many discontinue their policies in the early years.

The "retention method" is used in this book. It is the same as the other methods, except that it takes account of both interest and probabilities in evaluating what the policyholder pays in and what he gets back.

Stocks versus mutuals.—Most of the life insurance in the United States is sold either by stock companies or by mutual companies. A stock life insurance company is a corporation in which there are stockholders. A mutual life insurance company is a corporation in which there are no stockholders.

Some people argue that the mutual companies offer lower prices to their policyholders because there are no stockholders to take a cut. Implicit in such a view is the notion that other things are equal, but they never are. In Table 4–1, for example, some mutual companies' policies are at the high-retention end of the array. Also, although the policyholders in a mutual company are supposed to elect the members of the board of directors, policyholders do not have any effective control over such elections.

Some people argue that mutual companies are an anachronism in a capitalistic society. Nevertheless, mutual companies pay federal income taxes under the same law as stock companies, and they pay state premium taxes under the same laws as stock companies. Also, mutual companies pay large salaries to their top officials, and the prospect of even larger salaries certainly provides a profit motive.

Mutual companies usually are associated with participating life insurance; however, a few mutuals also sell nonparticipating insurance. Stock companies usually are associated with nonparticipating life insurance; however, many if not most stock companies also sell participating policies, and a few sell only participating policies. Thus, your decision on whether to buy participating or nonparticipating insurance is quite different from a decision with respect to stock companies versus mutual companies.

Other than the presence or absence of stockholders, differences between these two forms of organization are hard to identify. The prospective buyer should not be concerned about whether a company is stock or mutual. For example, if you decide to buy $25,000 of participating straight life, you should consider primarily those companies whose policies have low retentions in Tables 4–1, D–1, D–2, and D–3, regardless of their form of organization. For this reason, the various tables in this chapter and in Appendix D do not indicate whether the companies are stock or mutual in form.

Pro rata refund of premium.—Some companies pay at death, in addition to the face amount of the policy, the unearned portion of the premium. Suppose, for example, the policyholder pays a $400 annual premium on its due date and then dies three months later. In this example, about three-fourths of the premium, or $300, would be paid in addition to the face amount.

The pro rata premium refund practice was not taken into account in the calculations for this book. Thus, the figures penalize slightly those companies that make the extra payment. The adjustment was not made because the effect was considered inconsequential. For example, in Table 4–1, the adjustment would have increased the value of the protection element and decreased the value of the company retention by about $9 for those companies that make the extra payment.

Terminal dividends.—Some of the companies that issue participating policies pay so-called terminal dividends in addition to annual dividends. In most cases, terminal dividends are payable when the policy terminates—whether by death or discontinuation—provided the policy has been in force for some minimum period, such as ten or fifteen years. Terminal dividends were taken into account in the calculations. The procedure is shown in the explanation in Appendix H.

Rounding.—All of the values in the various tables are rounded to the nearest dollar. Such rounded figures are sufficiently accurate, and this procedure saved a great deal of space in the tables. However, such rounding produces some apparent discrepancies. For example, when the values of the protection element, savings element, dividends, and company retention are added, the sum may differ from the value of the premiums by $1 (or, in a few instances, $2). Such discrepancies should be disregarded.

Chapter 5

Other sources and forms

The material in Chapters 3 and 4 on policy types and the selection of a company dealt only with straight life and five-year renewable term policies sold by companies that operate through agents. In the present chapter, several other sources of life insurance are discussed, including a few organizations that operate without agents, certain government agencies, group life insurance, and other sources of individual life insurance. The final section of the chapter describes several forms of individual life insurance other than straight life and five-year renewable term.

Non-agency organizations

The absence of agents is no guarantee of low prices, but some non-agency organizations do offer low-priced life insurance. In this section, information is presented relative to savings bank life insurance, the Teachers Insurance and Annuity Association, and the Ministers Life and Casualty Union. Included in the brief description of each organization are retention figures comparable to those shown in Chapter 4 for policies issued by the major agency companies.

Undoubtedly there are other non-agency organizations worthy of inclusion, but no current survey of them was undertaken. Those mentioned above were asked for policy information in connection with this book because they cooperated in an earlier study by the author and were found at that time to deliver low-priced life insurance coverage.[1]

Watch out for companies that solicit by direct mail or by newspaper advertisements. Many of these companies are not worthy of your serious consideration. Frequently they state or imply that they charge low prices because they do not employ agents, but upon analysis their prices may be quite high. Moreover, many of these companies do not qualify for a policyholders' recommendation in *Best's Life Insurance Reports*.

Savings bank life insurance

Life insurance is offered over the counter in mutual savings banks in three states—Massachusetts, New York, and Connecticut. To be eligible for savings bank life insurance (SBLI), a person must be either residing or working regularly in the particular state when the policy is purchased. The amount that may be purchased in this manner is strictly limited by the laws that permit SBLI.

The SBLI organizations are commented upon in *Best's Life Insurance Reports*, but no policyholders' recommendations are included. It is the author's understanding that the Alfred M. Best Company considers its analytical procedure to be inapplicable to SBLI organizations. Moreover, an independent authority on SBLI has stated that ". . . there seems to be no question but what each policyholder is adequately protected. . . ."[2] Under these circumstances, it appears that SBLI should be considered an exception to the general rule that the buyer should be wary in dealing with companies not recommended in *Best's Life Insurance Reports.*

Massachusetts SBLI, the oldest of the three organizations, went into operation in 1908. The system limit that may be issued on any one life is $1,000 times the number of banks offering the coverage. At present there are forty-one banks, so the system limit is $41,000. There is also a policy limit of $5,000, so a buyer desiring the maximum would have to obtain several policies; however, he may obtain them from one bank.

The retention for a $25,000 participating straight life policy issued in 1970 to men aged 35 by Massachusetts SBLI is $319. This is directly comparable to the retention figures in Table 4–1, which range from $652 to $1,481. Clearly, the Massachusetts SBLI policy retention is well below all of the forty-eight agency companies' policies shown in that table.

The retention for a $25,000 five-year renewable term policy issued in 1970 to men aged 35 by Massachusetts SBLI is $247. This is directly comparable to the retention figures in Table 4–3, which range from $657 to $1,285. Again, the Massachusetts SBLI policy retention is well below all of the forty-three agency companies' policies shown.

The breakdown of these retention figures, and additional Massachusetts SBLI data corresponding to the additional tables of price information in Appendix D, are shown in Appendix E.

New York SBLI went into operation in 1939. The system limit that may be issued on any one life is $30,000.

The retention for a $25,000 participating straight life policy issued in 1970 to men aged 35 by New York SBLI is $590. Although this is somewhat higher than the corresponding Massachusetts SBLI figure, it is below all of the forty-eight agency companies' policies shown in Table 4–1.

The retention for a $25,000 five-year renewable term policy issued in 1970 to men aged 35 by New York SBLI is $375. Again, this is somewhat higher than the corresponding Massachusetts SBLI figure, but it is below all of the forty-three agency companies' policies shown in Table 4–3.

The breakdown of these retention figures, and additional New

York SBLI data corresponding to the additional tables of price information in Appendix D, are shown in Appendix E.

Connecticut SBLI went into operation in 1942. The maximum amount that may be issued on any one life is $5,000.

Because of this relatively low limit, retention figures comparable to those in Chapter 4 cannot be shown. In an earlier study based on comparisons of $5,000 policies, however, the author found that the retention on Connecticut SBLI policies was somewhat above the corresponding figures for policies of Massachusetts SBLI and New York SBLI. They were also somewhat above the corresponding figures for the lowest retention policies among the major agency companies, but were below the corresponding figures for the policies of most of the major agency companies.[3]

Teachers Insurance and Annuity Association

Teachers Insurance and Annuity Association (TIAA), together with its companion organization, College Retirement Equities Fund, provides retirement plans for persons employed by colleges, universities, and certain other educational institutions. In addition, it offers individual life insurance to such persons and their spouses.

TIAA handles its life insurance operations by mail. Its address is 730 Third Avenue, New York, New York 10017.

The retention for a $25,000 participating straight life policy issued in 1970 to men aged 35 by TIAA is $49. This is a very low retention figure. It is far below the corresponding figures for all of the forty-eight agency companies' policies shown in Table 4–1, and well below the SBLI figures mentioned earlier in this section.

The retention for a $25,000 five-year renewable term policy issued in 1970 to men aged 35 by TIAA is $394. This figure is well below all of the forty-three agency companies' policies shown in Table 4–3.

The breakdown of these retention figures, and additional TIAA data corresponding to the additional tables of price information in Appendix D, are shown in Appendix E.

Among the TIAA data shown in Appendix E are two retention figures that are negative. These, together with the very low retention figure referred to above, illustrate an important point that bears repeating. The interest, mortality, and lapse assumptions used in the calculations were selected by the author as reasonable from the buyer's point of view. Thus, it is entirely possible for a company to enjoy experience more favorable than the combination of interest, mortality, and lapse assumptions used by the author in the calculations for this book.

Ministers Life and Casualty Union

The Ministers Life and Casualty Union offers life insurance to clergymen, certain other persons engaged primarily in religious work, and members of their immediate families. For many years the Ministers Life handled its business by mail, but in recent years has begun to transact business through agents as well. Its address is 3100 West Lake Street, Minneapolis, Minnesota 55416. It is recommended in the 1971 edition of *Best's Life Insurance Reports,* but in language slightly less than the strongest.

The retention for a $25,000 participating straight life policy issued in 1970 to men aged 35 by Ministers Life is $457. This figure is well below all of the forty-eight agency companies' policies shown in Table 4–1. The breakdown of the retention figure, and additional data corresponding to the additional tables of price information in Appendix D, are shown in Appendix E. The Ministers Life does not offer five-year renewable term.

Government agencies

Outside the private sector, life insurance is available through certain government agencies. Among these are the Social Security Administration, the Veterans Administration, and the Wisconsin State Life Fund.

Social Security

Nearly all Americans employed full-time are covered by Social Security. The program provides substantial life insurance benefits, particularly when the worker has young children. The level of these survivors' benefits makes Social Security an important part of the typical worker's life insurance program. Examples of these benefits, together with suggestions on how to obtain detailed information on the Social Security benefits for which you are eligible, are found in Chapter 2.

Veterans Administration

Servicemen and veterans have long enjoyed some form of government subsidized life insurance as one of the financial rewards for wartime service to the United States. The details of these coverages constitute a long and complex story, but an attempt is made in the following paragraphs to summarize the essential points.

Servicemen and veterans of World War I were offered up to $10,000 of United States Government Life Insurance (USGLI). Similarly, servicemen and veterans of World War II were offered up to $10,000 of National Service Life Insurance (NSLI). Both of these coverages were written through government agencies. Both were (and are) heavily subsidized, since claims arising from service-connected deaths, as well as the administrative expenses of the programs, were (and are) handled from general revenues rather than from the insurance funds. As a result, both coverages were extremely low-priced, and the only servicemen and veterans who failed to take full advantage of the insurance were those who had no need for life insurance, those who did not realize or were misinformed about the magnitude of the bargain to which they had access, and those who could not pay the premiums. Unfortunately, insurance-in-force figures on USGLI and NSLI suggest that these three categories together comprise the majority of those who were eligible for the coverages.

Servicemen in the Korean War were provided with $10,000 of life insurance at no cost to them. Upon discharge, they were offered the opportunity to obtain up to $10,000 of a new form of NSLI. Although not as favorable in certain respects as the coverages made available to their World War I and World War II counterparts, the newer NSLI was still a low-priced, subsidized form of coverage.

Servicemen in the Vietnam War are provided with $15,000 of life insurance for $3 per month, with premiums handled by payroll deduction. The coverage is optional, in that the serviceman may elect $10,000 (for $2 per month), $5,000 (for $1), or none. The insurance is written by a syndicate of more than five hundred life insurance companies, with the administration handled by the Prudential. The program is subsidized by the federal government, which reimburses the syndicate for claims arising from service-connected deaths. The overwhelming majority of servicemen have the maximum coverage under the program, although the excellent participation may be attributed to the "negative enrollment" technique. This means that the serviceman is automatically covered for the maximum unless he takes action to elect either less than the maximum or no insurance at all.

Following discharge, the Vietnam veteran has 120 days within which to convert all or part of his coverage without evidence of insurability. Unlike the veterans of earlier wars, however, he must buy a cash-value form of insurance. He cannot purchase term insurance, even if term is the most appropriate for his circumstances.

Also, unlike the veterans of earlier wars, he must buy the coverage from a life insurance company rather than from a government agency. He has his choice among a substantial number of companies that operate in his home state and are authorized to convert his coverage. He pays the regular rates of the company he selects, and the government subsidizes the program to the extent of the extra claims attributable to service-connected deaths.

When the Vietnam veteran inquires about his conversion privilege, he is furnished with an alphabetical list of 609 authorized companies. The requirements that must be met by the companies to qualify are minimal. No information about the financial strength of the companies is given to the veteran. Nor is he given any price information. In 1969, Senator Philip A. Hart (D., Mich.), chairman of the Subcommittee on Antitrust and Monopoly of the Senate's Committee on the Judiciary, asked the Veterans Administration to assemble life insurance price information and disseminate it to Vietnam veterans. The VA declined to do so.

In short, Vietnam veterans do not have access to heavily subsidized government life insurance of the type available to veterans of earlier wars. They do not have access to term insurance under the program, as the veterans of earlier wars had. (A bill presently being considered by Congress would provide five years of low-cost term insurance for Vietnam veterans, after which conversion would be available as described above.) And they have not been provided with price information that would allow them to select the companies offering relatively low-priced coverage.

Wisconsin State Life Fund

The Wisconsin State Life Fund is a state-operated organization that offers individual life insurance to persons in Wisconsin at the time the insurance is granted. Its operations are handled by mail, and its address is 4802 Sheboygan Avenue, Madison, Wisconsin 53702.

The maximum amount that may be issued on any one life is $10,000. Because of this limit, retention figures comparable to those in Chapter 4 cannot be shown. Furthermore, data for the State Life

Fund on most of the smaller policies of the type shown in Appendix
D were not sufficiently complete for the author's calculations. On the
basis of estimated results, however, the author has concluded that
the retentions for the participating straight life policies offered by
the State Life Fund are somewhat below the corresponding figures
for all of the major agency companies' policies shown. The State Life
Fund does not offer five-year renewable term policies.

Group life insurance

This book deals primarily with "individual life insurance"—that is,
life insurance purchased by individuals. This is in contrast to "group
life insurance," which in its most common form is purchased by an
employer to cover his employees. In this section, several forms of
group life insurance are discussed briefly.

Employer group life

Virtually all large employers and many small employers offer some
form of group life insurance to their employees. In terms of the way
in which it is paid for, there are two categories of group life
insurance—"noncontributory" and "contributory."

A noncontributory group life plan is one in which the employees
pay nothing. The entire cost of the plan is borne by the employer.
If you are an eligible employee, you are automatically covered in a
noncontributory plan.

A contributory group life plan is one in which the employees pay
a portion of the cost. The remainder of the cost is borne by the
employer. Most contributory plans provide that eligible employees
may enroll or refrain from enrolling for the coverage. If an employee
wishes to secure the coverage without evidence of insurability, however, he usually must enroll when he first becomes eligible or during
some special enrollment period announced by his employer.

Most group life plans consist of one-year renewable term insurance. The insurance company calculates the employer's premium on
the basis of amounts of insurance and ages of the covered employees.
However, the employees in many contributory plans pay a flat
amount per month per $1,000 of coverage regardless of age. The
maximum is 60 cents, except in hazardous occupations, but some
employers charge less.

The effect of the flat rate is that the older employees get a real bargain. The younger employees sometimes pay as much as they would to obtain individual one-year renewable term coverage, or perhaps a bit more. However, the flat contribution rate means that the price tends to look increasingly attractive as the years go by.

Perhaps the best way to view such a plan is that the older employees receive a substantial subsidy from the employer, while the younger employees pretty much pay their own way. Only the very young employees are effectively being overcharged relative to open market prices, and even there the amount of the overcharge usually is not enough to get concerned about.

An important aspect of group plans is the conversion privilege. Should your coverage terminate because you leave your employer or retire, such plans provide that you may convert to individual coverage within thirty days of the termination, without evidence of insurability. When you convert, you must pay the premium rate associated with your age at the time of conversion, but you can get the insurance with no questions asked. It would be a good idea to check on your conversion privilege now, so that you will know what to expect when your coverage terminates.

Some group life plans are written on a cash-value basis. These are rare, however, and are beyond the scope of this discussion.[4]

It is suggested that you enroll for the group life coverage made available by your employer. As a general rule, such coverage is reasonably priced from the employee's point of view.

Credit life

Many lending institutions have arranged for insurance on the lives of their borrowers. Usually this so-called credit life insurance is on a group basis and provides that any remaining indebtedness is cancelled at the death of the borrower.

In some instances credit life insurance is included automatically in loan transactions "without any specific extra charge." This is the case, for example, in many credit unions.

In most instances, however, credit life insurance is optional with the borrower, and he pays a specific premium for the coverage. There are some serious problems with this form of insurance.

First, the premium is designed so that the borrowers as a group will pay more than the cost of the coverage. The excess is then returned to the lender by the insurance company as a dividend or commission. (In some instances the insurance company itself is a wholly-owned subsidiary of the lending institution.) From the viewpoint of borrowers, therefore, credit life insurance is likely to be more expensive than employer group life, in which the employer pays at least a portion of the cost.

Second, the general nature of credit life insurance has led to a phenomenon referred to as "reverse competition." When insurance companies bid for the credit life insurance business of a lending institution, frequently the focus is upon the size of the dividend or commission to the lender, rather than upon the premium. The lender tends to buy the coverage from the insurance company that offers the largest dividend or commission, rather than from the insurance company that offers the lowest premium. Since the insurance company offering the largest dividend or commission is likely to be the one that charges the highest premium, the effect of the competition is to *increase* the cost of the coverage to the borrower—hence the phrase "reverse competition."

Third, although the coverage is optional with borrowers, lenders often give the impression that the coverage is mandatory. Thus, borrowers often enroll for the coverage without realizing it is optional and without knowing how its cost compares with other forms of insurance.

These problem areas are well known in the insurance business, and credit life insurance rates are subject to regulation by various state insurance commissioners. As in other areas, however, regulation is uneven and spotty.

Since credit life insurance usually is available without evidence of insurability, it should be considered seriously by someone with insurability problems. The net effect of credit life insurance, however, is to increase the effective rate of interest charged by the lender. You should include an appropriate provision for debts in the determination of your life insurance needs, as suggested in Chapter 2, and then decline to buy credit life insurance when you borrow.

Association group life

Many professional associations and other organizations make life insurance available to their members. Such coverage has some characteristics of individual life insurance and some characteristics of group life insurance.

Association group life coverage usually is term insurance. Premium rates are based on age and usually increase periodically as the individual gets older. The cost of the coverage is borne entirely by the member, who receives premium notices directly from the insurance company. Sometimes the premiums are set high enough so that the insurance company can pay dividends to the association, in which case the purchase of the coverage by a member is an indirect way of making a modest contribution to the organization. Often there is a requirement that the member show evidence of insurability in order to qualify for the coverage, and the available amounts are strictly limited.

Because the member pays the entire cost, association group life usually is more expensive than employer group life, in which at least a part of the cost has to be borne by the employer. The coverage may be less expensive than individual term life insurance, although this point should be checked.

Association group life coverage is not as flexible as a good five-year renewable term contract issued on an individual basis. Often the coverage can be continued only if you remain a member of the organization. The coverage can be terminated by the organization or by the insurance company. Unlike individual term policies, association group coverage may not be convertible. (The conversion privilege in individual term policies is explained in Chapter 7.)

Association group coverage is worth considering if you are a member of an organization that offers such coverage and if you intend to remain a member for a long period of time. Before enrolling, however, you should check the cost and terms of the coverage. Even then, if you decide to buy, you should not rely heavily upon association group coverage as a part of your life insurance program, because the coverage may be terminated for reasons beyond your control.

Other sources of individual life insurance

This book deals primarily with "ordinary life insurance" sold by "commercial companies." In this section, however, reference is made to "industrial life insurance" and also to "fraternal benefit societies."

Industrial life insurance

The word "ordinary" refers to the kind of life insurance in which policies usually have a face amount of at least $1,000, and in which premiums other than the first usually are paid by mail on an annual, semi-annual, quarterly, or monthly basis. In contrast, the word "industrial" refers to the kind of life insurance in which policies usually have a face amount smaller than $1,000, and in which premiums usually are collected at the homes of policyholders on a monthly or weekly basis.

Industrial insurance usually is sold to low-income persons who need the discipline of frequent premium collection at the home. The relatively small size of industrial policies and the home collection feature make this form of insurance quite expensive.

To illustrate, consider a $500 nonparticipating straight life industrial policy sold to a man aged 35 by The Independent Life and Accident Insurance Company (Jacksonville, Florida), one of the large writers of industrial insurance. According to the same kind of calculations described in Chapters 3 and 4, the twenty-year values of the components of the contract are as follows:

Protection element	$ 14
Savings element	40
Company retention	102
Premiums	$156

In short, about 65 cents of the premium dollar are retained by the company to cover its expenses and make a profit.

In a sense, "industrial" is to the life insurance business what the finance company is to the consumer credit business. It is argued that some persons would not have any insurance at all if it were not for industrial insurance, just as it is argued that some persons would not be able to borrow if it were not for finance companies. It is unfortunate that such a high price must be paid by those who can least afford it. You should avoid industrial life insurance.

Fraternal benefit societies

This book deals primarily with life insurance sold by commercial corporations—stock companies and mutual companies. Other sources of individual life insurance, however, are the various fraternal benefit societies that have grown out of religious organizations or fraternal groups.

Among the largest fraternal benefit societies are the Aid Association for Lutherans (Appleton, Wisconsin), the Knights of Columbus (New Haven, Connecticut), and the Lutheran Brotherhood (Minneapolis, Minnesota). The life insurance available from these and other fraternal benefit societies is beyond the scope of this book.[5]

Other forms of individual life insurance

This section of the chapter describes several forms of life insurance coverage other than straight life and five-year renewable term. Although the material presented here is not exhaustive, because of the large variety of available policies and riders, it touches on most of the widely sold forms of coverage.

Since your needs can be met with the two major forms described in Chapter 3, this material is included in the book primarily for reference purposes. You may have occasion to familiarize yourself with these forms, or you may have previously purchased one or more of these coverages.

Limited-payment life

A limited-payment life policy is similar to a straight life policy in that the contract runs to age 100 (in the case of modern policies) and has a level face amount for the entire duration of the contract. It differs from straight life, however, in that premiums are payable over a period of time shorter than the duration of the contract.

The premiums for a limited-payment life policy usually are level for the premium-paying period, and, other things equal, are larger than the premiums for a straight life policy. The savings element grows more rapidly during the premium-paying period, and therefore the protection element declines more rapidly than in a straight life policy.

Some limited-payment life policies have premiums payable for a specified number of years. Examples are thirty-payment life (in which premiums are payable for thirty years), twenty-payment life, fifteen-payment life, and ten-payment life. The extreme case is single-premium life, in which one large premium is paid.

Some limited-payment life policies have premiums payable to a specified age. Examples are life paid-up at age 60 (often called life 60), life 65, and so forth. When premiums are payable to an advanced age, such as 85, 90, or 95, the policy closely resembles straight life, and some companies offer such policies along with or instead of straight life. In the tables of straight life price information in this book, therefore, some of the policies are life 85, life 90, or life 95.

At the end of the premium-paying period, a policy is said to be "paid-up." This means that no more premiums are needed. The cash value at that time, however, does *not* equal the face amount. The cash value equals the face amount only at age 100. This point is illustrated in Figure 5–1, which is a simplified diagram of a twenty-payment life policy issued at age 35. After the premium-paying period, interest earnings on the large savings element take care of the protection and also cause the cash value to continue to increase.

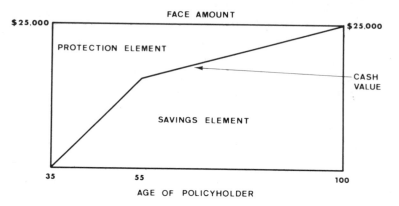

Figure 5–1
Rough diagram of a $25,000 twenty-payment life policy issued at age 35

The advantages of a twenty-payment life policy are that the policyholder "gets the premiums out of the way" and that the savings element grows more rapidly than in a straight life policy. Offsetting these advantages, however, are the substantially larger premiums and the more rapidly declining protection element in the twenty-payment life policy. Furthermore, although the premiums for a twenty-payment life policy are "out of the way" after twenty years, the policyholder continues to be charged, because a portion of the interest earnings on the savings element of the "paid-up" policy is used to pay for the continuing protection. Finally, there is some evidence to suggest that many if not most companies charge more for the protection in twenty-payment life policies than for the protection in straight life policies.[6]

Endowments

An endowment policy is one in which the cash value equals the face amount at the end of the policy's duration. (A semi-endowment policy is one in which the cash value equals half the face amount at the end of the policy's duration.) Some endowments run for a specified number of years; examples are thirty-year endowment, twenty-year endowment, and ten-year endowment. Some endowments run to a specified age; examples are endowment at 60 and endowment at 65.

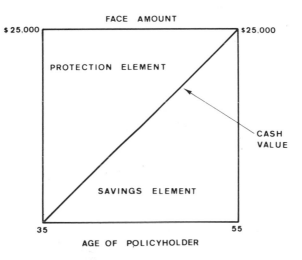

Figure 5–2
Rough diagram of a $25,000 twenty-year endowment issued at age 35

Endowment policies usually have a level face amount and level premiums for the entire duration of the contract. (There are exceptions, however. For example, a twenty-payment endowment at age 65 issued at age 35 has a thirty-year duration, but premiums are payable only for twenty years.) In this sense, a straight life policy may be viewed as an endowment at age 100. And when an endowment runs to an advanced age, such as 85, 90, or 95, the policy closely resembles straight life, and some companies offer such policies along with or instead of straight life. In the tables of straight life price information in this book, therefore, some of the policies are endowment at 85, endowment at 90, or endowment at 95.

The advantage of a twenty-year endowment is a very rapidly growing savings element. Offsetting this advantage, however, are very large premiums and a very rapidly declining protection element. Figure 5–2 is a simplified diagram of a twenty-year endowment.

The most serious drawback of a short-term endowment, such as a twenty-year endowment, is that the contract terminates and the protection ends completely at a time when the policyholder may still desire continued protection. The same could be said of a long-term endowment, such as an endowment at 85 or even a straight life policy, but a policyholder is likely to either die or terminate the policy voluntarily prior to age 85.

Retirement income

A retirement income policy (sometimes called "income endowment" or "retirement income endowment") is designed to generate a large enough cash value to produce a specified life income beginning at a specified age. Frequently the specified income is $10 per month for each $1,000 of face amount. A $25,000 retirement income at 65 policy, for example, might generate a cash value of about $40,000, which is the approximate amount needed to guarantee a life income of $250 per month for a man beginning at age 65. The premiums usually are level for the entire duration of the contract.

Such policies could be called "super endowments," because the cash values in the later years exceed the face amount. Should the policyholder die prior to the age at which the income commences, the beneficiary would receive the face amount or the cash value, whichever is greater. Should the policyholder survive to the age at which the income commences, he usually has the option to take the specified income, to take the cash value in a single sum, or to take any of the other settlement options provided in the contract. Should the policyholder elect to take the funds in installments, the amount payable to the beneficiary at the subsequent death of the policyholder would depend upon the provisions of the particular income arrangement the policyholder selected. Settlement options are discussed in Chapter 7.

The advantage of a retirement income policy is a very rapidly growing savings element. Offsetting this advantage, however, are very large premiums and a very rapidly declining protection element. Indeed, since the amount payable to the beneficiary in the event of the policyholder's death is equal to the cash value during the later years of the policy, there is no life insurance protection during that period. In short, during the early policy years a retirement income policy is like a short-term endowment; during the later policy years it is a pure savings plan providing no life insurance protection. Figure 5–3 is a simplified diagram of a retirement income at 65 policy.

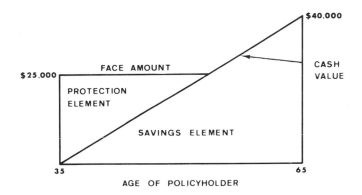

Figure 5–3
Rough diagram of a $25,000 retirement income at 65 policy issued at age 35

Level term

The word "term" refers to life insurance coverage that terminates without any cash value at the end of a specified number of years or at a specified age. In contrast, an "endowment," as mentioned earlier, also terminates at the end of a specified number of years or at a specified age, but its cash value at that time equals its face amount.

The word "level," when used with the word "term," means that the face amount of the term insurance is level for the duration of the coverage. Five-year renewable term, which was discussed earlier, is an example of level term coverage. The face amount is level for five years, and the insurance terminates at the end of five years without any cash value, although the policyholder has the privilege of renewing the coverage for another five years at a higher premium without evidence of insurability.

Other examples of level term insurance are one-year renewable term and ten-year renewable term. The reason for the emphasis on five-year renewable term in this book is that nearly all major companies offer such coverage. Relatively few companies offer renewable term coverages of other durations.

Many level term policies are not renewable; these expire at the end of the period of coverage without any cash value, and the policyholder would have to furnish evidence of insurability and obtain a new contract in order to extend his coverage. For example, there are five-year nonrenewable term policies and ten-year nonrenewable term policies. It is strongly suggested that these be avoided; you may be almost certain that a need for coverage is temporary, but a coronary can change your mind quickly. Other things equal, a renewable term policy costs more than a nonrenewable term policy. In a study several years ago, for example, it was concluded that the cost of five-year renewable term insurance, on the average, exceeded the cost of five-year nonrenewable term coverage by about 12 percent.[7] In the author's opinion, the renewal privilege is worth the higher price.

Other examples of level term insurance are fifteen-year term, twenty-year term, and term to age 65. These usually are nonrenewable. Also, premiums usually are level for the duration of the coverage. Other things equal, the longer the term, the higher the premium. Indeed, straight life may be viewed as term to age 100, with the proviso that anyone who survives to 100 is considered dead at that point and eligible to receive the face amount.

The premium for term to 65 falls between the premium for straight life and the initial premium for five-year renewable term. For that reason, it is sometimes suggested that a policy such as term to 65 be used rather than a combination of straight life and five-year renewable term. More flexibility can be achieved, however, with the combination of straight life and five-year renewable term.

Level term insurance is available in many companies, not only in separate policies but also in riders that may be attached to a basic policy such as straight life. The advantage of a level term rider, as contrasted with a separate level term policy, is that it is less expensive for a company to issue a rider than to issue a separate policy. This might result in cost savings to the policyholder. Unfortunately, it usually is difficult or impossible to determine whether such savings are passed on to policyholders, because companies rarely offer separate term policies that are directly comparable to their term riders. Moreover, the renewal and conversion privileges in term riders frequently are not as liberal as those found in separate term policies.

Decreasing term

In decreasing term insurance, the face amount of the coverage declines steadily until it reaches zero at expiration. Sometimes the decreases occur annually and sometimes monthly. Premiums usually are level and are payable either for the entire duration of the coverage or for a somewhat shorter period. In some companies, for example, the premiums for twenty-year decreasing term are payable for sixteen years.

The coverage may run for a specified number of years or to a specified age. Examples are ten-year decreasing term, twenty-year decreasing term, thirty-year decreasing term, and decreasing term to age 65. In a sense, straight life may be viewed as a combination of decreasing term to age 100 and an increasing savings element such that the sum of the two is always equal to the face amount of the straight life policy.

Decreasing term coverage, particularly for thirty years or less, is widely purchased. The reason may be that a relatively large amount of coverage is provided initially for a relatively small premium, but such coverage has important drawbacks.

The protection decreases rapidly, and this can be an important disadvantage. If the policyholder's health suddenly deteriorates, he might just as suddenly decide he does not like to see his life insurance protection declining rapidly. A level-term contract, such as five-year renewable term, can be decreased in amount if the policyholder wants it to decrease, but the protection remains unchanged unless the policyholder takes action to reduce it. And in straight life contracts, although the protection declines, the decrease is slow relative to that found in decreasing term coverage, and the protection does not reach zero until age 100.

It is sometimes said that a man's need for life insurance tends to decline as his family grows older, because of the decrease in the length of time over which income will be needed in the event of his death. This line of reasoning is used as an argument in favor of decreasing term insurance. Such reasoning, however, may be unsound. Although there may be a decline in the length of the period over which income is needed, there also may be an increase in the desired level of income because of the family's steadily improving standard of living. In a study several years ago, it was found that the increase in the desired level of income tends to more than offset the decreasing length of time over which the income is needed, with the result that a man's life insurance needs may increase for a considerable period of time before beginning to decline.[8]

Another important problem in some decreasing term coverage is found in the conversion clause. Some contracts provide that the policyholder may exchange the decreasing term coverage for a straight life or other cash-value policy without evidence of insurability, but the face amount of the converted policy may not exceed, say, 75 percent of the amount of decreasing term insurance in effect at the time of conversion. For example, suppose the policyholder becomes seriously ill, so that his insurability status is drastically altered. If he has decreasing term insurance with a 75 percent conversion clause, he would be faced with an impossible dilemma. If he converts, he would instantly lose one-fourth of his present insurance protection. On the other hand, if he does not convert, both the insurance and his conversion privilege would continue to decrease rapidly. Should you consider the purchase of decreasing term insurance, you should examine the conversion clause carefully and avoid any contract that provides less than 100 percent conversion of the amount of insurance in effect at the time of conversion. A more general discussion of the conversion clause in term policies is contained in Chapter 7.

Decreasing term insurance is available in many companies either in separate policies or in riders that may be attached to a basic policy such as straight life. Frequently, however, the coverage is available under another name, such as "family income" or "mortgage insurance."

A family income benefit, which is usually a rider to a basic policy, provides for the payment of a specified monthly income in addition to the face amount of the basic contract. In a twenty-year family income arrangement, for example, the income would be payable from the policyholder's death for the *remainder* of twenty years measured from the policy's issue date. Thus, the longer the policy-holder lives, the fewer would be the number of income payments. Hence, twenty-year decreasing term coverage is needed to provide the income payments.

Careful examination of a family income rider is needed to determine the exact amount of decreasing term coverage provided. Also, it is important to be sure that the beneficiary has the option to take a single sum settlement of the family income benefit, if the policy-holder desires such an option for the beneficiary. Some policies, unless specifically endorsed to the contrary, provide that the beneficiary must take the specified monthly income payments.

Mortgage insurance usually is decreasing term coverage under which the amount of protection is designed to parallel roughly the declining unpaid balance of a typical home mortgage. It is sometimes offered as a separate policy and sometimes as a rider to a basic policy such as straight life.

Increasing term

Increasing term coverage is issued invariably either as a rider to a basic policy, such as straight life, or as an integral part of a package policy. Most commonly, the coverage is called either a "return-of-premium benefit" or a "return-of-cash-value benefit." Frequently these benefits are limited to twenty years.

For example, a twenty-year return-of-premium benefit provides that the simple total of the premiums paid by the policyholder is paid to the beneficiary in addition to the face amount of the basic policy in the event of the policyholder's death during the first twenty years of the policy. The longer the policyholder lives (up to twenty years), the more is paid at death under the return-of-premium benefit. Hence, twenty-year increasing term coverage is needed to provide the benefit.

A return-of-premium benefit fits nicely into a sales presentation. It can be made to sound wonderful and as though the insurance company provides the benefit gratuitously. But the benefit costs money, and the policyholder pays for it.

A twenty-year return-of-cash-value benefit operates in much the same manner. It provides that the cash value of the basic policy is paid to the beneficiary in addition to the face amount in the event of the policyholder's death during the first twenty years of the policy.

The longer the policyholder lives (up to twenty years), the more is paid at death under the return-of-cash-value benefit. Hence, twenty-year increasing term coverage is needed to provide the benefit.

The return-of-cash-value benefit also fits well into sales presentations. Some critics of life insurance argue that a conventional straight life policy "should" pay the cash value to the beneficiary in addition to the face amount at the policyholder's death. The argument is based on a lack of understanding of life insurance arithmetic, but the return-of-cash-value benefit can be made to sound like the insurance company is doing the proper thing. Proper or not, though, the benefit costs money, and the policyholder pays for it.

Specialty policies

Some contracts involve a basic policy and several riders combined in such a way as to fit an elaborate sales presentation. These policies, often called "specialty policies," are so complex that meaningful analysis and understanding of the package is very difficult.

The President's Plan, which is sold by the Franklin Life Insurance Company (Springfield, Illinois), is perhaps the foremost example of specialty policies. The basic contract is a twenty-payment endowment at 65. Added to the basic policy is twenty-year increasing term coverage to provide a return-of-premium benefit. Also added to the basic policy is a "retirement annuity benefit," which is a pure savings plan. And other riders are often added. For example, a twenty-year decreasing term rider frequently is attached to the policy to provide a family income benefit.

What is the result of combining a level face amount policy containing cash values, an increasing term rider, a pure savings plan, and a decreasing term rider? In one case the result was a very slowly decreasing total death benefit and a steadily increasing savings element. Indeed, the result looked much like a straight life policy in terms of its protection-savings mix. The moral of the story is that a complex combination of coverages is unnecessary and serves only to confuse the consumer.

Many companies—particularly small, young companies—have developed specialty policies and marketing strategies similar to those of the Franklin Life. An example is the K–1832–B contract issued in recent years by the Life Insurance Company of Kentucky (Louisville, Kentucky). The name of the contract, although strange, communicates the same amount of information to the buyer as the name "President's Plan"—none. It should also be noted that many conventional policies—including straight life policies issued by major companies—have names that communicate no information. Examples of the latter are Economy Protector, Executive Equity, Executive Plan, Executive Preferred, Executive Special, Policy for Executives and Professionals, and Presidential Plus.

In the K–1832–B contract, the basic policy is twenty-payment life. Added to the package are a family income benefit (provided by decreasing term coverage), a return-of-premium benefit (provided by increasing term coverage), a "twentieth anniversary benefit" (provided by increasing term coverage), and a level term coverage that does not go into effect until the policy is twenty years old. The contract is incredibly complex. It is also misleading, because the wording of the contract exaggerates the death benefits provided.[9]

It has been suggested that specialty policies should be banned from the market by the state insurance commissioners.[10] Some attempts have been made to do so. Unfortunately, however, there is no reliable formula for distinguishing precisely between specialty policies and conventional policies. And it is possible that some specialty policies are low-priced, just as some conventional policies are high-priced. It would seem that disclosure of benefits and price is preferable to prohibition. If the price and true nature of specialty policies were made known to buyers, those specialty policies that are high-priced—along with high-priced conventional policies—would tend to disappear from the market.

Family policies

Up to this point, all of the coverages described are single life contracts; that is, they are based on one life. A family policy, however, covers more than one life.

Family policies are sold in "units." One unit might consist of $5,000 of straight life on the husband, $2,000 of term to age 65 on the wife, and $1,000 of term to age 25 on each of the children. The $1,000 of term coverage on a child usually is convertible to $5,000 of straight life without evidence of insurability when the child reaches 25.

A family policy is a convenient way to insure all the members of the family. But it is an extremely complex arrangement. The complexity becomes apparent when the policy is examined with regard to situations such as the following: husband dies and wife remarries; wife dies and husband remarries; or husband and wife each remarry following divorce.

Economies may be realized because, other things equal, it is less expensive for a company to cover several persons in one policy than to issue separate policies on each. But there is a lot to be said for simplicity, and for that reason it is suggested that you stick with single life policies.

Joint life

Another example of a policy covering more than one life is the so-called joint life contract. In its usual form, such a policy covers two lives—most frequently either a husband and wife or two business partners—and the face amount is payable at the first death. Such policies often contain a conversion clause allowing the survivor to buy a new policy on his own life without evidence of insurability within a specified time after the first death.

The premium for a $25,000 joint life policy, for example, is less than the combined premiums for otherwise comparable $25,000 policies on each life separately. The problem is that it is difficult to determine whether the price of a joint life policy is reasonable. To date, no price study of joint life contracts has been published. However, some of the companies currently promoting joint life policies offer relatively high-priced single life contracts. Until price information on joint life contracts becomes available, therefore, you should avoid them.

Split life

A recently developed product is split life insurance. Its name stems from the fact that the protection element and the savings element are in separate contracts. The two contracts are issued together and are tied in with one another.

The protection portion of the package is furnished by a one-year renewable term contract. The savings portion is provided by an annual premium retirement annuity contract, which is essentially a pure savings plan without life insurance protection.

The tie-in takes place in two ways. First, the relative proportions of term insurance coverage and retirement annuity premiums are prescribed. For each $10 of annuity premiums per year, up to $1,000 of term insurance coverage is available. For example, the purchase of an annuity with an annual premium of $500 permits the purchase of up to $50,000 of one-year renewable term insurance.

Second, the term insurance is "conditionally renewable," and the condition is that each annuity premium payable prior to age 65 must be paid in order for the term insurance to be renewed. At 65 the annuity matures and the owner begins receiving his retirement income payments, but the term insurance may be renewed continuously to an advanced age such as 95.

One interesting aspect of split life insurance is the fact that the one-year renewable term premium rates are very low relative to regular renewable term insurance rates. Furthermore, although the premium rates reach astronomical levels at the more advanced ages, the term insurance may be continued for many years longer than conventional term insurance contracts. The catch is that the annuity is a dismal savings plan. The combination of a low-priced term insurance contract and a high-priced annuity contract is a package whose price structure is not markedly different from that of a reasonably priced straight life contract. However, in terms of the protection-savings proportions of the package, the split life arrangement provides a larger protection element and a smaller savings element than a typical straight life policy.[11]

Comparisons of straight life and split life are complicated by the fact that the protection patterns are different. In the straight life contract, the face amount is level and the protection element steadily decreases. In split life, the face amount of the term insurance portion is level. The annuity portion provides a death benefit equal to the simple total of the annuity premiums paid, or the cash value of the annuity, whichever is larger. Therefore, the face amount of the package steadily increases, and the protection element is level.

Another interesting aspect of split life insurance is the fact that the annuity can be purchased by one person and the term insurance can be placed on someone else's life. The term insurance can even be "sprinkled" over several lives. For example, a man can buy an annuity with a premium of $2,000 per year, thus making possible the purchase of $200,000 of term insurance, which in turn can be issued in four $50,000 policies on the lives of his four sons. The sons then have the benefit of low-priced term insurance that is essentially subsidized by their father through his willingness to set aside funds in a low-yielding savings plan.

Many of the features of split life insurance can be duplicated through the use of conventional life insurance contracts. In the illustration above, for example, a similar result can be achieved if the father merely contributes toward the cost of conventional straight life or five-year renewable term policies purchased by his sons.

There are several problems with split life. It is so new that the "bugs" are not yet out of it. Some legal questions and tax questions are not yet resolved. And some insurance commissioners do not now permit its sale.

Finally, only a few companies presently offer split life. Among these are Executive Life Insurance Company (Beverly Hills, California), Hartford Life Insurance Company (Hartford, Connecticut), Life Insurance Company of California (San Francisco, California), and Louisiana and Southern Life Insurance Company (New Orleans, Louisiana). Of these, only Hartford Life is recommended in the strongest possible language in the 1971 edition of *Best's Life Insurance Reports*. Executive Life and Life of California are recommended, but in weaker language. And Louisiana and Southern, which is the company that first introduced split life, did not receive a policyholders' recommendation.

Variable life

The phrase "variable life insurance" has been applied to forms of life insurance in which the benefits fluctuate in accordance with the investment performance of an account consisting primarily of equity-type assets. At the time this book went to press, the complex question of whether such policies should be regulated as insurance by the state insurance commissioners or as securities by the federal Securities and Exchange Commission was not yet resolved. Thus, variable life insurance policies are not yet available in the United States, although they are being sold in several other countries including the Netherlands and the United Kingdom.

Several versions of variable life insurance have been proposed for sale in the United States, but the precise form that these policies will take is not yet known. Under such circumstances, it is not possible to provide guidance in this book relative to variable life insurance. But reference to the subject was considered appropriate because of the life insurance industry's current interest in it.

Chapter 6

The agent

Most of the life insurance in force in the United States has been sold through the efforts of life insurance agents. This chapter discusses the reasons for the existence of agents, what the agent does, what he costs, and how you should go about selecting an agent.

Why there are agents

There are many possible reasons for the involvement of agents in most life insurance sales. Four reasons, however, are perhaps the most significant.

First, life insurance is a financial service under which an insurance company promises future delivery of money. The delivery may take place only upon the death of an insured person, or the delivery may take place when the insured person cashes in or borrows against his policy. In either situation, life insurance requires the policyholder to forgo the present enjoyment of the things money will buy in exchange for that promise of future delivery. Many and perhaps most people recognize the need to buy life insurance next week, next month, next year, or at some vague future date. But it takes a high order of salesmanship to persuade people to take the plunge and buy life insurance *now.*

Second, the subject matter of life insurance is distasteful. No one enjoys discussing death and related topics. So there is a strong tendency to postpone the discussion of life insurance—sometimes until it is too late. Again, salesmanship is needed just to get people thinking about life insurance.

Third, the life insurance contract is a financial instrument, and most financial instruments are complex. Moreover, the life insurance company's promise is given in exchange for a premium payment that is small relative to the amount the insurance company obligates itself to pay in the event of the insured person's death. So a particularly complex document is needed to safeguard the interests of both parties and at the same time make the policy salable. A considerable amount of technical knowledge is necessary if life insurance is to be utilized most effectively by the policyholder.

The fourth reason for the predominance of agents in the sale of life insurance is their political prowess. They have been successful in persuading state legislatures to enact and retain restrictions that make it difficult to market life insurance other than through agents.

Consider the example of savings bank life insurance, which is sold over the counter—not through agents—in savings banks in Connecticut, Massachusetts, and New York. The maximum amount of savings bank life insurance that can be sold on any one life in Connecticut is $5,000. Attempts to relax that stringent limitation have met with strong opposition from the agents. The following excerpt from a newspaper story gives some of the flavor of that opposition:

> Insurance men Thursday gave the Capitol its biggest and noisiest hearing of this legislative session.
>
> About 500 of them showed up at a Banking Committee hearing to oppose a bill that would raise the ceiling on savings bank life insurance from the present $5,000 to $15,000.

They filled every seat in the Hall of the House and its gallery and stood as many as 10 deep in the aisles. And they cheered, applauded, booed, hissed and catcalled during testimony.

Attorney George Ritter, Hartford's deputy mayor, got the brunt of the hazing when he spoke out in favor of eliminating ceilings altogether on bank insurance. . . .[1]

What the agent does

The five functions of the agent are as follows:

- Persuade you to recognize and discuss the financial problems the future holds
- Help you evaluate your needs for life insurance protection
- Make sound recommendations in the light of your financial circumstances and objectives
- Persuade you to buy now
- Keep in touch with you so that your life insurance program will be updated frequently

The performance of these functions requires dedication and competence on the part of the agent.

The dedication is needed because companies place overwhelming emphasis on selling rather than servicing policyholders. The agent compensation system is based on commissions. A large commission is paid at the time of sale—frequently 55 percent or more of the first year's premium. Small commissions—often 5 percent of subsequent premiums—are paid on business that stays in force. Thus the primary incentive to take care of old policyholders is the hope that additional new business will result. That this may not be enough incentive in many cases is suggested by a study in which it was reported that only 13 percent of the policyholders surveyed said that an agent had ever been of service after the sale.[2]

The competence is needed because of the complexity of life insurance. Here you cannot rely upon the agent licensing procedures of the various state insurance departments. Licensing examinations require only a bare minimum of life insurance knowledge. Many life insurance companies oppose the upgrading of examinations, perhaps because they fear that tougher examinations would make recruiting of agents even more difficult than it is now.

Nor can you rely upon the agent training programs of the companies, because most of them fail to educate their men in the technicalities of life insurance. Most of the available time is used to teach effective selling techniques. Furthermore, as among salesmen in other fields, there is a high rate of turnover among life insurance agents. Such turnover compounds the difficulties faced by the companies in trying to develop competence in their agents.

Nor can you rely upon industry-wide training programs. The best known is the Life Underwriter Training Council (LUTC), a program sponsored by the National Association of Life Underwriters. LUTC provides some technical education, but, like many company programs, is heavily oriented toward the techniques of selling.

The most rigorous educational experience available to life insurance agents is the Chartered Life Underwriter (CLU) program administered by the American College of Life Underwriters. Even in this program there is a considerable amount of sales material, although some technical knowledge is required for successful completion. Included in the program is some general education in areas related to life insurance, such as finance, accounting, business law, and economics. Those who complete the program successfully are awarded the CLU designation and are eligible for membership in the American Society of Chartered Life Underwriters. Possession of the CLU designation indicates that the holder has passed a series of examinations, met a three-year experience requirement, and taken the following pledge:

> In all my relations with clients I agree to observe the following rule of professional conduct: I shall, in the light of all of the circumstances surrounding my client, which I shall make every conscientious effort to ascertain and to understand, give him that service which, had I been in the same circumstances, I would have applied to myself.

The holder of the CLU designation has demonstrated a willingness to undertake and carry to completion a voluntary course of study, and the experience requirement assures that he is no newcomer to the life insurance business. So he might be one with whom to do business.

But even here, you cannot be certain what kind of person you are dealing with. Neither the pledge nor the comprehensive code of ethics subscribed to by members of the American Society of Chartered Life Underwriters can guarantee the competence and sincerity of the individual. For example, an article written by a CLU and published in his company's magazine explained a sales technique that can only be called tricky and false. He acknowledged the "holes" in his technique, but said the technique was successful for him because his customers, although "rich," were not sufficiently "sophisticated" to spot the flaws.[3]

What the agent costs

Putting an appropriate price tag on the services of an agent is difficult because usually he can save you time. Moreover, a good agent may be in a position to save you money and to make your life insurance more effective than it might otherwise be.

Value of commissions

One way to measure the cost of the agent's services is to calculate the value of his commissions. These vary widely from company to company and from policy to policy, but a frequently cited schedule for straight life policies sold by some of the major companies is a commission of 55 percent of the first year's premium and 5 percent of each of the next nine years' premiums. Under the same interest, mortality, and lapse assumptions used in calculating the price data in Chapter 4, the value of such a commission schedule on policies issued to men aged 35 would be approximately 83 percent of one annual premium. The corresponding percentage figures for men aged 25 and men aged 45 would be approximately the same. If the annual premium for a $25,000 participating straight life policy issued to men aged 35 were $540, for example, the value of the agent's commissions under these assumptions would be about $448.

This calculation leaves something to be desired, not only because of commission variations among companies and policies, but also because the commission factor cannot be detached from the policy. In other words, you cannot decide on the company and policy you desire and then purchase the policy "net of commissions." The commission factor is an integral part of the price of a policy.

Difference in retention

Another way to measure the cost of the agent's services is to compare the retention for a policy issued by an agency company with the retention for a policy issued by a non-agency company. When the latter is the lower figure, as is sometimes the case when the non-agency organization is a well established, reputable company, the difference between the two figures may be viewed by the buyer as a measure of the cost of the agent.

For example, suppose that the retention for a $25,000 participating straight life policy issued at age 35 by a major agency company is $800, and that the retention for a similar contract issued by a non-agency company is $300. It might be said that the cost of the agent's services in this situation is $500.

This calculation also leaves something to be desired, because the lower retention in the non-agency company may be attributable not only to the absence of an agent but also to the absence of a number of other characteristics of the agency company, such as a branch office in or near the buyer's home town. Furthermore, there is the large variation in retention among the agency companies.

For example, suppose a comparison were being made between a non-agency company's policy with a retention of $300 and two agency companies' policies with retentions of $800 and $1,300. It might be reasonable to infer that the agent selling the higher retention agency company policy costs $1,000 while the agent selling the lower retention agency company policy costs $500, particularly if the agency company with the higher retention policy pays higher commission rates. On the other hand, the commission rates might be about the same in both companies, and the agency company with the higher retention policy might be less efficient in other areas.

How to select an agent

A competent and dedicated agent probably is worth more than he costs, no matter how this cost is calculated. On the other hand, an incompetent agent is worth little or nothing and more than likely has a negative value to the buyer. The trick, then, is to locate a competent and dedicated agent.

The most important point is that *you* must take the initiative and seek out your agent. If you wait to be called upon, your chances of winding up with a highly qualified agent are drastically reduced. Generally, the best qualified agents deal with people in the upper income brackets. One can hardly blame them for this, because the upper income people are capable of buying larger amounts of insurance, yielding the agent more income.

Here are a few suggestions to follow in your search for a competent agent:

- Ask those friends, relatives, or business colleagues whose judgment you respect for the names of the life insurance men they regard as the outstanding agents in the community.
- Ask your attorney, accountant, or banker for similar suggestions, emphasizing that competence is the criterion, rather than friendships or other special loyalties.
- Get acquainted with some of these highly recommended agents; see how you get along with them.
- Ask these men to show you testimonial letters from some of their policyholders, and pay particular attention to comments about service after the sale. You might even wish to talk to some of their policyholders.
- Ask each one about his educational background and qualifications. In doing so, keep in mind the limitations discussed earlier about licensing procedures, company training programs, and industry-wide training programs.
- Ask each one about his philosophy and freedom with respect to placing business with companies other than his primary company, because many companies prohibit or strongly discourage their agents from placing business with other companies.

This latter point may be important if the agent's primary company is noncompetitive for a particular need. It is even more important if the primary company does not offer the kind of contract desired by the agent for his prospective policyholder. It is fine for the agent to be loyal to his primary company, but if that loyalty requires him to do an inferior job for his policyholders, you should seek another agent.

As mentioned in Chapter 4, it is sometimes said that "you get what you pay for." As regards the agent's services, the phrase should be "the lower the price you pay, the better you are likely to be served." For example, it is well known that some of the companies with the low retention policies shown in Chapter 4 have relatively high proportions of their agents holding the CLU designation. Conversely, some of the companies with the high retention policies shown in

Chapter 4 have relatively few CLU's among their agents. In short, it is possible for you to secure a combination of a highly qualified agent, a financially strong company, and policies with relatively low retentions. If you succeed in obtaining such a combination, you will have done well in planning your life insurance affairs.

Chapter 7

The fine print

The life insurance policy contract is a complex legal document. Many volumes have been written about it, and even these have not explored all the interesting facets of the instrument. No attempt is made here to present a thorough analysis of the contract; rather, the purpose of this chapter is to point out some of the more important aspects that the buyer should understand. Many if not most of the points discussed are unlikely to come up in the typical sales interview unless you bring them up.

Contract provisions generally

Consistent with other parts of this book, this chapter deals only with straight life and five-year renewable term policies. This first section of the chapter contains discussions of several clauses that are common to both straight life and five-year renewable term policies.

Insuring agreement

Perhaps the heart of any life insurance contract is the insuring agreement. This clause spells out the insurance company's promise to pay the funds to the beneficiary "immediately upon receipt of due proof of the death of the insured while the policy is in force." The word "insured" refers to the person on whose life the policy is based.

Brief description of policy

An important thing to look for is the description normally found at the bottom of the first page of the policy. Although the description may be difficult to understand if the reader is unfamiliar with life insurance jargon, it is the one place where an attempt is made to describe briefly the major characteristics of the policy.

To illustrate, the following description is found at the bottom of the first page of the straight life policy issued by Connecticut Mutual:

> Whole life policy. Payable at death. Premiums payable for life unless previously paid-up by dividends. Annual dividends.

Death benefit

This clause, found in some contracts, spells out in some detail the amount payable upon the death of the insured. An important aspect of this clause is the question of interest between the date of death and the date of settlement. Some contracts, for example, provide for interest on the funds for that period, but for not to exceed, say, one year.

Some contracts, on the other hand, are silent on this point. This means that the company would not be obliged to pay interest from the date of death, although it might do so as a matter of practice. Be sure to check on this point. If the company does not pay such interest routinely, it should be possible to arrange things under a settlement option (to be discussed later) so that interest will accrue from the date of death. This is no small item. If the funds payable were $25,000 and if the applicable interest rate were 5 percent, the interest would amount to about $100 per month. If the beneficiary delays a couple of months in filing the claim, the interest is something to consider.

Another aspect of the death benefit clause is the question of the so-called unearned portion of the premium. Suppose the policy-holder pays a $400 annual premium on its due date and then dies three months later. Under such circumstances, some companies pay, in addition to the face amount of the policy, the unearned portion of the premium. In this example, about three-fourths of the premium, or $300, would be paid in addition to the face amount.

Some companies, on the other hand, consider the premium fully earned when paid. These companies argue that the extra payment is nothing more than additional protection, which can be provided only at a cost. Although this is a technically sound argument, the facts are that some companies make the extra payment while others do not.

At this point you may feel that undue emphasis has been placed on a couple of minor points. That may be true, but these two points are evidence of the quality of the contract and the quality of the company from the buyer's point of view. Ironically, you are at least as likely, and perhaps more likely, to find favorable provisions re-garding areas such as these in contracts with relatively low retentions than in contracts with relatively high retentions. This is another indication of the way in which life insurance contradicts the saying that "you get what you pay for."

The beneficiary

In a sense, the beneficiary clause is the heart of the contract. It identifies the person or persons to receive the funds at the insured's death.

One alleged advantage of the life insurance contract is the relative ease with which a beneficiary may be designated. It is simple, when compared with the formalities that surround the preparation of a will. Unfortunately, the simplicity of life insurance in this respect leads to carelessness in the designation of beneficiaries.

Consider, for example, the case of John Smith, who has a wife and three young boys. After a long session with an agent, John signs up for $50,000 of life insurance. With both John and his agent getting tired, they quickly dispose of the beneficiary question by using that common arrangement: "Mary Smith, wife of the insured, if living; otherwise, their children equally."

Now suppose one of the boys turns out to be a lazy, shiftless bum who likes to spend money on souped-up cars. The second turns out to be a conscientious student who wants to attend law school. And the third develops a serious medical problem that will require substantial sums of money. If both John and Mary were dead, it might or might not be appropriate for the three boys to share the life insurance funds equally.

One way to handle a situation like this is to have the funds payable to Mary, if living, but otherwise to a trustee (normally a commercial bank with a trust department). Then, through the terms of John's will and Mary's will, or through a separate trust instrument drafted by their attorney, the trustee can be given discretion in the use of the funds.

The trust arrangement frequently is appropriate because it is the one way to achieve flexibility and discretion concerning the funds. These characteristics are important when children are the beneficiaries, because the parents cannot know what the future holds. When they establish a trust, they are in effect hoping the trustee will do what they would have done.

Normally the beneficiary designation is revocable. This means that the owner reserves the right to change the beneficiary designation.

It is also possible to designate the beneficiary *irrevocably,* but this arrangement is rarely used. It means that the owner cannot change the beneficiary designation without the approval of the beneficiary. Nor can the owner exercise certain other ownership rights, such as cashing in or borrowing against the policy, without the approval of the beneficiary. In effect, then, the owner and the irrevocable beneficiary are both part owners of the policy. An irrevocable designation may be appropriate in some special situations, such as a divorce situation, or where a charitable organization is the beneficiary. Under no circumstances, however, should you designate a beneficiary irrevocably without thought and consultation with your attorney.

The disastrous consequences of an irrevocable beneficiary designation may be illustrated by the Woodruff case. Mr. and Mrs. Woodruff, owners of a small but successful business, were killed simultaneously in an automobile accident. They left four boys. Jack, the oldest, was 23 when his parents died, and he took over the business. The other three boys were minors. Since the family's financial affairs were in a state of flux following his parents' deaths, Jack bought $25,000 of straight life insurance on his own life for the benefit of his three young brothers.

Normally an irrevocable beneficiary designation requires a special written request, but the application in this case had "yes" and "no" boxes following the question about whether the owner reserves the right to change the beneficiary designation. The agent accidentally checked the "no" box, and Jack signed the application without realizing what he had done. The agent subsequently demonstrated his incompetence when he failed to detect the irrevocable designation in the policy and delivered it routinely to Jack.

A few years later, Jack married. By that time, the family's financial affairs had been straightened out, and a trust had been established for the benefit of Jack's brothers. Since there was no further need for the life insurance to be payable to his brothers, Jack routinely asked the company to designate his new bride as the beneficiary. He was then informed of the irrevocable designation of his brothers. On checking with his attorney, Jack discovered that there was no way to effect the change of beneficiary. His brothers, as minors, had no legal capacity to agree to the change, and no judge would stand by and allow minors to have their rights impaired. To add insult to injury, Jack was told that he could not cash in or borrow against the policy, since the minors had no legal capacity to agree and no judge would sanction such an agreement.

Jack could have continued to pay premiums until his brothers became of age and then seen if they would agree to give up what amounted to a part ownership of the policy. But he decided instead to discontinue premium payments and let the policy go on extended term insurance automatically (as discussed later in this chapter). He then had to buy new insurance for the benefit of his bride; fortunately he was insurable and therefore able to do so.

Settlement options

The settlement options are the ways in which the beneficiary may receive the funds other than in a lump sum. These provisions are complex, and it is not uncommon for them to occupy two full pages of fine print in the contract.

Perhaps the most widely used of the settlement options is the "interest option" or "deposit option." Here the funds are left with the company and periodic interest payments are made to the beneficiary. It is possible to arrange for the beneficiary to have unlimited privileges of withdrawal, or limitations can be imposed. The beneficiary can be given unlimited privileges of switching to another option, or limitations can be imposed.

Mention was made earlier of the problem of interest from the date of death to the date of settlement. In policies that do not provide for such interest, it is frequently possible for the insured to accomplish the desired objective by electing the interest option with unlimited withdrawal privileges. Normally the settlement option agreement will then provide for interest from the date of death.

Another of the settlement options is the "fixed amount" or "installment amount" option. Here the funds are left with the company and periodic payments of a specified amount that includes both principal and interest are made to the beneficiary until the funds (together with interest) are exhausted. Again it is normally possible to arrange for the beneficiary to have limited or unlimited privileges of withdrawal and limited or unlimited privileges of changing to another option.

A third settlement option is the "fixed period" or "installment time" option. Here the funds are left with the company and periodic payments that include both principal and interest are made to the beneficiary for a specified period of time. Under this option, it may be possible to arrange things so that the beneficiary can take down all of the remaining funds, but normally the company will not allow the beneficiary to make partial withdrawals.

All three of these settlement options are sometimes described as "not involving life contingencies." This expression means that neither the amount of the payments nor the number of payments is contingent in any way upon the survival of the beneficiary. If the first beneficiary dies before receiving all of the funds, the remainder goes to the next beneficiary in line. With regard to these three options, then, the important factors are the withdrawal privileges and the interest rates.

Settlement options usually guarantee a minimum interest rate in the 2 to 3 percent range. Companies then declare additional interest from year to year in accordance with current economic conditions. Usually the total interest rates paid under settlement options are below the interest rates paid by most savings banks and savings and loan associations, and this may be one of the reasons why settlement options are not widely used by beneficiaries.

In addition to the three options not involving life contingencies, most policies provide for at least two or three options that do involve life contingencies. The latter are various kinds of life annuities that the beneficiary may receive. One of them, for example, might provide for the beneficiary (who we will assume is a woman aged 70) to receive $6.26 per month for life for each $1,000 of funds, but in no event for less than ten years. This means that if she dies before receiving 120 monthly payments, the company must continue the payments to the next beneficiary in line until a total of 120 monthly payments have been made, at which time the annuity would expire without value. On the other hand, if she lives to receive the 120 monthly payments, the company must continue the payments until she dies, at which time the annuity would expire without value.

Two points should be mentioned about life annuities. First, they rarely fit into the situation unless the beneficiary is at least 65 or 70 years of age. At younger ages, it is normally preferable to invest the funds in high quality corporate or government bonds, on which the beneficiary may receive the interest while preserving the principal.

Second, the selection of a life annuity option is the same as the purchase of a single premium life annuity. As such, it is a big purchase that should be made carefully. Suppose, for example, the settlement option rates are much more favorable to the beneficiary than current single premium life annuity rates. Under these circumstances, the setttlement option rates should be used.

On the other hand, suppose the settlement option rates are inferior to a company's current single premium life annuity rates. In this situation, some companies see to it that the beneficiary gets the benefit of the better rates, and some of these companies provide a slight discount from their current rates. But other companies apparently are willing to let the beneficiary suffer the consequences if she unknowingly elects a life annuity settlement option when the company's current single premium life annuity rates would have been more favorable to her.

Nor is the latter questionable practice the only consideration. Some companies are more aggressive and competitive in the single premium life annuity business than others. It is possible, therefore, that the beneficiary who wants a life annuity would be well advised to take the funds and buy a single premium life annuity from another company.

One additional point should be mentioned concerning the fixed amount, fixed period, and life annuity options. Each of these involves liquidation of both principal and interest. If the funds arise from the death of the insured, if the beneficiary is the insured's spouse, and if one of these liquidating options is selected, the beneficiary would be entitled to a $1,000 annual interest exclusion for federal income tax purposes. In other words, the first $1,000 per year of interest received by the beneficiary under one of these liquidating options would be excluded from the beneficiary's income for federal income tax purposes. This point might be a consideration if the beneficiary has enough income to create a significant income tax problem.

With the exception of the interest option, which some beneficiaries may utilize temporarily until they decide what to do with the funds, settlement options are not widely used. When small amounts of proceeds are involved, the beneficiaries tend to put the funds in a bank account for simplicity. When large amounts are involved, beneficiaries are rightly concerned about the relatively low interest rates generally paid by the insurance companies, and by the usual inappropriateness of the various life annuity options.

Even more important, however, when large amounts are involved, it is often essential to provide for discretion. Suppose, for example, you have $100,000 of life insurance payable to your wife, and you are thinking about settlement options. If you give her full withdrawal rights or impose high limits on her withdrawal rights, she might become the victim of bad investments, con men, or both. On the other hand, if you impose low limits on her withdrawal rights, she might have a desperate need to exceed these limits, perhaps because of an illness or other emergency. But the insurance company cannot exercise discretion in the distribution of funds to your beneficiary, because any restrictions imposed through the settlement options are unbreakable. In short, instead of using settlement options, you may be forced to have the funds payable to a trustee, in whom you can lodge discretion through your will or through a separate trust instrument.

Ownership rights and assignment

Among the ownership rights in a life insurance policy are the right to name and change the beneficiary designation, the right to cash in or borrow against the policy, the right to receive any dividends paid by the company, and the right to dispose of some or all of the ownership rights themselves. When a person possesses all of the ownership rights in a policy, he is the sole owner. (If he possesses some of the rights, he is a part owner or joint owner.) In most instances, the insured and the owner are the same person. In some policies, however, someone other than the insured is the owner. A typical policy contains several clauses dealing with ownership rights and assignments.

If the owner of a policy gives or sells all of the ownership rights to someone else, the transaction is known as a transfer of ownership or an absolute assignment. It is also possible for the owner to dispose of some but not all of the ownership rights. Commonly this occurs when the owner wishes to pledge the policy to a financial institution as collateral for a loan, in which case the transaction is known as a collateral assignment.

The assignment clause is an important one because it gives the life insurance contract flexibility that it would not otherwise have. Perhaps the classic example of a widely used financial instrument that lacks assignability is the United States government "E" bond, which is prominently identified on its face as nontransferable.

Should you ever have occasion to assign a life insurance policy as collateral for a bank loan, be sure that the assignment form you execute is the ABA assignment form. This is a document worked out by the American Bankers Association in consultation with representatives of the life insurance industry. Under the ABA form, you give the bank just enough of the ownership rights to protect its interests— not too many and not too few. Before the ABA form was developed, banks prepared their own assignment forms, under which they sometimes took more ownership rights than necessary. In some instances, they took all of the ownership rights—perhaps just to be on the safe side. The reason for this warning is that some financial institutions apparently are still using their own homemade assignment forms, the terms of which are likely to be less favorable to the borrower than those of the ABA form.

Grace period

Life insurance contracts provide a grace period—usually of thirty-one days—beyond the premium due dates. The policy continues in force during the grace period. If the insured dies during the grace period without having paid the premium, the unpaid premium usually is deducted from the amount payable under the policy. Then, if the company follows the practice of refunding at death the unearned portion of the premium, it is added to the amount otherwise payable under the policy.

Grace period clauses generally are silent on the question of interest from the premium due date, but companies usually forget about the interest when the premium is paid during the grace period. On the other hand, many companies charge interest for the grace period when the premium is paid in part or in full by the use of the automatic premium loan provision, which is discussed later.

Incontestability

The incontestability clause says that the company cannot "contest" the policy after it has been in force for two years. (In a few companies the period is one year.) This is a crucial policy provision. In the absence of such a clause, the company could deny a death claim, many years after the policy had been issued, on the grounds that the insured had made a misstatement on the original application, even though the misstatement may have been inadvertent. Such a denial might create a difficult situation for the beneficiary, not only because the insured is not alive to argue his case, but also because the beneficiary might be in need of the funds and thus at a disadvantage in a protracted legal dispute.

Over the years, the courts have broadened the effect of the clause so that it even protects a beneficiary when the insured had made apparently fraudulent statements to obtain the insurance. About the only situations in which insurance companies have been able to get around the clause are those in which the fraud is outrageous, as in the case of a policy taken out with the intent to murder the insured. In other words, the incontestability clause is a powerful form of protection for the beneficiary.

It is important, however, to distinguish between a contest and a denial of a claim under a policy provision. Suppose, for example, a policy is issued with an aviation restriction, under which the company does not have to pay the face amount if the insured dies in the crash of a private plane he was piloting. When the company denies the payment of a claim in this kind of situation, it is merely following a policy provision—the aviation restriction. Such a denial is not a "contest" and is not affected by the incontestability clause.

Suicide

The insuring agreement states that the company will pay the face amount upon receipt of due proof of the insured's death. In the absence of a clause to the contrary, therefore, the company would have to pay even if death resulted from suicide. To protect the companies from having to pay death claims on behalf of insureds who buy life insurance with the intent to commit suicide, the contracts contain a suicide clause that reduces the liability of the companies to a return of the premiums if suicide occurs within two years (or, in a few policies, one year) of the issue date of the policy.

The suicide clause also can be justified from the standpoint of public policy. In the absence of the restriction, the availability of the life insurance contract could be viewed as an inducement to suicide. For example, if a man is seriously depressed, the financial plight of his family in the event of his death might be the one thing that would prevent him from suicide. If he could buy a large amount of life insurance without a suicide restriction, however, he might obtain such coverage and promptly commit suicide.

Reinstatement

When a premium is not paid by the end of the grace period, and when the automatic premium loan provision (discussed later) is not operative, the policy lapses. The reinstatement clause spells out the requirements that would have to be met for the policy to be reinstated. Normally four conditions must be met: the policy must not have been surrendered for its cash value, the reinstatement must be carried out within a specified period (often five years) after lapse, the insured must produce evidence of insurability satisfactory to the insurance company, and the overdue premiums must be paid together with compound interest (usually 5 or 6 percent) from their respective due dates.

Misstatement of age

When the insured dies, a discrepancy is sometimes found between the age of the insured at death and his age at the date of issue. In such a situation, the misstatement of age clause provides for the face amount to be adjusted to what the premium would have bought at the correct age.

For example, suppose John Brown buys a $25,000 straight life policy at the stated age of 35. His annual premium is $462. He dies exactly ten years later, at which time it is found that he is 46. The premium he was paying would have bought a $24,081 policy at age 36, so the latter is the amount paid by the insurance company. The clause also operates in the opposite direction. For example, if it is found that John is 44 at death, the amount paid by the company would be $25,932.

This clause seems eminently fair, but in recent years it has been criticized. It has been argued that some companies use the clause only when it operates in their favor. Further, it has been argued that it is unfair to base a settlement on the age given in a death certificate, for three reasons. First, such a certificate comes into existence only at a time when the insured can no longer challenge it. Second, the age on a death certificate often is written in carelessly. Third, the effect of the practice is to place the burden upon the beneficiary to disprove the age on the death certificate. The beneficiary may need the funds in a hurry, may not be able to secure proof of the insured's age readily, and may be unable to afford the legal expense of fighting a relatively small reduction in the amount payable. Thus, it is argued that some companies use the misstatement of age clause to engage in a form of "clipping." [1]

How can you protect your beneficiary in this area? File a proof of age with the company during your lifetime. Get the company to acknowledge that such proof is satisfactory, and file the acknowledgement with the policy. Some companies' policies specifically refer to their willingness to receive and acknowledge a proof of age, but other companies probably would do the same.

This procedure is worth following. The size of the adjustment in the illustration above was substantial, and the discrepancy in the illustration was only one year. If the discrepancy were five or ten years, the reduction could be a substantial proportion of the amount otherwise payable at death.

Alteration of policy

The alteration clause states that no modification of the policy is valid unless it is accomplished in writing over the signature of a company officer. The moral is that you should not accept the verbal (or written, for that matter) assurances of an agent.

To illustrate, suppose the contract is silent on the question of interest between the date of death and the date of settlement (as discussed earlier). You ask the agent about it, and he assures you his company pays such interest. Do not take his word for it. Have him obtain for you a letter to that effect over the signature of a company officer, and file the letter with your policy.

Dividend options

When a policy is participating, the company contemplates the payment of periodic (usually annual) amounts that are unfortunately called "dividends." The terminology is unfortunate because the word "dividend" implies that the policyholder is receiving something that resembles the dividend paid to a corporate shareholder. It is more logical, however, to view a life insurance policy dividend as a refund of part of the premiums. This view is the one that has been adopted in the Internal Revenue Code and is the reason why life insurance policy dividends are not taxable income to the policyholder.

Regardless of how they are viewed or what they are called, life insurance policy dividends are simply periodic payments to the policyholder. Companies usually offer their policyholders a variety of ways in which to dispose of the dividends. In some sales interviews, the discussion of these dividend options consumes a disproportionate amount of time, perhaps because it is more pleasant to talk about dividends than to talk about death.

One of the dividend options is the cash option. Here the policyholder receives a check each year for the amount of the dividend. Another option is to use the dividend to reduce the premium. Here the dividend is applied against the premium that is due, and the premium notice asks the policyholder to remit the difference between the premium and the dividend.

Both of these options result in the policyholder's immediate receipt of the dividend. Other options involve the policyholder's leaving the dividends with the company.

The third option is to leave the dividends with the company to accumulate at interest. The result here is the establishment of what amounts to a savings account. The contract usually guarantees a minimum interest rate in the 2 to 3 percent range. Companies then declare additional interest from year to year in accordance with current economic conditions. Usually the total interest rate paid under the dividend accumulation option is below the interest rates paid by most savings banks and savings and loan associations.

In the event of the policyholder's death, any dividend accumulation is paid to the beneficiary in addition to the face amount; in the event that the policyholder cashes in the policy, any dividend accumulation is paid to the policyholder in addition to the cash value. The accumulation is withdrawable by the policyholder at any time, but normally cannot be put back. The interest on the dividend accumulations is taxable in the same manner as interest on a savings account.

The fourth common option is to use each dividend to buy a "paid-up addition" to the basic policy. This means that each dividend is used to buy a small single-premium life insurance addition to the basic policy. The amount of the paid-up addition is determined by the amount of the dividend, the age of the policyholder at the time the dividend is payable, and the company's premium rates for paid-up additions. The chief advantage of paid-up additions is that they are available without evidence of insurability. Therefore, they are advantageous to the policyholder who is no longer insurable, or to the policyholder who can qualify for life insurance only at a high rate.

It is sometimes said that another advantage of paid-up additions is that they are a low-priced form of insurance. This statement may or may not be true. The only way to find out is to do a price analysis of paid-up additions. In one such study several years ago, the author found that the paid-up additions offered by some companies were indeed low-priced, while the paid-up additions offered by other companies were quite high-priced.[2]

Aside from the possibility that the paid-up additions in a given company may be high-priced, another disadvantage of this option is the type of insurance represented by such additions. Rarely is single premium life insurance appropriate. If you want $100,000 of life insurance, would you pay a single premium of $40,000 to get it? If not, why would you use a $40 dividend to buy a $100 paid-up addition? As stated repeatedly in this book, the life insurance needs of most people can be met satisfactorily with straight life, five-year renewable term, or some combination of the two. Both of these are annual premium rather than single premium forms of insurance.

A few companies offer a "full term addition" option. Here the dividend is used to buy one-year term insurance. Again, the amount of a term addition is determined by the amount of the dividend, the age of the policyholder at the time the dividend is payable, and the company's premium rates on term additions. Although you should check on the price of such additions, the coverage is less likely to be overpriced than are paid-up additions. Moreover, unlike paid-up additions, the one-year term form of insurance often is appropriate. It is not uncommon for a $40 dividend to buy $10,000 or more of one-year term coverage under this option. It is unfortunate that the option is offered only by a handful of companies. Among the forty-five companies for which price data were assembled in this book, those offering the full term addition option are Home Life (New York), Lincoln National, and Occidental (California).[3]

Many companies offer one or more "split term addition" options that are some combination of the full term addition option and another option. For example, many companies offer an option under which a part of the dividend is used to buy one-year term insurance equal to the basic policy's cash value, and the remainder of the dividend is left with the company either to accumulate or to buy a paid-up addition.

The simplest thing to do is to take out each dividend as it arises, usually by applying it to the premium then payable. This approach may be satisfactory if you have carefully purchased the amount of life insurance you need and if you plan to review your needs frequently. Should you decide to leave your dividends with the company, however, the material in this section will help you understand some of the available options.

Straight life contract provisions

The first section of this chapter dealt with contract provisions found in life insurance policies of all kinds. This second section contains discussions of several provisions peculiar to cash-value policies, including, more specifically, straight life policies.

The loan clause

It has already been mentioned that the existence of the loan clause is an important factor in making the savings element of a cash-value life insurance policy a highly liquid asset from the policyholder's point of view. It is similarly important for the policyholder to understand how the clause operates.

Generally, the maximum amount that can be borrowed under the loan clause is the cash value. The loan value and the cash value are not always identical, but this generalization is sufficiently accurate for the purposes of this discussion.

The clause provides that, with the exception of loans granted for the purpose of paying premiums on the company's policies, the company may postpone the granting of the loan for up to six months. This provision is similar to the delay clause found in savings accounts, and both were instituted as a result of the traumatic bank runs of the Great Depression. The delay provision apparently has not been used by life insurance companies, and the potentially disastrous public relations effect of invoking it is likely to deter companies from using it except under the most extreme circumstances.

In the event that the insured dies with a loan outstanding against the policy, the amount of the loan and any unpaid interest is deducted from the funds payable to the beneficiary. Similarly, in the event that a loan is outstanding at the time the policyholder cashes in the policy, the amount of the loan and any unpaid interest is deducted from the cash value. With these exceptions, there is no requirement about repayment of the loan. The policyholder can pay off the loan in full whenever he wishes to do so, or he may send in partial payments at any time (although there usually is a minimum limit, such as $10, that the company will handle), or he may make no repayment.

This lack of a repayment requirement has been described accurately both as an advantage of policy loans and as a disadvantage. On the one hand, it is nice to be free from pressure to repay. On the other hand, it is argued that the absence of the pressure makes repayment less likely and that the lack of repayment may thus disrupt the systematic savings aspect of cash-value life insurance.

Some critics of life insurance argue illogically that the companies are treating policyholders unfairly by charging interest on policy loans. And, as explained in Chapter 3, it is also illogical to say that the payment of policy loan interest means that the policyholder is "paying interest on his own money." Interest is an important factor in the construction of life insurance premiums, cash values, and dividends, and it is assumed that the funds held by a life insurance company are placed in interest-bearing investments. When some of the funds are used by policyholders, therefore, it is appropriate for such policyholders to pay interest on such funds.

The policy loan interest rate is specified in the contract. For about thirty years prior to 1969, the policy loan interest rate was 5 percent in many of the major companies' policies. In the last few years, because of the rapid rise in interest rates generally, many companies have increased the rate to 6 percent on new policies currently issued. New policies issued in New York State, however, still carry a 5 percent rate because the New York Insurance Law still imposes an upper limit of 4.8 percent interest payable in advance (which is equivalent to a true annual interest rate of about 5.04 percent, as explained shortly). Intensive efforts by life insurance industry lobbyists to persuade the New York legislature to modify this limitation have not yet been successful.

The loan clause in some policies states that interest will be at the rate of 6 percent per annum and uses such language as "will be due and payable at the end of each policy year," or "will be due and payable annually, not in advance." In such policies, if $100 is borrowed at the beginning of the policy year and repaid at the end of the policy year, $6 of interest is also payable at the end of the policy year. Since the policyholder has the use of $100 for a year and pays $6 interest at the end of the year, the true annual policy loan interest rate is 6 percent ($6 divided by $100).

Some policies, however, state that interest will be at the rate of 6 percent per annum "payable in advance." Let's again assume that $100 is borrowed at the beginning of the year and repaid at the end of the year. In this case, however, the company would take out the $6 of interest at the beginning of the year, and the policyholder would receive $94. At the end of the year, the policyholder would pay $100. Thus, the policyholder in effect pays $6 at the end of the year for the use of $94 for the year, and the true annual policy loan interest rate is about 6.38 percent ($6 divided by $94).

When the life insurance companies are required to comply with truth-in-lending legislation, they will have to disclose the true annual interest rate on policy loans. Meanwhile, the wording of the loan clause must be examined in order to ascertain the true annual interest rate.

Automatic premium loans

Most cash-value policies now include an automatic premium loan (APL) clause. When operative, the clause states that the company will automatically make a policy loan to pay a premium that is not paid by the end of the grace period, provided that the policy contains a loan value sufficient to handle the premium. The clause is operative only if it has been elected by the policyholder, and the election may be made either at the time of application or at some later date. No charge is levied by the company for the clause itself.

The APL clause can be both valuable and convenient, but it also can be troublesome. It can be valuable because the policy is automatically kept in force even though a premium may have been left unpaid inadvertently by the policyholder. In the absence of APL, the policy would go into a state of lapse and would require reinstatement to be put back in full force.

It can be convenient because the policyholder may not have the funds readily available to pay a premium, and the APL clause means that he does not have to go through the mechanics of obtaining a policy loan. Similarly, he may have readily available only enough to pay part of the premium, in which case he can send in that portion and simply indicate that the balance is to be handled by APL.

The APL clause can be troublesome, however, because a policyholder may come to rely too heavily upon it. He may get in the habit of allowing premiums to be paid by APL, and this may tend to destroy the long-term systematic savings aspect of cash-value life insurance.

Despite this troublesome aspect, it usually is desirable to elect the APL clause. You should familiarize yourself with it, however. Some companies allow only one or two consecutive premiums to be handled by APL, while others allow any number of premiums to be so handled.

When a premium is paid by APL, the result is essentially the same as though the policyholder had borrowed under the loan clause and used the funds so obtained to pay the premium. The only exception to this generalization is that some companies charge interest on automatic premium loans beginning on the premium due date, although other companies charge interest beginning at the end of the grace period. When interest is measured from the premium due date, the effect is to charge interest for the use of the grace period, a charge which otherwise is not made. This is a relatively minor point; for example, one month's interest on an annual premium of $500 paid by automatic premium loan, with a policy loan interest rate of 6 percent, would be only about $2.50. It illustrates, however, the way in which money is sometimes extracted from policyholders in almost invisible ways.

Nonforfeiture options

An understanding of nonforfeiture options requires some explanation. And the explanation involves a discussion of some life insurance fundamentals.

Death rates (or mortality rates) are the raw materials from which life insurance is fashioned. A mortality table is a device used by life insurance companies in many of their calculations and is developed by observing death rates among a large number of people at various ages. Suppose, for example, that a mortality table shows a death rate of .00140 at age 35. This means that out of 100,000 persons aged 35 it is expected that 140 will die within one year. Now suppose an insurance company wishes to sell $1,000 one-year term life insurance policies to a number of persons aged 35. Disregarding the timing of deaths and the timing of the insurance company's receipts during the year, it would be necessary for each person to pay $1.40 just to cover the estimated mortality costs of the $1,000 one-year term policy.

Death rates, and therefore the mortality costs of life insurance, increase rapidly with age. For example, here are some of the death rates in a recent mortality table based on the combined experience of a group of large life insurance companies:

Age	Death Rate
25	.00125
35	.00140
45	.00396
55	.01100
65	.02799
75	.06336
85	.14917

Thus, while it would take only $1.40 per $1,000 to cover the estimated mortality costs at age 35, it would take $3.96 at age 45,

$11.00 at age 55, $27.99 at age 65, and so forth. In reality, it would be necessary for each person to pay more than these amounts, because the insurance company must add enough to the premiums to take care of its expenses and make a profit.

Now suppose a policyholder buys a one-year term life insurance policy. Further, suppose the policy is renewable, which means he is guaranteed the right to renew the coverage for additional one-year periods without having to requalify. The premiums under such a policy would increase as the policyholder ages, in a manner similar to the increase in mortality rates. These increasing premiums are disconcerting to the policyholder, and they also present a difficult problem for the insurance company. The problem results from the fact that there is an increasingly strong tendency for healthy persons to discontinue their insurance as the premium gets higher and higher and for unhealthy individuals to continue their coverage. This means that there is a tendency for the remaining group to "deteriorate." This phenomenon is referred to in life insurance jargon as "adverse selection" because it results in a higher level of death payments by the insurance company, relative to premium payments, than would be the case in the absence of the adverse selection.

To overcome this adverse selection, at least to some extent, and to keep premiums down in the later years, insurance companies devised an arrangement under which premiums remain unchanged as the policyholder gets older. This level-premium arrangement requires higher premiums in the earlier policy years than would be paid under a one-year renewable term plan of insurance, to make up for lower premiums in the later policy years. For example, if interest is not taken into account, the level annual premium for each $1,000 of straight life insurance issued to 35-year-olds under the mortality table shown above would be $25.63, which would cover just the mortality costs of the policy.

Because the life insurance contract usually is a long-term financial instrument, the interest factor plays a crucial and powerful role. Consider the foregoing level premium of $25.63, which is calculated without the interest factor. When 5 percent interest is brought into the calculations, the level annual premium drops to $10.56. Again, this covers just the estimated mortality costs, so it would have to be increased to permit the insurance company to cover its expenses and make a profit.

As mentioned earlier, the insurance company's promises under a life insurance contract are conditioned upon the payment of premiums, but policyholders do not *have* to pay their premiums. They are free to discontinue their payments at any time, and many do.

Under a one-year renewable term policy, with its increasing premiums, the policyholder who discontinues premium payments receives no cash value. Such a policyholder has paid for and received protection from year to year, just as in the case of a fire insurance policy or an automobile insurance policy.

Under a level-premium life insurance contract, however, the policyholder pays more in the early policy years than he would pay under a one-year renewable term plan. When such a policyholder discontinues premium payments, it is reasonable that he should receive a cash value payment from the insurance company and that the amount of the payment should represent roughly the amount of his overpayment (including interest). The word "roughly" is used here because it is necessary to adjust the cash value, particularly in the early policy years, to compensate for the company's initial expenses in writing the policy.

In the early days of life insurance in the United States, companies often paid nothing when a policyholder discontinued a level-premium contract. Critics of this practice referred to the policyholder as being forced by the company to "forfeit" the overpayments he had made relative to what he would have paid if he had bought one-year renewable term insurance instead. The laws introduced to require cash values for terminating policyholders were thus called "nonforfeiture laws." Similarly, the various ways in which terminating policyholders could obtain their cash values were called "nonforfeiture options" or "nonforfeiture values."

The typical straight life policy has three nonforfeiture options. One of these is the cash value, which is the single sum that the policyholder may receive when he terminates the policy. The cash values available at various points in time are shown in the table of nonforfeiture values in the policy.

Another of the nonforfeiture options is paid-up insurance. Here the policyholder leaves the cash value with the company and receives instead a paid-up life insurance policy. In effect the cash value of the straight life policy is used to buy a single premium life insurance policy. The face amount of the paid-up policy usually is well below the face amount of the original policy and is determined by the amount of the cash value, the age of the insured at the time the original policy is terminated, and the company's premium rates for paid-up insurance. The amounts of paid-up insurance available at various points in time are shown in the table of nonforfeiture values in the policy. For example, in a $25,000 straight life policy issued by Connecticut Mutual to males aged 35, the cash value at the end of the tenth policy year is $3,999, and the amount of paid-up insurance purchased by that cash value is $8,575.

As in the case of the paid-up additions dividend option discussed earlier, it is difficult to generalize about whether the paid-up insurance nonforfeiture option is favorably priced. The option is available without evidence of insurability, but beyond that it should be viewed as a substantial purchase of single premium life insurance and evaluated as such in comparison with other single premium life insurance available in the market.

The other nonforfeiture option is extended term insurance. Here the policyholder leaves the cash value with the company and receives instead a paid-up term policy with a face amount equal to the face amount of the original policy. In effect the cash value of the original policy is used to buy a single premium term policy. The length of the term is determined by the amount of the cash value, the age of the insured at the time the original policy is terminated, and the company's premium rates for extended term insurance. The lengths of the term coverage available at various points in time are shown in the table of nonforfeiture values in the policy. For example, at the end of the tenth policy year in the above Connecticut Mutual policy issued at age 35, the length of the term is 15 years and 345 days. Thus the coverage would extend until the policyholder is about 61 (his age of 45 at the time the original policy terminated, plus almost 16 additional years). Should the policyholder die prior to 61, the full face amount would be payable to the beneficiary. If he survives to 61, the term coverage would expire without any cash value.

The price situation for extended term insurance is particularly difficult to assess, because single premium term insurance is not widely available in the market. Even if it were available, it is unlikely that it would be offered for the odd periods of time associated with the extended term insurance option. As with the other nonforfeiture options, the extended term insurance option is available to the policyholder without evidence of insurability.

In most straight life policies now being issued, the extended term insurance option is the one that goes into effect automatically if the policyholder fails to pay a premium by the end of the grace period, allows the policy to lapse, and fails to elect one of the other options. However, if the automatic premium loan clause is operative, the policy would not lapse, and the extended term insurance option would not go into effect.

When a policy with a loan outstanding goes on extended term, the face amount of the extended term insurance is reduced by the amount of the loan. Furthermore, the cash value used in determining the length of the extended term coverage is reduced by the amount of the loan. For example, assume the above-mentioned straight life policy issued by Connecticut Mutual has a $1,000 policy loan outstanding at the end of the tenth year, when the policyholder elects the extended term insurance option. The $25,000 face amount is reduced by $1,000, and the $3,999 cash value is reduced by $1,000. Then, the remaining cash value of $2,999 would be used as a single premium to buy $24,000 of term insurance for as long as the $2,999 would carry the coverage beginning at the insured's age of 45, when the original policy was terminated.

Settlement options

The settlement options that are available to the beneficiary were discussed in the first section of this chapter. In cash-value policies, the same settlement options generally are available to the policyholder with respect to the cash values. For example, a policyholder who discontinues premium payments could receive the cash value in installments under the fixed amount option. Or the policyholder who is well along in years might wish to receive the cash value under one of the life annuity options. The various considerations mentioned earlier with regard to the beneficiary apply with equal force to the policyholder who wishes to utilize the settlement options for himself.

Change of plan

Many straight life policies contain a change-of-plan provision under which the policy may be converted to a higher-premium plan of insurance, such as a limited-payment life or endowment policy, as of the issue date of the straight life policy. The financial adjustment required for such a change varies among companies. One common approach requires the policyholder to pay an amount equal to the difference between the cash values of the two plans, plus a carrying charge of 3 percent of that difference. Because the enlargement of the savings element reduces the amount of life insurance protection, such a change requires no evidence of insurability.

Conversely, higher-premium plans of insurance usually can be converted to a lower-premium plan, such as straight life, as of the issue date of the higher-premium policy. Here the common practice is for the insurance company to pay the policyholder the difference between the cash values of the two plans. Because the reduction in the savings element increases the amount of life insurance protection, companies usually require evidence of insurability to effect such a change.

Renewable term contract provisions

It is sometimes said that renewable term contracts are relatively simple in comparison with straight life contracts, but this observation fails to consider certain significant complexities in term policies. This section contains discussions of provisions peculiar to renewable term policies.

Sample policies were requested of the companies for which price data are shown in Chapter 4. At the time the data were being assembled, two of the companies—Franklin Life and Northwestern Mutual—did not issue five-year renewable term contracts. In addition, the author disregarded the five-year renewable term contract of the Western and Southern because of its extremely restrictive conversion clause, which is mentioned later. The references to companies in this section, therefore, pertain to the other forty-two companies whose sample five-year renewable term contracts were examined.

Renewability

The renewability clause spells out the duration of the coverage available under a term policy without evidence of insurability. The clause can be quite tricky. It is not enough to know merely that a five-year renewable term policy is "renewable to age 65." Some contracts so described can be renewed for an additional five-year term at any time up to age 65; thus, a contract bought at a quinquennial age (such as 30, 35, 40, and so forth) could be continued to age 70, while a contract bought at age 43, for example, could be continued to age 68.

On the other hand, some five-year renewable term contracts described as "renewable to age 65" can be renewed for an additional term at any time prior to 65, but only for a period such that coverage will expire at 65. For example, a contract bought at a quinquennial age would expire at 65; a contract bought at age 43, for example, could be renewed at age 63, but only for a two-year term that would expire at 65.

Among the forty-two policies studied, and assuming purchase at one of the quinquennial ages, twenty-four were continuable to age 65 and eighteen were continuable to 70. These figures are shown in the second column in Table 4–3.

In short, it is important to note the precise wording of the renewability clause in order to know to what age the coverage may be continued without evidence of insurability. Indeed, to be even more precise, you should pin down the exact date on which coverage expires without a continuation privilege. This determination necessarily differs between companies that classify applicants by age nearest birthday and those that classify applicants by age last birthday.

Premiums

Under five-year renewable term policies, the premium increases each time the policy is renewed for an additional five-year term. In most policies, the future premiums that will be charged are shown in the contract. In some policies, however, the renewal premiums are not shown.

Among the forty-two policies studied, all but three showed what the renewal premiums would be. The three policies that did not disclose this information were those issued by American National, Business Men's, and Great-West Life.

Information about future premiums is something that the buyer should have. In the absence of such information in the contract, the company could modify its premium rates substantially at some later date. You should check into this point if you buy a five-year renewable term contract.

Grace period

The grace period was discussed in the first section of this chapter. A special problem may exist in five-year renewable term policies, however, because technically the coverage expires at the end of each term. The question, then, is whether the coverage continues in effect for thirty-one days following the expiration date if the first premium for the subsequent term period is not paid on time.

Among the forty-two policies studied, twenty-four specify in the contract that the coverage remains in force during the thirty-one days following expiration of the term period. In other words, a grace period for the first premium of a subsequent term is allowed in such policies just as it is for other premiums.

In the other eighteen policies, however, the wording of the contract did not seem clear on this point. As a result of correspondence with these companies, it appears that sixteen of them interpret the contract as allowing a grace period for the first premium of a subsequent term. The other two—American National and New England Life—apparently do not provide for such a grace period.

You should check on this point if you buy a five-year renewable term policy. It presents no problem if you follow the practice of paying premiums on or before their due dates. But if you follow the practice of utilizing all or part of the grace period, it is possible that a five-year renewable term contract would be ineffective during a period of up to thirty-one days following the expiration of each five-year term. If you should die during such a period of ineffectiveness, it would be a disaster for your beneficiary.

Convertibility

The convertibility clause spells out the conditions under which the term policy may be exchanged for a straight life or other cash-value policy without evidence of insurability. In the case of five-year renewable term policies, the period within which such conversion may be made sometimes runs to the end of the period of coverage provided for in the renewability clause. More frequently, however, the conversion period ends some time prior to the end of the period of coverage.

Among the forty-two policies studied, the conversion periods end at various points. In five of the policies, the conversion period ends at age 60, in ten of the policies at 62, two at 63, one at 64, twenty at 65, one at 68, and three at 70. These figures are shown in the third column in Table 4–3.

There are two ways to convert. In one of these—called an "attained age conversion"—the new policy is written as of the time of conversion. In other words, the premium for the straight life policy is based on the age of the insured at the time of conversion, and the policy form is of the type written by the company at that time. This is the most common form of conversion and is provided for in all of the policies.

The other way to convert is under an "original age conversion." Here the new policy is written as of the issue date of the term policy. The premium is based on the age of the insured when he bought the term policy. To obtain the lower premium rate, however, a financial adjustment is necessary at the time of conversion. Frequently the policyholder must pay the company a sum equal to the difference in premiums since the issue date of the term policy, together with 5 or 6 percent interest compounded annually on such differences. Some of the term policies do not offer this type of conversion at all, and those that do usually limit the period (sometimes to five years) within which such a conversion may be made. In any case, the size of the financial adjustment represents a major barrier to this type of conversion, and it is not done frequently.

Five-year renewable term policies usually permit at least an attained age conversion at any time up to the end of the conversion period. The Western and Southern policy, however, is not convertible until age 65, at which time the coverage would otherwise terminate. This conversion privilege is so restricted as to make the contract not comparable to the others studied. It was for this reason that the price data for this contract were omitted from Table 4–3 and from the various renewable term tables in Appendix D.

Incontestability and suicide

The incontestability and suicide clauses were discussed in the first section of this chapter. The process of converting a five-year renewable term policy, however, creates certain additional considerations regarding these clauses.

To illustrate, let's assume that Tom buys a five-year renewable term policy on July 1, 1972. Exactly three years later—on July 1, 1975—he converts to straight life at attained age. Then, on February 1, 1976, Tom dies. The questions are these: Is the policy contestable? And is the suicide clause in effect?

The question about incontestability may be academic. When Tom converted, no evidence of insurability was required; therefore, with no questions having been asked and no answers having been given, no basis for a contest would exist.

The question about suicide, however, is far from academic. If Tom's death were the result of suicide, and if the suicide period of the new policy were measured from the date of conversion, then the company's liability would be limited to the return of any premiums paid on the new policy. On the other hand, if the suicide period were measured from the issue date of the original term policy, the company's liability would be the face amount.

Two of the forty-two term policies—those issued by Massachusetts Mutual and Nationwide Life—provide specifically for the incontestability and suicide clauses of a new policy to be endorsed so that the periods run from the issue date of the original term policy. Although the other forty term policies are silent on this point, the comments of the companies' officials suggest that many of them endorse the new contract routinely by company practice. Some officials argued that the companies would be hard pressed—legally, morally, and on the basis of "common sense"—to deny liability in such a situation. One official—indicating that his company followed the practice of endorsing the new policy—suggested that the point should be irrelevant for a policyholder acting in good faith. This latter comment would be of little consolation to Tom's widow if he were to convert with no intention of committing suicide, if the company were to fail to endorse the contract, if he were to go berserk and commit suicide, and if the company's liability were to be limited to a return of any premiums paid on the new policy.

You should check on this point when you buy a five-year renewable term policy. If a company does not provide for such an endorsement in its term policy, and if it follows the practice of endorsing the new policy upon conversion, it should be willing to guarantee such an endorsement by letter. If a company does not provide for such an endorsement in its term policy, and if it does not follow the practice of endorsing the new policy upon conversion, you are then forewarned about the possibility of a new suicide period under the new policy.

The waiver-of-premium clause

The waiver-of-premium clause, under which premiums are waived in the event of a total and permanent disability of the insured, has been discussed in earlier chapters. When such a clause is attached to a term policy, however, there are several different practices concerning the inclusion of the clause in a new policy obtained under the conversion clause of the term policy. Indeed, the practices in this area are so complex and varied that only a superficial examination is possible here.

Suppose Bill buys a five-year renewable term policy with a waiver-of-premium clause, converts a few years later to straight life at attained age, is not disabled at the time of conversion, and desires to include the waiver-of-premium clause in the new policy. One of the forty-two companies—National Life and Accident—will not allow inclusion of the waiver-of-premium clause without evidence of insurability. Although the other forty-one companies will allow such inclusion without evidence of insurability, they differ in certain other respects.

Four of the companies—Business Men's, Connecticut General, Great-West Life, and Southwestern Life—provide that the waiver-of-premium clause is operative only with respect to disabilities that are not the result of an injury sustained or disease contracted prior to the date of conversion. For example, if Bill suffered a disability traceable to an illness that he had contracted prior to the date of conversion, the waiver-of-premium clause of his straight life policy would not be operative. This shows that the infamous "pre-existing conditions" clause, which has been severely criticized in the field of health insurance, is also to be found in the life insurance business.

Six of the companies—Equitable (New York), Great-West Life, Home Life (New York), National Life (Vermont), Nationwide Life, and Penn Mutual—provide that the waiver-of-premium clause may be included in the new policy without evidence of insurability only if conversion is made prior to age 55. The effect of this provision is to shorten Bill's conversion period if he wishes to have the waiver-of-premium clause included in the new contract without evidence of insurability.

Provided that the insured is not disabled at the date of conversion, most of the companies studied allow the waiver-of-premium clause to be included in the new policy without evidence of insurability, without any "pre-existing conditions" clause, and without any additional age restrictions. This is the most desirable approach from the buyer's point of view.

Now suppose Bill buys a five-year renewable term policy with a waiver-of-premium clause, becomes totally and permanently disabled a few years later, and wants to convert to straight life at attained age. Would he be able to obtain the waiver-of-premium clause in the straight life policy without evidence of insurability, which he would be unable to provide?

About one-third of the companies provide that the waiver-of-premium clause may be included in the straight life policy only if the conversion is postponed until a specified age. In each of these cases, the specified age is 55 or older. In these companies, for example, if Bill wishes to convert immediately after becoming disabled, or at some point prior to the specified minimum age, the waiver-of-premium clause would not be included in the new straight life policy. This provision discourages conversion by disabled policyholders, because premiums would be waived if the coverage were continued as term insurance, but would not be waived if the policy were converted to straight life.

Most of the companies studied, however, would allow Bill to convert at any time within the conversion period and would include the waiver-of-premium clause in the straight life policy without evidence of insurability. This approach is far more desirable from the buyer's point of view. Conversion by disabled policyholders would actually be encouraged, because the higher premiums for the straight life policy would be waived and the cash value would begin to accumulate for the benefit of the policyholder.

Summary

The points discussed above relating to five-year renewable term contracts are complex. At the same time, they can be quite important, and the buyer should know where he stands with respect to them. By way of summary, the following is a list of questions to which you should have the answers before you buy a five-year renewable term policy:

- To what age can coverage be continued without evidence of insurability?
- Is the premium rate for each renewal period specified in the contract?
- If the insured dies within thirty-one days after the expiration of a five-year term period, and if the first premium for the subsequent five-year term period has not been paid, would the insurance coverage still be in effect?
- To what age can the policy be converted to straight life at attained age without evidence of insurability?
- Does the five-year renewable term contract guarantee that, if the insured converts to straight life at attained age, the suicide and incontestability clauses in the straight life policy would be modified to provide that the periods be measured beginning with the issue date of the term policy?
- If the insured is not disabled at the time of conversion, and if he converts to straight life at attained age, would the waiver-of-premium clause be included in the straight life contract without evidence of insurability?
- If the insured is disabled at the time of conversion, and if he converts to straight life at attained age, would the waiver-of-premium clause be included in the straight life contract without evidence of insurability?

Chapter 8

As and after you buy

Earlier chapters have dealt with such questions as how much to buy, what kind to buy, what company to choose, and what the contractual fine print is all about. This chapter deals with several miscellaneous topics that should be considered as you buy life insurance and after your purchase.

Applying for life insurance

When you apply for life insurance, there are several points to keep in mind. These are discussed in this first section of the chapter.

The application

The application for life insurance usually consists of two parts. The first part requires such information as your address, date of birth, and amount and kind of insurance you desire, the premium, the initial beneficiary designation, whether you desire the automatic premium loan clause to be in effect, and so forth. This is the sort of information needed by the company in order to prepare the policy.

The second part of the application requires information about your health, habits, and occupation, on the basis of which the company decides whether it is willing to write the insurance. Sometimes this second part of the application is completed by a physician in the course of a medical examination of you. Such an examination usually is required when the amount of insurance is large, when you are well along in years, or when your medical history is complex.

In many applications, however, the second part is completed by an agent, in which case it is called a "nonmedical application." Here the agent asks a long series of medical-type questions and records the answers. Most companies use the nonmedical application form when the amount of insurance is $25,000 or less, when the applicant is 40 or younger, and when the applicant's medical history is fairly clean. The company will require a medical examination if it is not satisfied with the results of the nonmedical application. The reason for the nonmedical approach is that the companies save more money by eliminating the medical examination than they lose by way of additional death claims.

The insurance company has other sources of information about you. Sometimes the company will request an inspection report from an organization such as the Retail Credit Company. The report the insurance company receives may be based in part on information about you that the inspection company has in its files from previous investigations and in part on information obtained in a new investigation. This is why you may sometimes hear from friends or neighbors that someone has been asking questions about you.

Another source of information is the Medical Information Bureau (MIB), which is an information clearinghouse operated by a large number of insurance companies on a cooperative basis. On the one hand, it is sometimes said that the insurance companies are "ganging up" on individual applicants. On the other hand, the insurance companies argue that such a clearinghouse is needed because of the substantial number of applicants who submit fraudulent information in an attempt to obtain coverage. The companies argue that the MIB helps protect them from such applicants, thereby keeping the price of insurance reasonable for the applicants who are acting in good faith.[1]

When you apply for insurance, you should tell the company the truth about yourself. Beware of the agent who advises you to play fast and loose on the second part of the application. If he is the kind who condones a few little falsehoods on the application, he is probably the kind who will tell you a few little falsehoods about the coverage you are buying. Don't stoop to his level. It is important to have the life insurance you need, but it is not worth turning yourself into a dishonest person to get it.

First premium

There are two ways in which to put life insurance into effect. One is to complete the two parts of the application, wait for the company to approve the insurance, and then pay the first premium upon delivery of the policy. When this procedure is followed, the insurance does not take effect until the policy has been delivered and the first premium has been paid. The result can be disastrous. You might change to a more hazardous occupation between the date of application and the date of delivery. You might suffer a coronary or develop some other serious health problem during the interval. Or you might even die. If there is any significant change in your health, habits, or occupation between the date of application and the date of delivery, the agent would have to withhold delivery and inform the company.

The other approach is far more preferable because it avoids all such possible complications. The two parts of the application are completed and the first premium is sent to the company along with the application. When this procedure is followed, the insurance, if approved by the company exactly as applied for, would take effect on the last of three dates: the date the first part of the application is completed, the date the second part of the application is completed, and the date the check is written. If the application is declined by the company, the applicant would get his money back. If the company offers the coverage but at a premium higher than that applied for, the applicant would have the choice of getting his money back or making up the balance upon delivery of the policy. In the latter case, the insurance takes effect at the time of delivery and payment of the balance.

Under this second approach, the insurance company is bound to consider the applicant in terms of the situation at the time of application. If the applicant is acceptable, the insurance would take effect at the time of application. There are cases on record in which the applicant died in an accident almost immediately after completing the application, so that the death claim went in with the application. In such a situation, if the applicant was acceptable at the time of application and if a check went in with the application, the company would have to pay the face amount.

When you have decided to buy the insurance, you might as well get it into effect at the earliest possible moment. In some companies, it is necessary to send in the full amount of the first premium with the application to bind the coverage. In other companies, however, it may be possible to bind the coverage by sending in merely a portion of the first premium, with the balance payable upon delivery of the policy.

The only possible disadvantage of this approach is that all or a portion of the first premium is paid before you see the policy. This drawback can be offset by examining a sample policy. Any company worthy of your patronage makes sample policies available to its agents. If the agent does not have a sample policy, you should get another agent.

Quantity discounts

Years ago, life insurance companies usually charged the same premium rate per $1,000 of face amount regardless of the size of the policy. Today, however, most companies charge lower premium rates on large policies than on otherwise comparable small policies. Thus life insurance is subject to what may be referred to as "quantity discounts."

There are three ways in which companies may differentiate by size of policy. The first is to offer different policies in various size ranges. For example, a company might offer an endowment at age 85 policy if the face amount is under $10,000, and a straight life policy if the face amount is $10,000 or more.

A second approach is to offer the same policy regardless of size, but to charge different premium rates in various size ranges. For example, under this "band" approach, a company might charge a premium rate of $25 per $1,000 of face amount if the face amount is in the $2,000 to $4,999 range, $23 in the $5,000 to $9,999 range, $22 in the $10,000 to $24,999 range, and $21.50 if the face amount is $25,000 or more.

A third approach, and the one that is probably the most common today, is to offer the same policy regardless of size, but to charge different premium rates for every policy size. This is accomplished by establishing a "basic" premium rate and an annual "policy fee." To determine the premium for a policy, the basic rate is multiplied by the number of thousands of face amount, and then the policy fee is added. For example, a company might have a basic premium rate of $21 per $1,000 of face amount for straight life policies issued to men aged 35, and an annual policy fee of $10. The premium for a $5,000 policy would be $115 ($21 multiplied by 5, plus $10), or $23 per $1,000 of face amount. At $10,000, the premium rate would be $22 per $1,000 of face amount; at $25,000, the premium rate would be $21.40; and so forth.

You should consider quantity discounts when you select the exact size of policy to buy. For example, you might be contemplating the purchase of $10,000 in a company with a lower-rate policy issued from $12,500 up; you should consider upping your purchase to $12,500. Or you might be contemplating the purchase of $20,000 in a company whose next higher band begins at $25,000; you should consider upping your purchase to $25,000. In general, it might be said that quantity discounts are of considerable importance below $10,000, of some importance between $10,000 and $25,000, and of little significance above $25,000.

Insurability problems

Most life insurance applicants qualify for "standard" coverage. This means that they pay the regular premium rates charged by the company. Some applicants, however, qualify for "substandard" insurance (sometimes called "special class" insurance), which means that they pay premium rates that are higher than the company's standard rates. The reason for the higher rates is that the insured's characteristics suggest that he is a member of a group likely to experience higher mortality rates than are found among standard policy-holders. Among such characteristics might be a health impairment or a relatively hazardous occupation.

There are many substandard categories. Some involve premiums only slightly higher than standard, while others involve premiums substantially higher than standard. And then, some policyholders have problems so acute that they do not qualify for life insurance at all.

If you have an insurability problem, causing you to be offered substandard coverage or to be declined altogether, there is no substitute for a competent agent who knows the life insurance business well. Companies differ substantially in liberality with respect to various insurability problems. Some do better than others with diabetes; some do better than others with heart problems; and so forth.

Do not be taken in by glamorous claims of liberal treatment. Remember that companies differ widely in terms of price for standard coverages, as discussed in Chapter 4. Since companies also differ widely in terms of liberality on substandard coverage, the result is a completely unpredictable market for a person with an insurability problem.

Consider the case of Mary Richards, who is 52 and overweight. She wanted $10,000 of nonparticipating straight life. Knowing she probably would qualify only for substandard insurance among the major companies, her agent tried the Summit National Life Insurance Company (Akron, Ohio), which was reputed to be very liberal. (The Company began operations in 1963 and did not receive a policyholders' recommendation in the 1971 edition of *Best's Life Insurance Reports.*) Back came a policy labeled on the front as "standard" insurance. Under the same interest, mortality, and lapse assumptions used in Chapter 4, the retention for the Summit National policy was $2,110. By way of contrast, the retention for a similar standard policy in the Aetna Life (a major company) was $1,066. Under a modified mortality assumption, reflecting Mary's higher probabilities of death, the substandard policy for which Mary probably would qualify in the Aetna Life had a lower retention than the so-called standard policy in the Summit National. The moral of the story is that the superficially attractive offer may not be so attractive under careful scrutiny.

Paying the premiums

The simplest way to handle life insurance premiums is to pay them annually and in full. Since things are not always that simple, two deviations—fractional premiums and financed insurance—are discussed here.

Fractional premiums

Instead of annually, premiums usually may be paid semi-annually, quarterly, or monthly. The only exception to this is that companies normally specify a minimum premium—most commonly $10.

Companies usually impose a "carrying charge" for paying premiums other than annually. For example, the semi-annual premium might be 52 percent of the annual premium. Such an arrangement is sometimes described as a "4 percent carrying charge," but in fact it resembles an interest charge of about 16.7 percent. This latter figure may be arrived at without resort to complex formulas. If you pay a $52 semi-annual premium instead of a $100 annual premium, you defer the payment of $48. Six months later you pay the $48, along with a $4 carrying charge. This means that you pay $4 for the use of $48 for six months, which is the same as paying $8 for the use of $48 for one year. Dividing $8 by $48 yields an annual interest rate of about 16.7 percent.

Here again, as in the case of those companies that charge interest "in advance" on policy loans, the insurance companies are failing to disclose the effective interest rate to policyholders. Until such disclosure is required, it is important that you realize the financial implications of paying premiums other than annually. Some of the common factors applied to annual premiums, and the associated annual percentage rates (to use the truth-in-lending terminology), are shown in Table 8–1.

Technically, the carrying charge is not precisely the same as an interest charge. The carrying charge contains a mortality factor, because companies usually cancel any remaining fractional premiums if the policyholder dies. For example, if a policyholder pays the first quarterly premium in a given policy year and dies before paying the second one, the remaining three quarterly premiums usually are cancelled.

Nevertheless, you should be aware of the carrying charge expressed as an annual percentage rate. Frequently you are better off paying premiums annually even if you have to borrow the money to do so. In the first place, the gross cost of borrowing is often less than the carrying charge. In the second place, the interest you pay is deductible for federal income tax purposes (if you itemize your deductions), while the carrying charge is not.

Table 8–1
Factors commonly applied to annual premiums and the associated annual percentage rates

	Factors	Annual Percentage Rates
Semi-annual premium:		
	.51	8.2%
	.515	12.4
	.52	16.7
Quarterly premium:		
	.26	10.7%
	.2625	13.4
	.265	16.1
Monthly premium:		
	.0875	10.8%
	.0883	12.8
	.09	17.2

To illustrate this point, suppose your annual premium is $500 and your semi-annual premium is $260. If you pay semi-annually, you would incur nondeductible carrying charges of $20. Now suppose you pay $260 toward the annual premium and borrow the remaining $240. Let's say the interest rate is 6 percent, either under your policy loan clause or from a bank. If you pay off the loan six months later, you would pay $247.20, including interest. In other words, you would have incurred deductible interest of $7.20, rather than nondeductible carrying charges of $20.

The major drawback of the borrowing approach is that the insurance company does not send you a reminder about repayment of the loan. In the preceding illustration, for example, you would not receive a reminder to pay the $247.20 at the end of six months. On the other hand, if you pay premiums semi-annually, you would receive a premium notice each time. But you should be willing to keep track of your life insurance premiums, particularly when you see the substantial savings that can accrue from a little effort.

If you contemplate paying premiums other than annually, you should find out how the fractional premiums are calculated by the company you are considering. It is the author's understanding that some companies impose carrying charges even larger than those shown in Table 8–1. All of the price figures in Chapters 4 and 5 and in Appendixes D and E are based on annual premiums, and it would be possible to go astray by paying fractional premiums in a company that imposes large carrying charges.

Financed insurance

In these days of "buy now, pay later," it is possible to buy just about any commodity or service and finance the purchase. Since life insurance itself is an important financial instrument, it is not surprising to find various schemes for financing it. "Financed insurance" refers to any arrangement under which all or part of a life insurance premium is paid by borrowing.

Unquestionably the biggest problem with financed insurance is that the financing scheme often seems to dominate the entire discussion. Many life insurance agents preach the advantages of financed insurance without going into any detail about the amount of insurance needed, the type of insurance that is appropriate, or the underlying price and quality of the contract. The most important thing to remember about financing, therefore, is that it should be discussed only as a final step in the purchase of life insurance.

The most common form of financed insurance today is often called "minimum deposit." The plan frequently is based on a straight life policy, and each year the policyholder pays just enough to keep the policy going with a maximum policy loan against it. Specifically, each year the policyholder pays the annual premium, plus the interest on the accrued loan, minus the increase in the policy's loan value. The effect of the arrangement is to transform a straight life policy (which contains a decreasing protection element and an increasing savings element) into a decreasing term policy with no savings element.

The amount payable to the beneficiary at the death of the insured is the face amount of the policy minus the amount of the policy loan outstanding. To make things seem even more attractive, however, most companies offer a dividend option under which enough one-year term insurance is purchased to cover the amount of the policy loan. (This option was mentioned briefly in Chapter 7.) When this option is elected, the amount payable to the beneficiary is level—a result accomplished by superimposing an increasing amount of one-year term insurance on top of a decreasing amount of protection.

Years ago, when bank loan interest rates typically were below policy loan interest rates, the corresponding arrangement was called "the bank loan plan." It worked the same way, except that the borrowing was done at a bank through a collateral assignment of the policy, rather than directly from the insurance company under the policy loan clause.

There are two advantages usually alleged to be associated with the minimum deposit plan. The first is that the price of the protection may be lower in a straight life policy than in a term policy. In other words, it is argued that the policyholder who wants only protection and no savings element may do better in terms of price by buying straight life and using the minimum deposit plan than by buying term insurance.

This may or may not be the case in a given situation, and it is difficult to determine. For example, it cannot be judged by comparison of the retention figures in Tables 4–1, 4–2, and 4–3. A decreasing amount of protection is involved in the straight life policies in Tables 4–1 and 4–2, while a level amount of protection is involved in the term policies in Table 4–3.

Instead, a careful year-by-year price analysis must be performed. When this is carried out, it may be found that the alleged price advantage of the straight life protection is a small one at best, provided that a low-priced term contract is used in the analysis. And the straight life protection may be more costly than the term insurance if a high-priced straight life policy is the subject of the analysis.

The other alleged advantage of the minimum deposit plan is the income tax situation. As a general rule, policy loan interest paid is deductible by the policyholder who itemizes his deductions. At the same time, the inside interest in cash-value life insurance is essentially tax-exempt, as explained in Chapter 3. The result is a powerful form of tax leverage, with the amount of the power directly related to the policyholder's income tax bracket.

The Internal Revenue Service is well aware of the implications of this tax leverage and for many years has been playing a kind of game with the life insurance industry. Early in the game some life insurance agents got the idea of selling single premium life insurance to high tax-bracket policyholders who would borrow the full amount of the premium. This was a bonanza for such policyholders (and got their agents some large commissions, too), because the interplay between the tax-exempt inside interest and the tax-deductible loan interest gave the policyholder his protection at a very low and often negative net outlay. The IRS response was to change the rules so that interest on a loan taken for the purpose of buying single premium life insurance was no longer deductible.

Undaunted, some agents got the idea of using limited-payment life policies (such as ten-payment life or twenty-payment life) and having their policyholders pay all of the premiums in a single sum. When this is done, the insurance company offers a discount on premiums paid in advance of their due dates, which means that the advance premiums simply constitute an interest-bearing fund. The policyholders would obtain the single sum by borrowing. Again, the result was a bonanza for high tax-bracket policyholders (and their agents), because of the interplay between the tax-exempt inside interest and the tax-deductible loan interest. (In the early days of this arrangement, there was an extra bonanza because the interest on the premiums paid in advance was not taxable, but the IRS has since closed that loophole by making such interest taxable.) The IRS response was to change the rules again, so that interest on a loan taken for the purpose of paying a substantial number of premiums in advance was no longer deductible.

Still undaunted, some agents turned to the bank loan or minimum deposit plan. The arrangement involved borrowing only a part of each annual premium as it fell due, so that there were no large single sum borrowings. Nevertheless, the interplay between the tax-exempt inside interest and the tax-deductible loan interest created a bonanza for high tax-bracket policyholders. This time the IRS changed the rules so that interest on a loan taken as part of a systematic plan of borrowing to pay premiums was no longer deductible. However, the loophole was only partly closed, because the IRS ruled that an arrangement would *not* be construed as systematic borrowing if the policyholder paid in full (without borrowing) at least four of the first seven annual premiums.

It is important that you understand some of the agent's motivations in recommending minimum deposit insurance. Suppose you are 35 years old, have decided to increase your life insurance by $50,000, and do not wish to put any more of your savings into life insurance. If the agent sells you a $50,000 five-year renewable term policy, his first-year commission probably would be in the $100 to $125 range. If he sells you a $50,000 straight life policy on the minimum deposit plan, however, his first-year commission probably would be in the $500 to $600 range. This gives him a powerful vested interest in the minimum deposit approach. This is not intended to suggest that the agent necessarily will be giving you advice contrary to your best interests, but you should appreciate the pressures under which he operates.

You should avoid minimum deposit and other financing schemes unless three conditions are met. First, you should thoroughly understand the plan. Second, the amount of insurance should be substantial and you should be in a fairly substantial tax bracket, so that the tax leverage has a significant value for you. Third, you should be willing to put up with the complexities of the minimum deposit plan and be willing to "play the game" with the IRS. This last point is important because a large and growing interest deduction may attract attention to your income tax return.

Financed insurance often is used to obscure a fundamentally high-priced life insurance contract. Beware of the sales pitch that focuses primarily on the financing scheme. As mentioned earlier, the subject of financing should not be discussed until the amount of insurance, the type of insurance, and the company have been selected.

Classic examples of the use of financed insurance to obscure the nature of the contract are found in the practices of some companies on college campuses. Frequently undergraduate students are sold a policy on the basis of "$10 down and no further payments until after graduation." It is the rare student who thoroughly understands the implications of the contract into which he has entered. The author has seen examples of inappropriate, high-priced contracts sold to students. And some students do not realize until it is too late that they signed a promissory note and are legally obligated to pay it off.[2]

Nor is campus solicitation limited to undergraduates. Graduate students are intensively solicited. And particularly elaborate financing schemes have been developed for young professionals—such as budding physicians serving as interns or residents. Frequently such men are married and need large amounts of life insurance. The financing arrangements go well beyond minimum deposit, since a young doctor may borrow the entire premium each year for several years—"nothing to pay until you get into practice." Invariably the sale is straight life, so he may build up a large amount of indebtedness that he must begin to repay while he is going through the trials and tribulations of starting practice. A young doctor with large life insurance needs and limited funds is a candidate for five-year renewable term insurance. He may even have to finance the premiums; but by buying term insurance he would build up a much smaller amount of indebtedness.

After the purchase

Following the purchase of life insurance, several important points should be kept in mind. These are discussed in this final section of the chapter.

Periodic review

Circumstances sometimes change rapidly, so it is essential that your life insurance program be reviewed periodically. Ideally, you should plan to review your life insurance program once a year. Failing that, try to do a thorough review at least once every two years. If you perform the review carefully, you may be surprised at the number of changes you will want to make.

If you have selected a good agent, he will encourage you to review your program periodically. But if he fails to take the initiative, you should get in touch with him and urge him to do his job. Even if no additional sale materializes, he should help with your review. He owes such service to you because of the commissions he earns when you buy life insurance.

Beneficiary changes

The beneficiary designation is one area that most often requires periodic review, because of changes in family relationships. Consider, for example, the case of Tom and Mary Jones and their two young sons. Tom designated Mary as beneficiary, if living, otherwise their two sons equally, or the survivor. This means that if Mary and one of their sons were to predecease Tom, the other son would receive all of the funds at Tom's death.

Years later, both sons were married and had children of their own. Should Tom fail to change the beneficiary designation, should Mary and one of their sons predecease Tom, and should Tom then die, all of the funds would go to the surviving son. The effect, then, would be to disinherit their widowed daughter-in-law and their fatherless grandchildren. Presumably this would not be Tom's and Mary's intent, but it would happen because they had failed to review the beneficiary designation.

Storage of policies

A common practice is to keep one's life insurance policies in a safe-deposit box at a bank. There are some disadvantages to this procedure, however.

There may be some delay in getting at the policies in the event of the insured's death. Frequently it is necessary for a representative of the state to inventory the contents of a deceased's safe-deposit box before making it accessible to the deceased's family.

Second, policies kept in a safe-deposit box may be looked at only rarely. Periodic review of one's policies is hampered when the policies are relatively inaccessible.

For these reasons, it may be preferable to keep one's policies at home in a desk drawer or filing cabinet. Should the policies be destroyed, stolen, or lost, it is a simple matter to obtain duplicate copies from the respective insurance companies. To expedite matters, it would be desirable to have a list showing the names of the companies and the policy numbers. Such a list—rather than the policies themselves—might be kept in a safe-deposit box. The policyholder who follows this procedure would have his policies more accessible and also might require a smaller, less expensive safe-deposit box.

The replacement problem

The word "replacement" refers to the act of discontinuing a life insurance policy and taking out a new one in its place. A policyholder has a right to accomplish a replacement if it is his desire to do so. There is nothing inherently wrong or immoral about a replacement, but as will be explained shortly, it is sometimes contrary to the policyholder's best interests to accomplish a replacement.

From the viewpoint of the life insurance industry as a whole, replacements are counterproductive. They tend to increase certain expenses—commissions and other expenses associated with the issuance of new policies—without increasing the amount of life insurance in force. As a result, companies are sensitive about replacements and try to discourage them in various ways.

A life insurance agent is said to be "twisting" if he uses misrepresentation or an incomplete comparison to induce a replacement to the detriment of the policyholder. State laws or regulations prohibit twisting and frequently require the disclosure of certain information in a replacement situation. For example, when a replacement is proposed, the agent making the suggestion may be required to furnish the policyholder with certain information about the existing policy and about the proposed replacement policy. Presumably the purposes of such requirements are to spell out the kind of information the agent must furnish in order to avoid being accused of making an incomplete comparison, and to provide the policyholder with the information he needs to make an intelligent decision. Unfortunately, the requirements seem to result in nondisclosure, because the mass of required data is neither condensed nor interpreted so that the policyholder can digest it. Furthermore, the completion of the necessary forms is such a difficult task that agents are discouraged from suggesting a replacement even when it may be justified.

The disclosure aspect of replacement regulations is an anomaly in another way. When a replacement is proposed, the various disclosure requirements pertain. But no such disclosure is required when a person simply wants to buy a life insurance policy. In other words, the life insurance industry and the regulatory agencies are quite paternalistic about protecting policyholders from possible errors in a replacement situation, but show no such concern about protecting buyers from errors in the choice of policy when no replacement is involved.

One of the most powerful arguments against replacement is that the policyholder is thus subjected to the acquisition costs (or "front-end load") a second time, after which he has only one policy. This argument is valid as far as it goes, but those using it usually fail to mention the very large price differences among policies. It is possible for a policyholder with a high-priced policy to be better off by incurring a second set of acquisition expenses in order to obtain a low-priced contract.

Another argument against replacement is that the incontestability and suicide periods begin again. This is a valid argument. Also, it is interesting to note that replacement regulations generally do not frown upon replacement of term policies—but only replacement of cash-value policies. The incontestability and suicide situations are just as important in term policies as in cash-value policies, as evidenced by the discussion of this point in the third section of Chapter 7.

A third argument against replacement is that the existing policy may contain certain clauses more favorable to the policyholder than the proposed policy. This is a reasonable argument, although it is just as likely for the proposed policy to have the more favorable clauses. And often it is difficult to determine the relative value of the various clauses.

About the only generalization possible in the replacement area is that it is difficult or impossible to generalize. The author has seen cases in which replacement was detrimental to the policyholder, cases in which replacement was justified, and cases in which it made little difference one way or the other.

Replacement of a low-priced policy is almost certain to be detrimental to the policyholder. Replacement of a medium-priced policy is likely to be detrimental to the policyholder. Replacement of a high-priced policy may be advantageous to the policyholder if the new policy is a low-priced one. But determining whether a given policy is low-priced, medium-priced, or high-priced is tricky. In short, any given replacement situation must be evaluated on the basis of its own set of facts.

In the face of this uncertainty, you should not replace a policy unless you are convinced that the replacement is to your advantage. Since the agent who recommends replacement has a vested interest in it—in the form of a new first-year commission—you should seek the advice of the company that wrote the original policy. You should do this even if the proposed policy is in the same company that wrote the original policy. If you decide to replace, you should be sure the new policy is in effect before you discontinue the old one. And above all—when in doubt, keep the old policy.

Of one thing you can be reasonably sure. If you follow carefully the suggestions in this book on selection of policy and company, you probably would never have occasion to replace the policy. You probably would have acquired a relatively low-priced contract in a financially strong company.

Sometimes an existing policy is no longer appropriate. For example, a policyholder may have purchased a retirement income policy when he was single and now considers straight life more appropriate because he is married and raising a family. Under these circumstances, instead of replacing the retirement income policy, he should consider changing it to a straight life policy as of the issue date of the retirement income policy. Such a policy change is referred to in Chapter 7.

The death claim

When the insured dies, the beneficiary should take her time and not do anything hurriedly. In the usual situation, it is not necessary for her to pay anyone anything to collect the funds payable under a life insurance policy.

Unless there is some dispute concerning the policy, it would be wasteful for the beneficiary to retain an attorney and pay him a fee simply to obtain the funds for her. All she needs to do is notify the company—or its agent—of the insured's death. She will receive the necessary forms and instructions. If she decides upon a single sum settlement, she would receive the check shortly after she sends in the policy, the death certificate, and the death claim. If she decides upon a settlement option, she would receive a so-called supplementary contract that spells out the terms of the agreement between her and the company.

If the insured had selected and worked with a good life insurance agent, the beneficiary should turn to him. An agent can handle the details and provide guidance for the beneficiary at no cost to her.

Complaint procedure

When a dispute arises between an insurance company and a policyholder (or beneficiary), an appropriate first step is to contact the insurance commissioner in the insured's state of residence. The addresses of the various state insurance commissioners are listed in Appendix F.

You should not hesitate to contact your state insurance department, because it is equipped to handle complaints. It can act as an intermediary between the policyholder (or beneficiary) and the insurance company and often can resolve disputes quickly and to the satisfaction of both parties.

Chapter 9

Some illustrative cases

Previous chapters have provided information on measuring life insurance needs, deciding on policy forms, selecting a company, choosing an agent, and understanding the fine print in life insurance contracts. The purpose of this chapter is to describe the decisions made by several hypothetical families, in the hope that the descriptions will help you achieve a better understanding of the suggestions contained in earlier chapters.

In most of the illustrative cases, certain companies are mentioned. The fact that the hypothetical individuals are willing to deal with certain companies does not necessarily mean that you should deal with those companies. Similarly, the fact that the hypothetical individuals decide against dealing with certain companies does not necessarily mean that you should avoid those companies. The company references are included so that you can follow the entire sequence of decisions in each case.

The Adams case

Allan Adams is a 25-year-old accountant in Ohio. He is employed by a large public accounting firm and earns $13,500 per year. He expects that his income will increase fairly rapidly in the future.

Allan is single and has no marriage plans. He has $13,500 of group life insurance. He has $5,000 in savings and no debts of any consequence.

Allan estimates his final expense needs to be $2,000. Although his savings alone substantially exceed his final expense needs, he feels a strong obligation to his parents, who financed his college education and his graduate study at considerable sacrifice to themselves. Also, he feels it would be a good idea to start building a life insurance program while he is able to qualify for life insurance easily.

He has studied the characteristics of the savings element of cash-value life insurance, as described in Chapter 3, and has decided to put about $200 per year into that kind of savings. He also has noted the rule of thumb that, beginning at age 25, an average of about $8 goes into the savings element of a straight life policy each year for each $1,000 of face amount. So he decides to buy $25,000 of straight life, including the waiver-of-premium clause and the guaranteed insurability rider. He decides on the latter because he anticipates buying more life insurance later on, particularly if he should marry and start raising a family. He is fairly optimistic about future economic conditions and future interest rates, so he decides to buy participating insurance.

Allan already knows three agents pretty well—one representing the Nationwide Life Insurance Company (Columbus, Ohio), one representing the Sun Life Assurance Company of Canada (Toronto, Ontario), and the other representing the Western and Southern Life Insurance Company (Cincinnati, Ohio). He first consults Appendix B and notes that all three companies are among those receiving the strongest possible recommendations in the 1971 edition of *Best's Life Insurance Reports*. He then consults Table 4–1 and notes that the $25,000 participating straight life policies issued by Nationwide Life and Sun Life are near the low-retention end of the array and that the $25,000 participating straight life policies issued by Western and Southern are at or near the high-retention end of the array. He next consults Tables D–1, D–2, and D–3 and observes the relative positions of the companies' straight life policies on the basis of historical dividends. He concludes that he is willing to buy from either Nationwide Life or Sun Life, and decides to deal with the agent he feels is the more capable of the two.

The Baker family

Bart Baker is a 35-year-old high school teacher in Indiana. He earns $12,500 per year and expects that his income will increase slowly in the future. Bart and his 30-year-old wife Barbara have two children, ages 8 and 5, and they own a $25,000 home with a $19,000 mortgage. Bart has $16,000 of life insurance—$10,000 of group life insurance, $5,000 of straight life he bought several years ago, and $1,000 of straight life his parents bought for him many years ago. The family has $1,000 in savings and $3,000 in debts (in addition to the mortgage).

Before their marriage, Barbara was a nurse. They have agreed, however, that if Bart should die now, it would be better for the children if Barbara were to refrain from returning to work for at least the next ten years. They also have agreed that, if the home were free and clear, Barbara would need about $8,000 per year for that ten-year period. Referring to Appendix A (Example 1), and assuming 2 percent interest (5 percent interest minus 3 percent inflation), they estimate the present value of their income needs to be $73,000.

They estimate their final expense needs to be $3,000. In consultation with the local Social Security office, they estimate their Social Security survivors' benefits for the next ten years to be $5,000 per year. Then, referring to Appendix A (Example 1), and using the same 2 percent interest assumption mentioned above, they estimate the present value of Social Security survivors' benefits for the next ten years to be $46,000. They then estimate that they need $35,000 of additional life insurance, as summarized in Table 9–1.

Bart and Barbara feel that the combination of Social Security retirement benefits and Bart's pension plan will come reasonably close to meeting their retirement needs. Moreover, they feel they are unable to save much out of their current income. They have

Table 9–1
Summary of data on illustrative cases

	Baker	Clark	Donaldson	Elliott	Fischer	Gilbert	Harris
Financial Requirements at Death							
Final expenses	$ 3,000	$ 3,000	$ 6,000	$ 5,000	$ 7,000	$ 8,000	$ 60,000
Income needs	73,000	28,000	110,000	145,000	85,000	219,000	365,000
Mortgage on home	19,000	–	23,000	22,000	25,000	35,000	20,000
Other debts	3,000	3,000	2,000	3,000	2,000	40,000	95,000
Total	$ 98,000	$ 34,000	$141,000	$175,000	$119,000	$302,000	$540,000
Financial Resources at Death							
Life insurance	$ 16,000	$ 16,000	$ 40,000	$ 50,000	$ 55,000	$ 65,000	$200,000
Social Security	46,000	20,000	44,000	43,000	40,000	35,000	21,000
Other assets	1,000	1,000	7,000	2,000	4,000	2,000	219,000
Total	$ 63,000	$ 37,000	$ 91,000	$ 95,000	$ 99,000	$102,000	$440,000
Additional Life Insurance Needed	$ 35,000	–	$ 50,000	$ 80,000	$ 20,000	$200,000	$100,000

studied the characteristics of the savings element of cash-value life insurance, as described in Chapter 3, and have decided to put about $100 per year more into that kind of savings. They also have noted the rule of thumb that, beginning at age 35, an average of about $10 goes into the savings element of a straight life policy each year for each $1,000 of face amount. So they decide to buy $10,000 of straight life and $25,000 of five-year renewable term, including the waiver-of-premium clause in both instances, to meet their needs for additional life insurance. They are fairly optimistic about future economic conditions and future interest rates, so they decide to buy participating insurance.

Bart and Barbara already know two agents pretty well—one representing the Bankers Life Company (Des Moines, Iowa), and the other representing the Confederation Life Insurance Company (Toronto, Ontario). They first consult Appendix B and note that both companies are among those receiving the strongest possible recommendations in the 1971 edition of *Best's Life Insurance Reports*. They then consult Tables 4–1 and D–6 and note that the $25,000 and $10,000 participating straight life policies issued by both companies are at or near the low-retention end of the arrays. They next consult

Table 4–3 and note that the $25,000 five-year renewable term policies issued by both companies are near the low-retention end of the array. Finally, they consult Tables D–1, D–2, and D–3 and observe the relative positions of the companies' straight life policies on the basis of historical dividends. They conclude that they are willing to buy from either of these companies, and decide to deal with the agent they feel is the more capable of the two.

The Clark family

Carl Clark is a 35-year-old bank loan officer in California. He earns $12,500 per year and expects that his income will increase slowly in the future. Carl and his 30-year-old wife Connie have two children, ages 8 and 5, and they own a $25,000 home with a $19,000 mortgage. Carl has $16,000 of life insurance—$10,000 of group life insurance, $5,000 of straight life he bought several years ago, and $1,000 of straight life his parents bought for him many years ago. The family has $1,000 in savings and $3,000 in debts (in addition to the mortgage).

Before their marriage, Connie was a computer programmer. They have agreed to assume that, if Carl should die now, Connie would return to work within one year. They have decided to omit specific reference to the mortgage among their financial requirements at Carl's death, and to consider the mortgage payments as a part of their income needs. They have agreed that, with the mortgage still outstanding, Connie would need about $9,000 for the first year, and about $5,000 per year for the subsequent four years to supplement her income. They feel that her financial adjustments would be completed satisfactorily within five years after Carl's death. Referring to Appendix A (Example 2), and assuming 2 percent interest (5 percent interest minus 3 percent inflation), they estimate the present value of their income needs to be $28,000.

They estimate their final expense needs to be $3,000. In consultation with the local Social Security office, they estimate their Social Security survivors' benefits for the next five years to be $5,000 for the first year and $4,000 per year for the subsequent four years. Then, referring to Appendix A (Example 2), and using the same 2 percent interest assumption mentioned above, they estimate the present value of Social Security survivors' benefits for the next five years to be $20,000. They conclude that they do not need any additional life insurance at the present time, as summarized in Table 9–1.

In terms of family status, income, assets, and liabilities, the Clark family is the same as the Baker family. However, the perceived financial requirements of the two families are quite different. These results illustrate the importance of a family's perceived financial needs, the personal nature of a life insurance program, and the futility of attempts to generalize with rules of thumb about the amount of life insurance various families should own.

The Donaldson family

David Donaldson is a 35-year-old college professor in Texas. He earns $18,500 per year. He expects that his income will increase slowly in the future. David and his 30-year-old wife Diana have two children, ages 8 and 5, and they own a $35,000 home with a $23,000 mortgage. David has $40,000 of life insurance—$25,000 of group life insurance, $10,000 of straight life he bought a few years ago, and $5,000 of straight life he bought several years ago when he was single. The family has $2,000 in savings accounts and $5,000 in mutual funds. They owe $2,000 (in addition to the mortgage).

Before their marriage, Diana was a teacher. They have agreed, however, that if David should die now, it would be better for the children if Diana were to refrain from returning to work for at least the next five years. They also have agreed that, if the home were free and clear, Diana would need about $12,000 per year during that five-year period. They have agreed that, after that period, Diana would need about $5,000 per year for the subsequent fifteen years to supplement her teacher's salary. Referring to Appendix A (Example 2), and assuming 3 percent interest (5 percent interest minus 2 percent inflation), they estimate the present value of their income needs to be $110,000.

They estimate their final expense needs to be $6,000. In consultation with the local Social Security office, they estimate their Social Security survivors' benefits for the next twenty years to be $5,000 per year for the first five years, $4,000 per year for the subsequent five years, $2,000 per year for the next subsequent three years, and zero for the final seven years. Then, referring to Appendix A (Example 2), and using the same 3 percent interest assumption mentioned above, they estimate the present value of Social Security survivors' benefits to be $44,000. They then estimate that they need $50,000 of additional life insurance, as summarized in Table 9–1.

David and Diana feel that the combination of Social Security retirement benefits and David's pension plan will take care of a substantial portion of their retirement needs. In addition, they have already embarked on a systematic accumulation of mutual fund shares. They believe, however, that they should balance their savings program by setting aside some additional fixed-dollar savings. They have studied the characteristics of the savings element of cash-value life insurance, as described in Chapter 3, and have decided they should put about $250 per year more into that kind of savings. They also have noted the rule of thumb that, beginning at age 35, an average of about $10 goes into the savings element of a straight life policy each year for each $1,000 of face amount. So they decide to buy $25,000 of straight life and $25,000 of five-year renewable term, including the waiver-of-premium clause in both instances, to meet their needs for additional life insurance. They also plan to convert the term insurance to straight life within the next few years. They are fairly optimistic about future economic conditions and future interest rates, so they decide to buy participating insurance.

David and Diana already know two agents pretty well—one representing the American National Insurance Company (Galveston, Texas) and the other representing the Republic National Life Insurance Company (Dallas, Texas). They also realize they are eligible to buy life insurance from the Teachers Insurance and Annuity Association of America (TIAA). They first consult Appendix B and note that all three companies are among those receiving the strongest possible recommendations in the 1971 edition of *Best's Life Insurance Reports.* They then consult Table 4–1 and note that the $25,000 participating straight life policies issued by both American National and Republic National are near the high-retention end of the array. They then look at Table 4–3 and note that the $25,000 five-year renewable term policies of the two companies are in the high-retention half of the array. Next, they consult Tables D–1, D–2, and D–3, seeking information on the companies' straight life policies on the basis of historical dividends. They find that American National did not issue participating policies in 1950, 1940, or 1930. As for Republic National, dividend data were not available for participating policies issued in 1950, and the Company did not issue conventional participating policies in 1940 and 1930.

David and Diana then consult Appendix E and compare the TIAA figures shown there with the figures in Tables 4–1 and 4–3. They next compare the TIAA figures in Appendix E with those in Tables D–1, D–2, and D–3. They are impressed by the low-retention figures and decide to buy their additional life insurance from TIAA.

The Elliott family

Edward Elliott is a 35-year-old engineer in New York. He is employed by a large power company and earns $20,000 per year. He expects that his income will increase slowly in the future. Edward and his 30-year-old wife Elaine have one child, age 2, and they own a $30,000 home with a $22,000 mortgage. Edward has $50,000 of life insurance—$40,000 of group life insurance, and $10,000 of twenty-payment life he bought when he was single. The family has $2,000 in savings and $3,000 in debts (in addition to the mortgage).

Before their marriage, Elaine was a librarian. They have agreed, however, that if Edward were to die now, it would be better for their child if Elaine were to refrain from returning to work for the next ten years. They also have agreed that, if the home were free and clear, Elaine would need about $10,000 per year for that ten-year period. They have agreed that, after that period, Elaine would need about $5,000 per year for the subsequent twenty years to supplement her librarian's salary. Referring to Appendix A (Example 2), and assuming 3 percent interest (5 percent interest minus 2 percent inflation), they estimate the present value of their income needs to be $145,000.

They estimate their final expense needs to be $5,000. In consultation with the local Social Security office, they estimate their Social Security survivors' benefits for the next thirty years to be $4,000 per year for the first ten years, $2,000 per year for the subsequent six years, and zero for the final fourteen years. Then, referring to Appendix A (Example 2), and using the same 3 percent interest assumption mentioned above, they estimate the present value of Social Security survivors' benefits to be $43,000. They then estimate that they need $80,000 of additional life insurance, as summarized in Table 9–1.

Edward and Elaine are concerned about the twenty-payment life policy he bought several years ago. They realize that the annual premium is high, and that a substantial amount is going into the savings element each year, relative to the face amount of the policy. They decide to ask the insurance company that issued the policy to change it to straight life as of Edward's age at the time he bought the policy. This change will reduce the premium, reduce the annual amount going into the savings element, and reduce the current cash value. The amount of the reduction in cash value will be refunded to Edward, and he can put the refund into their savings account.

Edward and Elaine have studied the characteristics of the savings element of cash-value life insurance, as described in Chapter 3. They also have noted the rule of thumb that, beginning at age 35, an average of about $10 goes into the savings element of a straight life policy each year for each $1,000 of face amount. Since changing the twenty-payment life policy to straight life will reduce the amount going into the savings element of the policy, they decide to put about $300 per year into the savings element of a new straight life policy. So they decide to buy $30,000 of straight life and $50,000 of five-year renewable term, including the waiver-of-premium clause in both instances, to meet their needs for additional life insurance. They are fairly optimistic about future economic conditions and future interest rates, so they decide to buy participating insurance.

Edward and Elaine already know two agents pretty well—one representing the Crown Life Insurance Company (Toronto, Ontario), and the other representing the Provident Mutual Life Insurance Company of Philadelphia (Philadelphia, Pennsylvania). They first consult Appendix B and note that both companies are among those receiving the strongest possible recommendations in the 1971 edition of *Best's Life Insurance Reports*. They then consult Table 4–1 and note that the $25,000 participating straight life policies issued by both companies are in the low-retention half of the array. They next consult Tables 4–3 and D–15 and note that the $25,000 and $100,000 five-year renewable term policies issued by both companies are in the low-retention half of the arrays. Then they consult Tables D–1, D–2, and D–3 and observe the relative positions of the companies' straight life policies on the basis of historical dividends.

They also realize they are eligible to buy up to $30,000 of New York Savings Bank Life Insurance (SBLI). They consult Appendix E and compare the New York SBLI figures shown there with the figures in Table 4–1. They next compare the New York SBLI figures in Appendix E with those in Tables D–1 and D–2. They are impressed by the low-retention figures, and decide to buy $30,000 of straight life from New York SBLI. They also conclude that they should buy the $50,000 of five-year renewable term from either Crown Life or

Provident Mutual, and decide to deal with the agent they feel is the more capable of the two.

The Fischer family

Frank Fischer is a 35-year-old chemist in Maryland. He is employed by a large manufacturing firm and earns $22,500 per year. He expects that his income will increase slowly in the future. Frank and his 30-year-old wife Frieda have two children, ages 9 and 7, and they own a $35,000 home with a $25,000 mortgage. Frank has $55,000 of life insurance—$45,000 of group life insurance, and $10,000 of straight life he bought when he was single. The family has $4,000 in savings and $2,000 in debts (in addition to the mortgage).

Before their marriage, Frieda was a bookkeeper. They have agreed, however, that if Frank should die now, it would be better for the children if Frieda were to refrain from returning to work for at least the next five years. They also have agreed that, if the home were free and clear, Frieda would need about $10,000 per year for that five-year period, and then about $5,000 per year for the subsequent ten years to supplement her income. Referring to Appendix A (Example 2), and assuming 3 percent interest (5 percent interest minus 2 percent inflation), they estimate the present value of their income needs to be $85,000.

They estimate their final expense needs to be $7,000. In consultation with the local Social Security office, they estimate their Social Security survivors' benefits for the next fifteen years to be $5,000 per year for the first five years, $4,000 per year for the subsequent four years, $2,000 per year for the next subsequent two years, and zero for the final four years. Then, referring to Appendix A (Example 2), and using the same 3 percent interest assumption mentioned above, they estimate the present value of Social Security survivors' benefits to be $40,000. They then estimate that they need $20,000 of additional life insurance, as summarized in Table 9–1.

Frank is a diabetic. He has the condition well under control, but he and Frieda realize that he probably will not be able to obtain life insurance at regular rates from a well-established company. They decide to seek out an experienced and knowledgeable agent, using the suggestions mentioned in Chapter 6. They plan to pay particular attention to the agent's ability and willingness to place business with various companies, since it is possible that the agent's primary company will not do as well for Frank as another company. Until they learn more about Frank's eligibility for life insurance, they decide to withhold judgment on the kind of life insurance to buy.

The Gilbert family

George Gilbert is a 35-year-old pediatrician in Pennsylvania. He spent a few years in military service and many years in school, and is just getting his practice started. He earned about $25,000 last year after payment of his professional expenses, and he expects his income to increase rapidly in the next few years. George and his 30-year-old wife Greta have three children, ages 6, 4, and 1. They just bought a $40,000 home with a $35,000 mortgage. George has $65,000 of life insurance—$15,000 of five-year renewable term that he bought several years ago, and $50,000 of five-year renewable term that he bought last year. The family has $2,000 in savings, but George's debts—incurred during his years in school and in the process of getting established in practice—amount to $40,000 (in addition to the mortgage).

Before their marriage, Greta was a dental hygienist. They have agreed, however, that if George should die now, it would be better for the children if Greta were to refrain from working for the next five years. They also have agreed that, with the house free and clear, Greta would need $15,000 per year during the five years. In addition, they feel she would need $10,000 per year for the subsequent fifteen years to supplement her income, and that it would be desirable to provide enough funds to give her $5,000 per year for the next subsequent twenty years. Referring to Appendix A (Example 2), and assuming 3 percent interest (5 percent interest minus 2 percent inflation), they estimate the present value of their income needs to be $219,000.

They estimate their final expense needs to be $8,000. In consultation with the local Social Security office, they estimate their Social Security survivors' benefits for the next forty years to be $2,500 per year for the first fourteen years, $1,000 per year for the subsequent three years, zero for the next subsequent thirteen years, and $1,000 per year for the final ten years. Then, referring to Appendix A (Examples 2 and 4), and using the same 3 percent interest assumption mentioned above, they estimate the present value of Social Security survivors' benefits to be $35,000.

They feel that Greta might decide to sell their home and move into a smaller house, but decide to disregard that possibility in estimating their resources. They also feel that some of George's office equipment, as well as the practice itself, might be salable in the event of his death. Because of the uncertainty of the value, however, they decide to disregard those items in estimating their resources. They then estimate that they need $200,000 of additional life insurance, as summarized in Table 9–1.

At first they are stunned by the amount of additional life insurance they apparently need. But then they realize that they have substantial debts, that George has been delayed quite a number of years in getting his career going, that George's income potential in the next fifteen or twenty years is very large, and that under the circumstances George should have a substantial amount of life insurance protection. They decide that George should now buy an additional $200,000 of life insurance, including the waiver-of-premium clause.

George and Greta have not yet been able to start a systematic savings program. Nor do they feel it is appropriate to begin such a program at this time. They feel they will have to start saving substantial amounts within the next few years, but the primary need now is protection. So they decide that George should buy $200,000 of five-year renewable term insurance, including the waiver-of-premium clause. To avoid "putting all their eggs in one basket," they feel it would be appropriate to divide the insurance between two companies.

They feel that George will be converting at least part of his coverage to straight life within a few years. Also, they are fairly optimistic about future economic conditions and future interest rates, so they assume the conversion will be to participating straight life.

The Gilberts already know four agents pretty well—one representing the Connecticut General Life Insurance Company (Hartford, Connecticut), one representing the Home Life Insurance Company (New York, New York), one representing the Massachusetts Mutual Life Insurance Company (Springfield, Massachusetts), and one representing The Prudential Insurance Company of America (Newark, New Jersey). They first consult Appendix B and note that all four companies are among those receiving the strongest possible recommendations in the 1971 edition of *Best's Life Insurance Reports.*

They then consult Table D–15 and note that the $100,000 five-year renewable term policies issued by all four companies are around the middle of the array. Also, they are impressed by the low premiums and low retention for the $100,000 five-year renewable term policy issued by the North American Life Assurance Company (Toronto, Ontario). They then consult Table D–7 and note that the $100,000 participating straight life policies issued by Home Life, Massachusetts Mutual, and North American are in the low-retention half of the array, while the corresponding policies issued by Connecticut General and Prudential are in the high-retention half. They consider the information on straight life important because of their conversion expectations.

Finally, they consult Tables D–1, D–2, and D–3 and observe the relative positions of the companies' straight life policies on the basis of historical dividends. They conclude that George should buy $100,000 of five-year renewable term from either Home Life or Massachusetts Mutual, depending on which agent they consider the more capable of the two, and $100,000 of five-year renewable term from North American. They decide to ask the agent they select if he can handle the entire transaction for them.

The Harris family

Harold Harris is a 45-year-old physician in Illinois. His general practice is well established and provided him with a net income of about $60,000 last year. He expects his income to continue to rise for the next several years, but not rapidly.

Harold and his 40-year-old wife Hilda have three children, ages 18, 15, and 12. They own a $60,000 home with a $20,000 mortgage. Harold owns $200,000 of life insurance purchased over a period of years—$100,000 of straight life (with a current cash value of $20,000), and $100,000 of five-year renewable term insurance. The family has $10,000 in savings accounts, $4,000 in United States government "E" bonds, and $5,000 in miscellaneous debts. They own $40,000 in common stock (at current market value) and $150,000 in income-producing real estate (at current market value), with $90,000 of indebtedness against it. In addition, as a self-employed individual, Harold has been putting the maximum of $2,500 per year into a tax-deferred retirement plan for several years. The deposits have been invested in mutual funds and their current market value is $15,000.

Before their marriage, Hilda was a secretary. They have agreed, however, to disregard the possibility of her earning any significant income after Harold's death. She has developed certain health problems and they doubt that she would be able to work effectively. They have agreed that, if the indebtedness were taken care of, an income of $20,000 per year would be adequate for the next ten years, and an income of $15,000 per year after that. To approximate the present value of a life income for Hilda, they assume she would need the $15,000 income until age 85. Referring to Appendix A (Example 1), and assuming 4 percent interest (6 percent interest minus 2 percent inflation), they estimate the present value of their income needs to be $365,000. They use the fairly high interest rate of 6 percent because of the common stock and income-producing real estate among their assets.

They estimate their final expense needs to be $60,000. In consultation with the local Social Security office, they estimate their Social Security survivors' benefits for the next forty-five years to be $2,500 per year for the first six years, zero for the subsequent fourteen years, and $1,000 per year for the final twenty-five years. Then, referring to Appendix A (Examples 1 and 4), and using the same 4 percent interest assumption mentioned above, they estimate the present value of Social Security survivors' benefits to be $21,000.

They feel that Hilda might decide to sell their home and move into a smaller house, but decide to disregard that possibility in estimating their resources. They also feel that some of Harold's office equipment, as well as the practice itself, might be salable in the event of his death. Because of the uncertainty of the value, however, they decide to disregard those items in estimating their resources. They then estimate that they need $100,000 of additional life insurance, as summarized in Table 9–1. They decide to buy an additional $100,000 of life insurance, including the waiver-of-premium clause.

Harold and Hilda have studied the characteristics of the savings element of cash-value life insurance, as described in Chapter 3. They are particularly interested in the income tax treatment of the savings element. They feel their savings program is fairly heavy on the equity side, in view of their common stock, mutual fund, and real estate investments. So they decide to put some more into the fixed-dollar side of their program.

They also have noted the rule of thumb that, beginning at age 45, an average of about $13 goes into the savings element of a straight life policy each year for each $1,000 of face amount. They feel they can put aside an additional $1,300 per year in this form of savings, so decide to buy the new insurance on a straight life basis, with the idea of converting the previously purchased renewable term insurance within a few years. They are fairly optimistic about future economic conditions and future interest rates, so they decide to buy participating insurance.

Harold and Hilda already know three agents quite well—one representing the Berkshire Life Insurance Company (Pittsfield, Massachusetts), one representing the Connecticut Mutual Life Insurance Company (Hartford, Connecticut), and one representing The Northwestern Mutual Life Insurance Company (Milwaukee, Wisconsin). They first consult Appendix B and note that all three companies are among those receiving the strongest possible recommendations in the 1971 edition of *Best's Life Insurance Reports.*

They then consult Tables D–5 and D–7, note that no data are provided for Berkshire Life, and note that the straight life policies issued by Connecticut Mutual and Northwestern Mutual are near the low-retention end of the arrays. They next consult Tables D–1, D–2, and D–3 and observe the relative positions of Connecticut Mutual and Northwestern Mutual straight life policies on the basis of historical dividends.

They decide to ask the Berkshire Life agent for the figures corresponding to those in Tables D–1, D–2, D–3, D–5, and D–7. They refer to Chapter 4, where it is mentioned that the figures should be developed at the Company's home office by the use of the formulas in Appendix H. They note the warning that they should insist on receiving the figures in writing over the signature of a Company officer. If the figures are not made available, they plan to deal with either the Connecticut Mutual agent or the Northwestern Mutual agent. If the Berkshire Life figures are made available, and if they are reasonably close to the corresponding figures for the other two companies, Harold and Hilda plan to deal with the agent they feel is the most capable of the three.

Chapter 10

Conclusion

Ignorance, complexity, and apathy are the three words that best characterize the life insurance market. The purpose of this chapter is to describe these characteristics, show how their combined effect produces fertile ground for the exploitation of consumers, and outline what is being done to improve the life insurance market.

Ignorance

Most prospective buyers do not understand the different kinds of life insurance policies. They do not know some life insurance companies are operating on a shoestring. They do not know there are very large differences in price among life insurance companies for essentially the same coverage. They do not understand the financial implications of the death of a breadwinner, nor do they appreciate fully the important role of life insurance at such a time. It is hoped that this book will dispel some of the ignorance among consumers.

Nor is ignorance confined to life insurance buyers. Many if not most life insurance agents are ill-equipped to provide reliable financial advice for their customers. State licensing examinations require a minimum of knowledge about life insurance. Company training programs and most industry-wide training programs place the emphasis on sales skill rather than technical knowledge. The Chartered Life Underwriter (CLU) program contains a considerable amount of sales material, although some technical knowledge is required for successful completion; and the holders of that designation still comprise a small minority of the life insurance agents, despite a rapid growth in the CLU movement in recent years.

Nor is ignorance confined to life insurance buyers and life insurance agents. Many life insurance company home office executives have only a superficial knowledge of life insurance. Life insurance company investment officers and many life insurance company attorneys are engaged in specialized work that has only an indirect effect on the life insurance market. And those responsible for sales development generally have come up through the sales ranks. Many of these sales executives were successful in the field, but sales success is not synonymous with technical knowledge. Indeed, it is often argued that technical knowledge tends to hamper sales efforts.

Those who know the most about life insurance, and who must therefore assume the primary responsibility for the ignorance in the life insurance market, are the actuaries. These are the technicians of life insurance. They are responsible for the calculation of premiums, cash values, and dividends. They do the technical work in the development of new policies. Their knowledge and expertise are used in virtually every aspect of life insurance company operations. Although they are company employees, they are also professionals. The ones who complete a comprehensive series of examinations become Fellows of the Society of Actuaries and are allowed to display the FSA designation after their names.

In defense of the actuaries, many of them are not in a strong enough position to affect company policy. Let's assume an actuary decides to make a recommendation that would benefit consumers.

If implementation of the recommendation might have an adverse effect on the company's profit picture or sales volume—even if the adverse effect were expected to be temporary—the recommendation might be sidetracked at the insistence of other executives. If an actuary's recommendations are repeatedly sidetracked, he is likely to become less enthusiastic about making recommendations. Also, repeated rejections of his recommendations might undermine his position in the company, and he may decide that it is safer to follow the path of least resistance. The result is likely to be a preservation of the status quo.

Complexity

The complexity of life insurance reinforces the ignorance referred to earlier. There are two kinds of life insurance complexity, however, that relate directly to consumers.

The first of these is the complexity that is inherent in life insurance because of its nature and purpose. Death rates increase with advancing age; therefore, in the absence of special arrangements, premiums increase with advancing age. When special arrangements are made to avoid increasing premiums, the resulting level premiums involve an overcharge in the early policy years that gives rise to a savings element. The life insurance policy is thus transformed into a complex package consisting of life insurance protection and a savings medium.

Furthermore, because premiums are small in relation to face amounts, safeguards must be incorporated into life insurance to protect the companies and their policyholders from attempts to defraud. The effect of these safeguards is an increase in complexity. It is hoped that this book will help consumers deal with the complexity that is inherent in life insurance.

The second kind of life insurance complexity stems from the proliferation of policy types. It is not surprising that there is virtually an infinite variety of life insurance policy types, because businesses in every industry (other than the monopolies) engage in product differentiation in an attempt to avoid price competition.

But the proliferation in life insurance has reached very large proportions. There are many so-called specialty policies. These usually are designed to fit an elaborate sales presentation, rather than to perform real services for the buyer. There are also many different policies of the so-called conventional type—so many, indeed, that it is difficult to distinguish between conventional policies and specialty policies.

Here again, it is hoped that this book will help consumers. One of the major premises of the book is that the life insurance needs of virtually all buyers can be met satisfactorily by just two policy forms—straight life and five-year renewable term—or some combination of the two.

Apathy

The apathy in the life insurance market is widespread. It is also important in at least two respects.

First, apathy on the part of buyers is at least partially responsible for what happens in the life insurance market. The typical person does not like to talk about life insurance, perhaps because it forces him to think about his own death. People would rather spend their leisure time discussing automobiles, sports, politics, social problems, or the state of the economy.

The effect of the apathy is to make life insurance very difficult to sell. This difficulty, in turn, makes it necessary for life insurance companies to provide intensive sales training for their agents. Since the companies want to get their agents into production quickly, there is not enough time to give them a thorough grounding in the technical aspects of life insurance. Moreover, there is a strong feeling that technical knowledge does not assist, and may actually hinder, sales efforts.

Once an agent starts to sell, he is likely to encounter difficulty in maintaining satisfactory production. His selling problems usually stem from apathy on the part of prospective buyers. So he must be provided with constant encouragement and more sales training. The constant emphasis on sales techniques, moreover, probably tends to harden the resistance of buyers. So the agents are given more and more sales training to overcome the sales resistance of their prospects. In short, apathy on the part of buyers is at least partially responsible for the emphasis on sales tactics as well as for the kind of sales tactics employed by life insurance companies and their agents.

The second important effect of apathy on the life insurance market is that it tends to perpetuate ignorance. When people are not interested in discussing life insurance, they do not find out how it operates or how it can be useful to them. They do not learn of major differences among policies and among companies. They get the idea that all life insurance is the same.

Thus, there is a circular characteristic to the ignorance, complexity, and apathy that permeate the life insurance market. The apathy fosters ignorance and complexity, because consumers generally are not interested enough in life insurance to try to dispel their ignorance and cut through the complexity. At the same time, ignorance and complexity foster apathy, because consumers generally do not realize the extent to which they are being penalized by ignorance and complexity and therefore are not interested in life insurance.

The results

In such an atmosphere of ignorance, complexity, and apathy, there are ample opportunities for the exploitation of consumers. Some companies train their agents to use a single sales presentation designed to sell one particular policy, without consideration of the suitability of the policy for a particular buyer. Many such policies are high-priced as well as unsuitable, and their primary redeeming virtues are a large agent's commission and an even larger profit for the insurance company.

Some companies are allowed to continue operations even though they are in a precarious financial condition. As long as buyers think all insurance companies are financially strong, and as long as the insurance commissioners in many states are unable or unwilling to do an adequate job in this area, such companies will continue to take premium dollars from unsuspecting consumers.

Even if they acquire suitable life insurance from companies that are reasonably strong, many policyholders are overcharged, in the sense that they could have bought comparable coverage at much lower prices. How can large price differences exist? The market for individual life insurance is characterized by an absence of reliable price information. As long as buyers do not have good information, and as long as buyers *think* all life insurance companies charge about the same price, companies that charge high prices can sell just as successfully as companies that charge low prices.

Fortunately, some companies that are financially strong also sell life insurance at relatively low prices, and some agents do a reasonable job of selecting suitable policies to meet the needs of buyers. Hopefully this book will help you find such companies, agents, and policies.

The life insurance market is characterized not only by an absence of reliable price information, but also by the presence of deceptive price information. The word "deceptive," as used here, refers to information that tends to give the buyer an erroneous impression of important relationships. The emphasis is on the buyer, and it is not intended to suggest that the deception is necessarily deliberate on the part of the agent. Many agents do not realize they are engaging in deceptive sales practices.

Suppose a 25-year-old person has decided to buy $25,000 of life insurance to cover the next forty years. He is told he can pay $250 per year for the forty years, a total of $10,000; or he can pay $500 per year for the first ten years and nothing thereafter, a total of $5,000. The agent tells him he should take the second payment arrangement because it is half as costly as the first arrangement. However, when the timing of the payments is considered, by using a reasonable interest assumption and reasonable assumptions about the respective probabilities of payment, the two payment arrangements have about the same value.

Even more serious is the price information given to consumers regarding one policy year at a time. An agent might say that in the tenth year of a given policy the premium (minus the dividend, if any) is smaller than the amount by which the cash value increases that year. He then states that the policyholder's cost that year is negative. The deception stems from an improper handling of the interest factor. For example, if a depositor puts $1,000 each year into a savings account, the account might increase in the tenth year by $1,629. If it is implied that all of the $629 of interest arose from the tenth year's deposit of $1,000, the implication would be that the depositor earned 62.9 percent interest on that deposit. If the interest were allocated properly, however, most of it would be allocated to earlier deposits, and the correct interest rate would be 5 percent.

These and other deceptive practices are widespread. They are so varied and often so complex that it is impractical for the layman to attempt to equip himself to recognize all of them. It is suggested that the buyer follow carefully the procedures described in this book and that he disregard any figures that deviate from those procedures.

What is being done?

The only effective way to make reliable price information widely available at the point of sale is a rigorous system of price disclosure for the life insurance industry. In a 1966 study, I suggested the need for such a disclosure system so that careful buyers could make reasonably informed purchase decisions.[1] Since that time, some progress has been made, but it has been slow.

In 1967, a front page story in *The Wall Street Journal* dealt with the price disclosure problem.[2] Prior to the story, the subject had been discussed solely among persons within or close to the life insurance industry. The story was significant because it transformed the subject into one of interest to the public at large.

October 1, 1968, was the effective date of a Washington State insurance department administrative rule requiring that certain price information be disclosed to the buyer when an agent recommends the replacement of one policy with another. Although the rule pertained only to replacement situations, it was significant because it represented the first strong life insurance price disclosure requirement by a regulatory agency.

On October 15, 1968, United States Senator Philip A. Hart (D., Mich.), chairman of the Subcommittee on Antitrust and Monopoly of the Committee on the Judiciary, mentioned the possibility of "truth in life insurance" legislation. In a speech before a life insurance industry group, he made the following statements:

> Obviously, if it makes sense to tell consumers how much of what is in a package on a supermarket shelf, or how much interest they will pay for using someone else's money, it makes sense to tell them how much they are paying for death protection and how much they are saving when they plunk down a life insurance premium.
>
> Hopefully your industry will think so too—and start supplying the information.
>
> If not—watch for Truth in Life Insurance to follow Truth in Packaging and Truth in Lending through the legislative mill.
>
> Because that's the way people are thinking in consumerland.[3]

Early in 1969, as a result of Senator Hart's admonition, three life insurance trade associations appointed a prestigious industry committee to look into the price disclosure problem. The report of the committee was released in May 1970.[4] On the one hand, it contains suggestions that, if implemented, would represent a major forward step by a conservative industry. On the other hand, the report leaves several crucial areas untouched.

The major recommendation of the committee is that the traditional net cost method, which involves the simple addition of amounts payable at different points in time, should be replaced by the interest adjusted method, which recognizes the timing of payments by taking interest into account. The report is silent, however, on the problem of price information for one policy year at a time—a problem that is even more serious than the one to which the committee addressed itself. Furthermore, the report fails to deal with one major aspect of Senator Hart's admonition—the need to inform the buyer about the extent to which he is buying protection and the extent to which he is putting away savings when he buys a cash-value life insurance policy.

Knowledgeable persons in the life insurance industry have strongly urged the companies to implement the recommendations of the committee voluntarily in order to forestall price disclosure legislation. The National Underwriter Company, a major insurance trade publisher, has developed a comprehensive volume of price information based on the interest adjusted method recommended by the committee. One company—Bankers Life (Iowa)—supported the committee's recommendation by adopting the interest adjusted method in some of its sales material. A few other companies began furnishing interest adjusted cost figures to their agents. At the urging of Mrs. Virginia H. Knauer, President Nixon's special assistant for consumer affairs, a number of additional companies indicated that they plan to furnish interest adjusted cost figures to their agents.

The reaction of most of the rest of the industry has been silence. The Alfred M. Best Company, the other major insurance trade publisher, apparently is planning to do nothing. A few persons—mostly agents and others representing the agents' point of view—have reacted with hostility. The rest of the industry—about 1,700 companies and about 200,000 agents—have not reacted at all.

In the face of the life insurance industry's apathy, and perhaps in part because of it, price disclosure legislation appears imminent. The Wisconsin insurance department has proposed an administrative rule that would require life insurance companies to make interest adjusted price figures available to their agents. (Unfortunately, the proposed rule provides that the information must be furnished to prospective buyers only when they request it.) The Pennsylvania insurance department has issued "A Shopper's Guide to Life Insurance," which shows interest adjusted price figures for numerous major companies. The National Association of Insurance Commissioners is studying the problem. Several federal agencies are taking a close look at the life insurance market.

The precise form that price disclosure legislation will take is not yet known. To do the job, however, the following kinds of information about a policy would have to be furnished to the consumer at the point of sale: (1) year-by-year information on the premiums to be paid by the policyholder, the amount payable at death, the amount payable on discontinuation of the policy, and the dividends payable under the company's current scale; (2) year-by-year information on the amount of life insurance protection provided, and the price of each $1,000 of protection; (3) summary information so that the consumer would be able to compare similar policies in different companies and so that he would be able to see the proportion of the premium dollar going into life insurance protection, the proportion going into the the savings element, the proportion coming back in the form of dividends, and the proportion being retained by the company; and (4) a system for consistently disclosing the relationship between year-by-year dividends paid and those illustrated at the time of sale. The technology for such a disclosure system is available; all that is required is its implementation.[5]

The life insurance industry, with its powerful lobbies at both the state and federal levels, is likely to argue against such disclosure in a variety of ways. It is not needed, it would confuse buyers rather than help them, buyers have not requested it, it would be expensive administratively, it would hinder sales, it would lead to keen price competition, and it would be inconsistent with our enterprise system.

Those favoring price disclosure legislation are likely to respond directly to such arguments. Price disclosure in life insurance is urgently needed, it would help buyers, it is being requested by buyers, it would be inexpensive in this computer era, it would help sales by giving consumers more confidence in what they are buying, keen competition is an integral part of an enterprise economy, and price disclosure thus is consistent with our enterprise system.

A broadening of disclosure requirements has taken place in every area of business activity in recent decades and has been accompanied by a growing sophistication among American consumers. It is unlikely that the life insurance purchases of an increasingly knowledgeable public will support a satisfactory growth rate for the life insurance industry in the face of inadequate and often deceptive price information. Life insurance price disclosure should raise the stature of the industry and strengthen public confidence in the institution of life insurance.

Appendixes

Appendix A
Computation of Present Values

The purpose of this appendix is to explain how to calculate the present value of your income needs and the present value of your estimated Social Security survivors' benefits. The phrase "present value" means the amount of funds which, if available at the beginning of a time period and invested consistently at the assumed interest rate, would be precisely sufficient to produce the given yearly payments. For example, Table A–1 shows that $10,899 would be the present value of $1,000 per year for fifteen years at 5 percent interest. In other words, $10,899 would be precisely sufficient to produce payments of $1,000 per year for fifteen years (with the payments at the beginning of each year), if the remaining funds were consistently invested at 5 percent interest.

Table A–1 shows the present value of $1,000 per year (with the payments at the beginning of each year) for various numbers of years at various interest rates. The table can be used to calculate not only the present value of a series of equal payments but also the present value of a series of unequal payments. Some of the uses of the table are illustrated by the following four examples.

Example 1—Equal payments

Suppose the objective is to determine the present value of an income of $8,000 per year for fifteen years at 5 percent interest. Table A–1 shows that the present value of $1,000 per year for fifteen years at 5 percent is $10,899. The present value of $8,000 would be eight times that, or $87,192. In other words, the present value of the desired yearly income is determined by multiplying the appropriate figure from Table A–1 by the number of thousands of dollars of desired yearly income.

Example 2—Decreasing payments

Suppose the objective is to determine the present value of an income of $12,000 per year for ten years, followed by an income of $9,000 per year for the subsequent twenty years, at an interest rate of 4 percent. The over-all income pattern may be viewed as $9,000 per year for the entire thirty years, plus an additional $3,000 per year for the first ten years. The present value of $9,000 per year for thirty years at 4 percent interest is $161,856 ($17,984 multiplied by 9). The present value of $3,000 per year for ten years at 4

191

Table A–1
Present value of $1,000 per year
(Payable at beginning of each year)

Number of Years	Interest Rate						
	0%	1%	2%	3%	4%	5%	6%
1	$ 1,000	$ 1,000	$ 1,000	$ 1,000	$ 1,000	$ 1,000	$ 1,000
2	2,000	1,990	1,980	1,971	1,962	1,952	1,943
3	3,000	2,970	2,942	2,913	2,886	2,859	2,833
4	4,000	3,941	3,884	3,829	3,775	3,723	3,673
5	5,000	4,902	4,808	4,717	4,630	4,546	4,465
6	6,000	5,853	5,713	5,580	5,452	5,329	5,212
7	7,000	6,795	6,601	6,417	6,242	6,076	5,917
8	8,000	7,728	7,472	7,230	7,002	6,786	6,582
9	9,000	8,652	8,325	8,020	7,733	7,463	7,210
10	10,000	9,566	9,162	8,786	8,435	8,108	7,802
11	11,000	10,471	9,983	9,530	9,111	8,722	8,360
12	12,000	11,368	10,787	10,253	9,760	9,306	8,887
13	13,000	12,255	11,575	10,954	10,385	9,863	9,384
14	14,000	13,134	12,348	11,635	10,986	10,394	9,853
15	15,000	14,004	13,106	12,296	11,563	10,899	10,295
16	16,000	14,865	13,849	12,938	12,118	11,380	10,712
17	17,000	15,718	14,578	13,561	12,652	11,838	11,106
18	18,000	16,562	15,292	14,166	13,166	12,274	11,477
19	19,000	17,398	15,992	14,754	13,659	12,690	11,828
20	20,000	18,226	16,678	15,324	14,134	13,085	12,158
25	25,000	22,243	19,914	17,936	16,247	14,799	13,550
30	30,000	26,066	22,844	20,188	17,984	16,141	14,591
35	35,000	29,703	25,499	22,132	19,411	17,193	15,368
40	40,000	33,163	27,903	23,808	20,584	18,017	15,949
45	45,000	36,455	30,080	25,254	21,549	18,663	16,383
50	50,000	39,588	32,052	26,502	22,341	19,169	16,708
55	55,000	42,569	33,838	27,578	22,993	19,565	16,950
60	60,000	45,405	35,456	28,506	23,528	19,876	17,131
65	65,000	48,103	36,921	29,306	23,969	20,119	17,266
70	70,000	50,670	38,249	29,997	24,330	20,310	17,368

percent interest is $25,305 ($8,435 multiplied by 3). The sum of these two results is $187,161 ($161,856 plus $25,305), which is the present value of an income of $12,000 per year for ten years, followed by an income of $9,000 per year for the subsequent twenty years, at 4 percent interest.

Example 3—Increasing payments

Suppose the objective is to determine the present value of an income of $9,000 per year for ten years, followed by an income of $12,000 per year for the subsequent twenty years, at an interest rate of 4 percent. The over-all income pattern may be viewed as $12,000 per year for the entire thirty years, *minus* $3,000 per year for the first ten years. The present value of $12,000 per year for thirty years at 4 percent interest is $215,808 ($17,984 multiplied by 12). The present value of $3,000 per year for ten years at 4 percent interest is $25,305 ($8,435 multiplied by 3). The difference between these two results is $190,503 ($215,808 minus $25,305), which is the present value of an income of $9,000 per year for ten years, followed by an income of $12,000 per year for the subsequent twenty years, at 4 percent interest.

Example 4—Delayed equal payments

Suppose the objective is to determine the present value of an income of $7,000 per year for fifteen years, with the income to start twenty years from now, at an interest rate of 4 percent. The over-all income pattern may be viewed as $7,000 per year for the entire thirty-five years, *minus* $7,000 per year for the first twenty years. The present value of $7,000 per year for thirty-five years at 4 percent interest is $135,877 ($19,411 multiplied by 7). The present value of $7,000 per year for twenty years at 4 percent interest is $98,938 ($14,134 multiplied by 7). The difference between these two results is $36,939 ($135,877 minus $98,938), which is the present value of an income of $7,000 per year for fifteen years, with the income to start twenty years from now, at 4 percent interest.

Appendix B
Alphabetical Listing of Companies with Most Strongly
Worded Recommendation in 1971 Edition of *Best's Life
Insurance Reports*

(Companies marked with an asterisk are those for which price data are included in the
tables in Chapters 4 or 5 and in Appendixes D or E.)

Full Name of Company	Home Office Location
*Aetna Life Insurance Company	Hartford, Connecticut
American General Life Insurance Company	Houston, Texas
American General Life Insurance Company of Delaware	Wilmington, Delaware
American Mutual Life Insurance Company	Des Moines, Iowa
*American National Insurance Company	Galveston, Texas
*American United Life Insurance Company	Indianapolis, Indiana
*Bankers Life Company	Des Moines, Iowa
Bankers National Life Insurance Company	Parsippany, New Jersey
Beneficial Life Insurance Company	Salt Lake City, Utah
Berkshire Life Insurance Company	Pittsfield, Massachusetts
*Business Men's Assurance Company of America	Kansas City, Missouri
California-Western States Life Insurance Company	Sacramento, California
*The Canada Life Assurance Company	Toronto, Ontario, Canada
Central Life Assurance Company	Des Moines, Iowa
The Columbus Mutual Life Insurance Company	Columbus, Ohio
Commonwealth Life Insurance Company	Louisville, Kentucky
*Confederation Life Insurance Company	Toronto, Ontario, Canada
*Connecticut General Life Insurance Company	Hartford, Connecticut
*Connecticut Mutual Life Insurance Company	Hartford, Connecticut
Continental American Life Insurance Company	Wilmington, Delaware
*Continental Assurance Company	Chicago, Illinois
Country Life Insurance Company	Bloomington, Illinois
*Crown Life Insurance Company	Toronto, Ontario, Canada
The Dominion Life Assurance Company	Waterloo, Ontario, Canada
*The Equitable Life Assurance Society of the United States	New York, New York
Equitable Life Insurance Company	Washington, D.C.
Equitable Life Insurance Company of Iowa	Des Moines, Iowa

Appendix B—Continued

Full Name of Company	Home Office Location
Farm Bureau Life Insurance Company	Des Moines, Iowa
The Fidelity Mutual Life Insurance Company	Philadelphia, Pennsylvania
Fidelity Union Life Insurance Company	Dallas, Texas
*Franklin Life Insurance Company	Springfield, Illinois
General American Life Insurance Company	St. Louis, Missouri
Government Employees Life Insurance Company	Washington, D.C.
Great Southern Life Insurance Company	Houston, Texas
*The Great-West Life Assurance Company	Winnipeg, Manitoba, Canada
Guarantee Mutual Life Company	Omaha, Nebraska
*The Guardian Life Insurance Company of America	New York, New York
Hartford Life Insurance Company	Hartford, Connecticut
Home Beneficial Life Insurance Company	Richmond, Virginia
*Home Life Insurance Company	New York, New York
The Imperial Life Assurance Company of Canada	Toronto, Ontario, Canada
Indianapolis Life Insurance Company	Indianapolis, Indiana
Integon Life Insurance Corporation	Winston-Salem, North Carolina
Interstate Life & Accident Insurance Company	Chattanooga, Tennessee
*Jefferson Standard Life Insurance Company	Greensboro, North Carolina
*John Hancock Mutual Life Insurance Company	Boston, Massachusetts
Kansas City Life Insurance Company	Kansas City, Missouri
Lafayette Life Insurance Company	Lafayette, Indiana
The Lamar Life Insurance Company	Jackson, Mississippi
Liberty Life Insurance Company	Greenville, South Carolina
Liberty National Life Insurance Company	Birmingham, Alabama
Life and Casualty Insurance Company of Tennessee	Nashville, Tennessee
Life Insurance Company of Georgia	Atlanta, Georgia
The Life Insurance Company of Virginia	Richmond, Virginia
*The Lincoln National Life Insurance Company	Fort Wayne, Indiana
Loyal Protective Life Insurance Company	Boston, Massachusetts
Lutheran Mutual Life Insurance Company	Waverly, Iowa
*The Manufacturers Life Insurance Company	Toronto, Ontario, Canada
*Massachusetts Mutual Life Insurance Company	Springfield, Massachusetts
*Metropolitan Life Insurance Company	New York, New York
The Midland Mutual Life Insurance Company	Columbus, Ohio

Appendix B—Continued

Full Name of Company	Home Office Location
Midwestern United Life Insurance Company	Fort Wayne, Indiana
The Minnesota Mutual Life Insurance Company	St. Paul, Minnesota
Monarch Life Insurance Company	Springfield, Massachusetts
Monumental Life Insurance Company	Baltimore, Maryland
*Mutual Benefit Life Insurance Company	Newark, New Jersey
*The Mutual Life Insurance Company of New York	New York, New York
Mutual Trust Life Insurance Company	Chicago, Illinois
National Fidelity Life Insurance Company	Kansas City, Missouri
National Guardian Life Insurance Company	Madison, Wisconsin
*The National Life & Accident Insurance Company	Nashville, Tennessee
*National Life Insurance Company	Montpelier, Vermont
*Nationwide Life Insurance Company	Columbus, Ohio
*New England Mutual Life Insurance Company	Boston, Massachusetts
*New York Life Insurance Company	New York, New York
North American Company for Life and Health Insurance	Chicago, Illinois
*North American Life Assurance Company	Toronto, Ontario, Canada
North American Reassurance Company	New York, New York
Northern Life Assurance Company of Canada	London, Ontario, Canada
Northern Life Insurance Company	Seattle, Washington
*The Northwestern Mutual Life Insurance Company	Milwaukee, Wisconsin
Northwestern National Life Insurance Company	Minneapolis, Minnesota
*Occidental Life Insurance Company of California	Los Angeles, California
Ohio National Life Insurance Company	Cincinnati, Ohio
Ohio State Life Insurance Company	Columbus, Ohio
Pacific Mutual Life Insurance Company	Los Angeles, California
Pan-American Life Insurance Company	New Orleans, Louisiana
The Paul Revere Life Insurance Company	Worcester, Massachusetts
*The Penn Mutual Life Insurance Company	Philadelphia, Pennsylvania
Philadelphia Life Insurance Company	Philadelphia, Pennsylvania
*Phoenix Mutual Life Insurance Company	Hartford, Connecticut
Pilot Life Insurance Company	Greensboro, North Carolina

Appendix B — Continued

Full Name of Company	Home Office Location
Presbyterian Ministers' Fund	Philadelphia, Pennsylvania
Protective Life Insurance Company	Birmingham, Alabama
°Provident Life and Accident Insurance Company	Chattanooga, Tennessee
°Provident Mutual Life Insurance Company of Philadelphia	Philadelphia, Pennsylvania
°The Prudential Insurance Company of America	Newark, New Jersey
Reliance Standard Life Insurance Company	Chicago, Illinois
°Republic National Life Insurance Company	Dallas, Texas
SAFECO Life Insurance Company	Seattle, Washington
Security Life and Accident Company	Denver, Colorado
Security Mutual Life Insurance Company of New York	Binghamton, New York
Shenandoah Life Insurance Company	Roanoke, Virginia
Southern Farm Bureau Life Insurance Company	Jackson, Mississippi
°Southwestern Life Insurance Company	Dallas, Texas
Standard Insurance Company	Portland, Oregon
°State Farm Life Insurance Company	Bloomington, Illinois
°Sun Life Assurance Company of Canada	Montreal, Quebec, Canada
Sun Life Insurance Company of America	Baltimore, Maryland
Sunset Life Insurance Company of America	Olympia, Washington
°Teachers Insurance and Annuity Association of America	New York, New York
Texas Life Insurance Company	Waco, Texas
°The Travelers Insurance Company	Hartford, Connecticut
The Union Central Life Insurance Company	Cincinnati, Ohio
Union National Life Insurance Company	Baton Rouge, Louisiana
°United Benefit Life Insurance Company	Omaha, Nebraska
United Farm Bureau Family Life Insurance Company	Indianapolis, Indiana
United Fidelity Life Insurance Company	Dallas, Texas
United Life and Accident Insurance Company	Concord, New Hampshire
United Services Life Insurance Company	Washington, D.C.
The United States Life Insurance Company in the City of New York	New York, New York
The Volunteer State Life Insurance Company	Chattanooga, Tennessee

Appendix B—Continued

Full Name of Company	Home Office Location
Washington National Insurance Company	Evanston, Illinois
West Coast Life Insurance Company	San Francisco, California
Western Life Insurance Company	St. Paul, Minnesota
°The Western and Southern Life Insurance Company	Cincinnati, Ohio
Wisconsin National Life Insurance Company	Oshkosh, Wisconsin

Appendix C
Policy Abbreviations Used
in Tables of Values

Abbreviation	Policy Name
AWL	Adjustable whole life
C95	Commercial 95
CL	Convertible life
CWL	Commercial whole life
E50WL	Estate 50 whole life
E85	Endowment at 85
E90	Endowment at 90
E95	Endowment at 95
EE	Executive equity
EOL	Executive ordinary life
EP	Economy protector
EPWL	Estatemaster preferred whole life
ES	Executive special
ESL95	Executive special life 95
ESpWL	Estatemaster special whole life
ESWL	Executive select whole life
EWL	Executive whole life
ExP	Executive plan
ExPf	Executive preferred
GWL	Guaranteed whole life
L85	Life 85
L90	Life 90
L95	Life 95
LL90	Leader life 90
LP	Life preferred
M3	Modified 3
OL	Ordinary life
OLPR	Ordinary life preferred risk
PEP	Policy for executives and professionals
PL	Preferred life

Appendix C—Continued

Abbreviation	Policy Name
PL85	Preferred life 85
PL90	Preferred life 90
PLM2	Protector life modified 2
POL	Preferred ordinary life
POL100	Presidential ordinary life 100
PP	Presidential plus
PPWL	Professional preferred whole life
PROL	Preferred risk ordinary life
PRWL	Preferred risk whole life
PtL	Protector life
PWL	Preferred whole life
PWLM3	Preferred whole life modified 3
S25L95	Signature 25 life 95
SE	Select economy
SL	Straight life
SL85	Special life 85
SL90	Standard life 90
SOL	Select ordinary life
SpOL	Special ordinary life
StOL	Standard ordinary life
SSL	Super select life
SpWL	Special whole life
SWL	Select whole life
WL	Whole life
WLIP	Whole life and indexed protection
WLP	Whole life preferred
5-YR RCT	Five-year renewable convertible term

Appendix D
Additional Tables of Price Information

This appendix contains fifteen tables of price information to supplement the three tables in Chapter 4. The discussion in that chapter explains the purpose of each of the supplemental tables.

Tables D–1, D–2, and D–3 show figures for certain participating straight life policies issued to 35-year-old men in 1950, 1940, and 1930, respectively, based on historical dividends. Tables D–4 and D–5 show figures for certain $25,000 participating straight life policies issued in 1970 to men aged 25 and 45, respectively. Tables D–6 and D–7 show figures for certain participating straight life policies issued to 35-year-old men in 1970, with face amounts of $10,000 and $100,000, respectively.

Tables D–8 and D–9 show figures for certain $25,000 nonparticipating straight life policies issued in 1970 to men aged 25 and 45, respectively. Tables D–10 and D–11 show figures for certain nonparticipating straight life policies issued to 35-year-old men in 1970, with face amounts of $10,000 and $100,000, respectively.

Tables D–12 and D–13 show figures for certain $25,000 five-year renewable term policies issued in 1970 to men aged 25 and 45, respectively. Tables D–14 and D–15 show figures for certain five-year renewable term policies issued to 35-year-old men in 1970, with face amounts of $10,000 and $100,000, respectively.

Table D–1
*Values for $10,000 participating straight life policies issued in 1950
to men aged 35*

Company	Policy	Premiums	Protection Element	Savings Element	Historical Dividends	Company Retention
Aetna Life	OL	$3,193	$317	$1,378	$ 851	$ 647
American National[a]	—	—	—	—	—	—
American United	OL m2½	3,022	323	1,290	690	720
Bankers Life (Iowa)	L85	3,240	318	1,351	896	675
Bankers Life (Iowa)	POL m5	3,110	318	1,344	1,024	423
Canada Life	E85	3,124	318	1,361	([b])	—
Canada Life	SSL m10	2,756	319	1,339	636	462
Confederation Life	L85	2,907	325	1,266	544	772
Connecticut General	OL	3,159	317	1,378	813	652
Connecticut Mutual	OL	3,194	317	1,354	1,090	433
Continental Assurance	OL	3,182	318	1,368	786	710
Crown Life	L85	2,880	327	1,226	553	774
Crown Life	OL m5	2,724	328	1,215	595	587
Equitable (N.Y.)	OL	3,357	318	1,359	900	780
Franklin Life	OL	3,266	330	1,178	713	1,044
Franklin Life	ESWL m10	2,891	320	1,339	732	500
Great-West Life	E85	3,074	318	1,366	723	667
Great-West Life	PROL m5	2,666	319	1,344	586	417
Guardian Life	OL	3,183	320	1,346	692	826
Guardian Life	PL85 m10	2,934	320	1,357	706	553
Home Life (N.Y.)	L85	3,148	321	1,346	734	747
Home Life (N.Y.)	PWL m5	2,867	321	1,343	633	571
Jefferson Standard	PROL m2½	3,057	328	1,222	803	704
Jefferson Standard	L85 m10	3,159	316	1,369	862	612
John Hancock	L85	3,173	320	1,389	764	700
John Hancock	PRWL m5	2,898	318	1,380	762	439
Lincoln National	OL	3,179	321	1,329	691	839
Manufacturers Life	OL	2,950	325	1,259	788	578
Massachusetts Mutual	OL	3,157	316	1,357	977	506
Metropolitan Life	L85	3,082	320	1,393	547	823
Metropolitan Life	WL m5	2,793	321	1,375	497	600
Mutual Benefit	OL	3,153	310	1,461	803	579
Mutual of New York	L85	3,358	319	1,401	932	706
National Life (Vt.)	OL	3,134	317	1,377	944	496
Nationwide Life[c]	OL m3	2,808	325	1,248	628	607
New England Life	L85	3,148	316	1,380	912	540
New England Life	OL m5	2,994	317	1,370	866	441
New York Life	L85	3,366	313	1,430	879	744
New York Life	OL m5	3,210	314	1,419	935	542
North American (Can.)	L85	2,917	325	1,262	407	925
North American (Can.)	LP m5	2,648	325	1,251	513	559
Northwestern Mutual	OL	3,156	311	1,442	1,012	391

Table D–1 — Continued

Company	Policy	Premiums	Protection Element	Savings Element	Historical Dividends	Company Retention
Occidental (Calif.)ᵈ	OLPR m5	3,133	325	1,283	914	612
Penn Mutual	OL	3,250	313	1,403	858	675
Phoenix Mutual	OL	3,197	315	1,391	909	582
Provident Mutual	OL	3,254	313	1,409	975	557
Provident Mutual	PtL m5	3,208	318	1,343	998	548
Prudential	L85	3,196	319	1,366	599	912
Prudential	M3 m5	2,911	323	1,320	665	608
Republic National	OL	3,197	325	1,248	(ᵇ)	—
State Farm Life	L85	3,358	326	1,311	743	977
State Farm Life	SOL m5	2,745	327	1,301	531	586
State Mutual	WL	3,153	317	1,351	854	631
Sun Life (Can.)	OL	3,091	321	1,335	861	574
Sun Life (Can.)	PL m5	2,908	321	1,335	810	443
Western & Southern	L85	3,089	325	1,259	478	1,027
Western & Southern	CWL m5	2,808	325	1,249	426	807

ᵃ Company did not issue participating policies in 1950.

ᵇ Dividend data are not available.

ᶜ Name of company in 1950 was Farm Bureau Life Insurance Company.

ᵈ Company did not issue participating policies smaller than $5,000 in 1950.

Note: The symbol m2½ means that the minimum policy of the specified type issued by the company was $2,500. The symbols m3, m5, and m10 similarly refer to minimum policy limits of $3,000, $5,000, and $10,000.

SUMMARY

Company Retention	Number of Policies
$ 380–$ 419	2
420– 459	5
460– 499	2
500– 539	2
540– 579	10
580– 619	8
620– 659	3
660– 699	3
700– 739	5
740– 779	4
780– 819	2
820– 859	3
860– 899	0
900– 939	2
940– 979	1
980– 1,019	0
1,020– 1,059	2
	54

Table D-2
*Values for $5,000 participating straight life policies issued in 1940 to men
aged 35*

Company	Policy	Premiums	Protection Element	Savings Element	Historical Dividends	Company Retention
Aetna Life	OL	$1,638	$188	$754	$357	$339
American National[a]	—	—	—	—	—	—
American United	OL	1,408	192	690	106	422
Bankers Life (Iowa)	E85	1,659	186	767	322	384
Bankers Life (Iowa)	SOL m5	1,651	187	758	394	312
Canada Life	OL	1,532	187	752	219	373
Confederation Life	L85	1,420	188	748	168	316
Connecticut General	OL	1,574	188	754	259	374
Connecticut Mutual	OL	1,625	186	763	387	289
Continental Assurance	OL	1,651	188	750	384	329
Crown Life	OL	1,442	188	749	168	338
Equitable (N.Y.)	OL	1,733	189	752	493	300
Franklin Life	OL	1,717	191	709	311	506
Franklin Life	PROL m2½	1,637	190	738	244	465
Great-West Life	E85	1,543	185	814	252	293
Great-West Life	PROL m5	1,336	187	766	181	202
Guardian Life	OL	1,625	187	763	256	418
Home Life (N.Y.)	E85	1,633	186	773	221	454
Home Life (N.Y.)	PWL m5	1,412	189	720	158	344
Jefferson Standard	PROL m2½	1,586	188	750	354	293
John Hancock	E85	1,607	187	771	273	376
John Hancock	PRWL m5	1,495	187	763	315	229
Lincoln National[b]	OL m5	1,514	192	689	334	300
Manufacturers Life	OL	1,443	187	758	214	283
Massachusetts Mutual	OL	1,625	186	763	324	351
Metropolitan Life	L85	1,563	192	757	285	329
Metropolitan Life	WL m5	1,391	192	754	259	186
Mutual Benefit	OL	1,625	184	794	319	328
Mutual of New York	OL	1,733	191	753	411	377
National Life (Vt.)	OL	1,625	186	762	415	262
Nationwide Life[c]	OL	1,469	189	731	204	346
New England Life	OL	1,665	186	771	377	331
New York Life	OL	1,733	192	752	405	385
North American (Can.)	L85	1,537	184	810	190	353
North American (Can.)	LP m5	1,387	184	806	183	214
Northwestern Mutual	OL	1,658	186	763	473	235
Occidental (Calif.)[b]	OLPR m5	1,423	187	757	239	240

Table D-2—Continued

Company	Policy	Premiums	Protection Element	Savings Element	Historical Dividends	Company Retention
Penn Mutual	OL	1,625	186	765	329	345
Phoenix Mutual	OL	1,516	189	735	215	377
Provident Mutual	OL	1,596	186	762	348	300
Provident Mutual	PtL m5	1,580	188	738	379	274
Prudential	E85	1,567	190	779	245	353
Prudential	M3 m5	1,425	192	749	266	218
Republic National[d]	—	—	—	—	—	—
State Farm Life	OL	1,708	192	739	293	485
State Mutual	OL	1,625	186	763	270	405
Sun Life (Can.)	OL	1,720	185	773	412	349
Western & Southern[a]	—	—	—	—	—	—

[a] Company did not issue participating policies in 1940.
[b] Company did not issue participating policies smaller than $5,000 in 1940.
[c] Name of company in 1940 was Farm Bureau Life Insurance Company.
[d] Company did not issue conventional participating policies in 1940.
Note: The symbol m2½ means that the minimum policy of the specified type issued by the company was $2,500. The symbol m5 similarly refers to a minimum policy limit of $5,000.

SUMMARY

Company Retention	Number of Policies
$180–$199	1
200– 219	3
220– 239	2
240– 259	1
260– 279	2
280– 299	4
300– 319	5
320– 339	6
340– 359	7
360– 379	5
380– 399	2
400– 419	2
420– 439	1
440– 459	1
460– 479	1
480– 499	1
500– 519	1
	45

Table D–3
*Values for $5,000 participating straight life policies issued in 1930
to men aged 35*

Company	Policy	Premiums	Protection Element	Savings Element	Historical Dividends	Company Retention
Aetna Life	OL	$1,442	$179	$709	$226	$328
American National[a]	—	—	—	—	—	—
American United	OL	1,323	180	689	107	347
Bankers Life (Iowa)	E85	1,530	177	723	269	360
Canada Life	OL	1,616	174	766	255	421
Confederation Life[b]	—	—	—	—	—	—
Connecticut General	OL	1,476	178	713	233	352
Connecticut Mutual	OL	1,526	175	761	304	287
Continental Assurance[a]	—	—	—	—	—	—
Crown Life	OL	1,355	176	745	125	308
Equitable (N.Y.)	OL	1,628	175	756	416	280
Franklin Life[a]	—	—	—	—	—	—
Great-West Life	OL	1,587	177	728	380	302
Guardian Life	OL	1,526	175	762	278	311
Home Life (N.Y.)	E85	1,534	175	766	238	355
Home Life (N.Y.)	PWL m5	1,326	178	714	179	255
Jefferson Standard	PROL m2½	1,490	175	759	335	221
John Hancock	E85	1,506	177	728	291	310
John Hancock	PRWL m5	1,326	177	721	242	186
Lincoln National[a]	—	—	—	—	—	—
Manufacturers Life	OL	1,355	174	775	134	273
Massachusetts Mutual	OL	1,526	175	763	295	294
Metropolitan Life	E85	1,390	178	729	214	270
Metropolitan Life	WL m5	1,239	178	721	185	155
Mutual Benefit	OL	1,526	174	783	307	262
Mutual of New York	OL	1,628	175	755	334	364
National Life (Vt.)	OL	1,526	175	761	336	255
Nationwide Life[c]	—	—	—	—	—	—
New England Life	OL	1,564	175	763	370	255
New York Life	OL	1,628	177	754	394	304
North American (Can.)	OL	1,587	175	763	344	305
Northwestern Mutual	OL	1,557	175	762	435	186
Occidental (Calif.)[d]	OLPR m5	1,249	176	750	([e])	—
Penn Mutual	OL	1,526	175	763	340	249
Phoenix Mutual	OL	1,338	178	715	148	297
Provident Mutual	OL	1,326	178	716	192	240
Prudential	E85	1,310	177	727	156	250
Prudential	M3 m5	1,217	179	699	142	198

Table D–3 – Continued

Company	Policy	Premiums	Protection Element	Savings Element	Historical Dividends	Company Retention
Republic National[f]	—	—	—	—	—	—
State Farm Life	OL	1,504	180	695	272	357
State Mutual	OL	1,526	175	762	309	281
Sun Life (Can.)	OL	1,616	174	764	337	340
Western & Southern[a]	—	—	—	—	—	—

[a] Company did not issue participating policies in 1930.
[b] Company did not issue participating policies in the United States in 1930.
[c] Company was not yet in business in 1930.
[d] Company did not issue participating policies smaller than $5,000 in 1930.
[e] Dividend data are not available.
[f] Company did not issue conventional participating policies in 1930.

Note: The symbol m2½ means that the minimum policy of the specified type issued by the company was $2,500. The symbol m5 similarly refers to a minimum policy limit of $5,000.

SUMMARY

Company Retention	Number of Policies
$140–$159	1
160– 179	0
180– 199	3
200– 219	0
220– 239	1
240– 259	6
260– 279	3
280– 299	5
300– 319	6
320– 339	1
340– 359	5
360– 379	2
380– 399	0
400– 419	0
420– 439	1
	34

Table D–4
*Values for $25,000 participating straight life policies issued in 1970
to men aged 25*

Company	Policy	Premiums	Protection Element	Savings Element	Illustrated Dividends	Company Retention
Aetna Life	WL	$4,329	$315	$1,913	$ 930	$1,171
Aetna Life	E95	4,453	311	1,990	1,139	1,013
American National	OL	4,154	313	1,916	872	1,053
American United	ESL95	4,198	311	1,940	1,025	922
Bankers Life (Iowa)	SpWL	3,174	317	1,752	489	616
Bankers Life (Iowa)	PWL	4,020	310	1,954	1,182	575
Canada Life	PL	3,815	311	1,944	734	825
Canada Life	ExPf	3,956	310	1,964	702	980
Confederation Life	WL	3,894	314	1,831	1,039	710
Confederation Life	SL85	4,305	305	2,141	1,054	805
Connecticut General	L90	3,820	308	2,061	495	956
Connecticut Mutual	WL	3,751	314	1,805	1,087	545
Continental Assurance	WL	4,223	311	1,966	1,058	888
Crown Life	SOL	3,191	320	1,607	485	780
Equitable (N.Y.)	AWL	4,171	311	1,941	989	930
Franklin Life	ESWL	4,035	314	1,867	909	946
Great-West Life	EPWL	4,057	311	1,940	968	839
Guardian Life	POL	4,005	311	1,942	929	823
Home Life (N.Y.)	WL	4,169	310	1,962	1,181	715
Jefferson Standard	WL	4,008	316	1,771	847	1,073
Jefferson Standard	L90	4,136	309	1,986	1,035	807
John Hancock	S25L95	4,282	309	2,062	810	1,101
John Hancock	PWLM3	3,978	312	1,970	913	782
Lincoln National	OL	4,206	312	1,917	1,029	947
Manufacturers Life	WL	3,469	321	1,581	695	872
Massachusetts Mutual	CL	4,258	309	1,997	1,244	708
Metropolitan Life	PL90	4,094	313	1,963	818	1,001
Mutual Benefit	OL	4,226	309	1,991	1,141	786
Mutual of New York	WL	4,080	312	1,950	862	955
National Life (Vt.)	OL	4,213	306	2,210	835	863
National Life (Vt.)	PEP	4,213	305	2,245	795	869
Nationwide Life	EE	3,961	309	1,965	867	820
New England Life	OL	4,258	309	1,991	1,143	814
New York Life	WL	4,174	313	1,828	1,160	872
North American (Can.)	WLIP	3,961	312	1,928	948	773
Northwestern Mutual	L90	4,292	308	2,059	1,212	713
Occidental (Calif.)	PWL	4,077	309	1,961	855	951
Penn Mutual	WL	4,186	309	1,983	1,005	889
Phoenix Mutual	OL	4,260	307	2,187	854	912
Provident Mutual	WL	4,089	309	1,987	1,058	735
Provident Mutual	PLM2	3,615	314	1,805	' 836	660
Prudential	EWL	4,065	312	1,972	711	1,069

Table D–4 – Continued

Company	Policy	Premiums	Protection Element	Savings Element	Illustrated Dividends	Company Retention
Republic National	L90	3,815	314	1,866	581	1,054
State Farm Life	SOL	3,864	317	1,771	881	894
State Mutual	WL	4,087	309	1,985	1,113	681
Sun Life (Can.)	WL	4,196	314	1,879	1,271	732
Western & Southern	EP	4,188	311	1,962	751	1,165
Western & Southern	SE	4,191	314	1,898	984	995

SUMMARY

Company Retention	Number of Policies
$ 500–$ 599	2
600– 699	3
700– 799	10
800– 899	14
900– 999	10
1,000– 1,099	6
1,100– 1,199	3
	48

Table D–5
*Values for $25,000 participating straight life policies issued in 1970
to men aged 45*

Company	Policy	Premiums	Protection Element	Savings Element	Illustrated Dividends	Company Retention
Aetna Life	WL	$7,817	$1,653	$3,120	$1,621	$1,424
Aetna Life	E95	8,061	1,626	3,255	1,944	1,236
American National	OL	7,668	1,627	3,156	1,227	1,659
American United	ESL95	7,787	1,620	3,182	1,684	1,301
Bankers Life (Iowa)	SpWL	6,319	1,660	2,977	805	878
Bankers Life (Iowa)	PWL	7,477	1,609	3,220	2,021	628
Canada Life	PL	7,257	1,625	3,151	1,252	1,229
Canada Life	ExPf	7,345	1,602	3,300	1,065	1,377
Confederation Life	WL	7,262	1,655	2,979	1,502	1,126
Confederation Life	SL85	7,614	1,577	3,417	1,539	1,081
Connecticut General	L90	7,399	1,598	3,316	949	1,536
Connecticut Mutual	WL	7,482	1,626	3,119	1,823	914
Continental Assurance	WL	7,971	1,623	3,163	1,869	1,317
Crown Life	SOL	6,333	1,689	2,793	885	967
Equitable (N.Y.)	AWL	7,730	1,628	3,169	1,607	1,326
Franklin Life	ESWL	7,619	1,647	3,043	1,497	1,431
Great-West Life	EPWL	7,619	1,615	3,188	1,704	1,111
Guardian Life	POL	7,430	1,632	3,208	1,333	1,257
Home Life (N.Y.)	WL	7,602	1,614	3,230	1,735	1,024
Jefferson Standard	WL	7,541	1,648	3,038	1,286	1,569
Jefferson Standard	L90	7,787	1,595	3,311	1,647	1,234
John Hancock	S25L95	7,881	1,605	3,375	1,402	1,500
John Hancock	PWLM3	7,503	1,620	3,236	1,683	963
Lincoln National	OL	7,775	1,627	3,140	1,673	1,335
Manufacturers Life	WL	6,534	1,690	2,805	985	1,054
Massachusetts Mutual	CL	7,801	1,596	3,313	1,949	943
Metropolitan Life	PL90	7,205	1,641	3,194	1,275	1,095
Mutual Benefit	OL	7,810	1,596	3,306	1,810	1,098
Mutual of New York	WL	7,583	1,624	3,224	1,478	1,257
National Life (Vt.)	OL	7,543	1,587	3,451	1,449	1,057
National Life (Vt.)	PEP	7,543	1,580	3,506	1,391	1,066
Nationwide Life	EE	7,576	1,607	3,237	1,778	954
New England Life	OL	7,683	1,603	3,306	1,762	1,011
New York Life	WL	7,683	1,633	3,151	1,757	1,143
North American (Can.)	WLIP	7,432	1,625	3,164	1,487	1,156
Northwestern Mutual	L90	7,775	1,593	3,346	1,947	889
Occidental (Calif.)	PWL	7,624	1,610	3,232	1,349	1,433
Penn Mutual	WL	7,853	1,599	3,270	1,752	1,232
Phoenix Mutual	OL	7,621	1,603	3,394	1,406	1,218
Provident Mutual	WL	7,640	1,600	3,283	1,704	1,053
Provident Mutual	PLM2	7,120	1,631	3,107	1,441	941
Prudential	EWL	7,642	1,626	3,255	1,449	1,312

Table D–5—Continued

Company	Policy	Premiums	Protection Element	Savings Element	Illustrated Dividends	Company Retention
Republic National	L90	7,555	1,644	3,059	945	1,906
State Farm Life	SpOL	7,349	1,673	3,003	1,463	1,210
State Mutual	WL	7,744	1,597	3,300	1,916	931
Sun Life (Can.)	WL	7,791	1,647	3,060	2,078	1,007
Western & Southern	EP	7,841	1,620	3,205	1,193	1,823
Western & Southern	SE	7,855	1,644	3,127	1,452	1,632

SUMMARY

Company Retention	Number of Policies
$ 600–$ 699	1
700– 799	0
800– 899	2
900– 999	7
1,000– 1,099	10
1,100– 1,199	4
1,200– 1,299	8
1,300– 1,399	6
1,400– 1,499	3
1,500– 1,599	3
1,600– 1,699	2
1,700– 1,799	0
1,800– 1,899	1
1,900– 1,999	1
	48

Table D–6
Values for $10,000 participating straight life policies issued in 1970 to men aged 35

Company	Policy	Premiums	Protection Element	Savings Element	Illustrated Dividends	Company Retention
Aetna Life	WL	$2,348	$263	$1,009	$498	$577
American National	OL	2,266	260	1,015	395	597
American United	OL	2,437	261	984	537	655
Bankers Life (Iowa)	SpWL	1,813	265	945	254	350
Bankers Life (Iowa)	PWL	2,209	257	1,033	612	308
Canada Life	PL	2,098	259	1,021	364	454
Confederation Life	WL	2,150	263	966	509	412
Confederation Life	SL85	2,305	253	1,107	522	424
Connecticut General	L90	2,160	255	1,076	257	572
Connecticut Mutual	WL	2,142	261	979	545	357
Continental Assurance	WL	2,364	259	1,029	567	510
Crown Life	SOL	1,823	269	879	253	422
Equitable (N.Y.)	AWL	2,286	259	1,022	497	507
Franklin Life	ESWL	2,218	262	985	451	520
Great-West Life	EPWL	2,245	258	1,023	514	449
Guardian Life	SOL	2,259	260	1,013	455	531
Home Life (N.Y.)	WL	2,266	259	1,022	558	426
Jefferson Standard	WL	2,219	263	962	411	583
Jefferson Standard	L85	2,254	256	1,047	462	490
John Hancock	L85	2,373	258	1,052	455	608
Lincoln National	OL	2,309	260	1,013	529	508
Manufacturers Life	WL	1,931	269	877	338	447
Massachusetts Mutual	CL	2,314	257	1,038	612	407
Metropolitan Life	SL90	2,342	261	1,034	413	633
Mutual Benefit	OL	2,340	256	1,055	564	465
Mutual of New York	WL	2,234	260	1,027	403	543
National Life (Vt.)	OL	2,257	253	1,124	437	442
Nationwide Life	WL	2,269	260	1,006	543	461
New England Life	OL	2,279	259	1,029	543	449
New York Life	WL	2,288	261	990	571	466
North American (Can.)	WLIP	2,194	259	1,020	467	448
Northwestern Mutual	L90	2,302	255	1,075	613	359
Occidental (Calif.)	PWL	2,289	257	1,038	429	564
Penn Mutual	WL	2,307	257	1,035	521	495
Phoenix Mutual	OL	2,290	255	1,120	422	493
Provident Mutual	WL	2,249	256	1,052	514	426
Provident Mutual	PLM2	2,045	261	979	419	385
Prudential	L85	2,289	260	1,037	386	605

Table D–6—Continued

Company	Policy	Premiums	Protection Element	Savings Element	Illustrated Dividends	Company Retention
Republic National	L90	2,176	262	988	286	641
State Farm Life	SpOL	2,152	266	956	446	483
State Mutual	WL	2,270	257	1,036	571	407
Sun Life (Can.)	WL	2,294	262	991	631	410
Western & Southern	EP	2,324	259	1,033	396	636

SUMMARY

Company Retention	Number of Policies
$300–$339	1
340– 379	3
380– 419	5
420– 459	10
460– 499	7
500– 539	5
540– 579	4
580– 619	4
620– 659	4
	43

Table D–7
*Values for $100,000 participating straight life policies issued in 1970
to men aged 35*

Company	Policy	Premiums	Protection Element	Savings Element	Illustrated Dividends	Company Retention
Aetna Life	E90	$23,349	$2,590	$10,704	$6,107	$3,948
Aetna Life	WL	22,594	2,634	10,090	4,980	4,891
American National	OL	22,001	2,597	10,148	3,952	5,304
American United	ESL95	22,290	2,587	10,243	5,372	4,089
Bankers Life (Iowa)	SpWL	17,428	2,647	9,446	2,540	2,795
Bankers Life (Iowa)	PWL	21,389	2,573	10,329	6,116	2,371
Canada Life	PL	20,183	2,588	10,213	3,639	3,744
Canada Life	ExPf	20,830	2,574	10,448	3,391	4,418
Confederation Life	WL	20,702	2,627	9,657	5,091	3,328
Confederation Life	SL85	22,261	2,527	11,069	5,220	3,446
Connecticut General	L90	20,722	2,551	10,765	2,568	4,838
Connecticut Mutual	WL	20,756	2,609	9,794	5,448	2,905
Continental Assurance	WL	22,584	2,586	10,286	5,668	4,045
Crown Life	SOL	17,350	2,688	8,794	2,531	3,337
Equitable (N.Y.)	AWL	22,173	2,591	10,222	4,973	4,387
Franklin Life	ESWL	21,545	2,619	9,852	4,720	4,355
Great-West Life	EPWL	21,653	2,581	10,229	5,144	3,700
Guardian Life	POL	21,330	2,596	10,282	4,546	3,906
Home Life (N.Y.)	WL	21,928	2,582	10,383	5,583	3,380
Jefferson Standard	WL	21,310	2,634	9,619	4,109	4,948
Jefferson Standard	L90	22,055	2,560	10,531	5,179	3,785
John Hancock	S25L95	22,516	2,571	10,856	4,170	4,919
John Hancock	PWLM3	21,166	2,590	10,409	4,798	3,369
Lincoln National	EOL	22,212	2,595	10,129	5,560	3,928
Manufacturers Life	WL	18,517	2,693	8,766	3,381	3,677
Massachusetts Mutual	CL	22,437	2,561	10,580	6,121	3,176
Metropolitan Life	PL90	21,487	2,611	10,342	4,133	4,401
Mutual Benefit	OL	22,614	2,561	10,554	5,637	3,863
Mutual of New York	WL	21,604	2,598	10,337	4,393	4,277
National Life (Vt.)	OL	22,065	2,529	11,344	4,375	3,817
National Life (Vt.)	PEP	22,065	2,522	11,527	4,200	3,816
Nationwide Life	EE	21,477	2,571	10,388	5,077	3,440
New England Life	OL	22,349	2,570	10,556	5,429	3,795
New York Life	WL	22,192	2,612	9,899	5,712	3,971
North American (Can.)	WLIP	21,055	2,592	10,198	4,667	3,599
Northwestern Mutual	L90	22,487	2,552	10,746	6,132	3,056
Occidental (Calif.)	PWL	21,565	2,574	10,381	4,292	4,317
Penn Mutual	WL	22,585	2,563	10,477	5,210	4,335
Phoenix Mutual	OL	22,192	2,549	11,196	4,220	4,227
Provident Mutual	WL	21,781	2,564	10,524	5,136	3,557
Provident Mutual	PLM2	19,740	2,614	9,794	4,186	3,147
Prudential	E50WL	20,693	2,609	10,282	3,803	3,999

Table D–7 — Continued

Company	Policy	Premiums	Protection Element	Savings Element	Illustrated Dividends	Company Retention
Republic National	L90	20,879	2,616	9,876	2,860	5,528
State Farm Life	SpOL	20,634	2,661	9,564	4,459	3,950
State Mutual	WL	21,967	2,562	10,531	5,706	3,168
Sun Life (Can.)	WL	22,153	2,620	9,910	6,309	3,314
Western & Southern	EP	22,580	2,586	10,332	3,959	5,702
Western & Southern	SE	22,609	2,619	10,067	5,057	4,867

SUMMARY

Company Retention	Number of Policies
$2,000–$2,399	1
2,400– 2,799	1
2,800– 3,199	5
3,200– 3,599	9
3,600– 3,999	14
4,000– 4,399	8
4,400– 4,799	2
4,800– 5,199	5
5,200– 5,599	2
5,600– 5,999	1
	48

Table D–8
*Values for $25,000 nonparticipating straight life policies issued in 1970
to men aged 25*

Company	Policy	Premiums	Protection Element	Savings Element	Company Retention
Aetna Life	WL	$2,937	$317	$1,756	$ 864
American National	EWL	3,248	312	1,988	948
Business Men's	PWL	3,224	315	1,849	1,060
Connecticut General	OL	3,135	319	1,737	1,079
Continental Assurance	WL	3,080	317	1,735	1,028
Crown Life	LL90	2,924	322	1,519	1,083
Crown Life	EWL	2,662	323	1,455	883
Franklin Life	PPWL	3,174	318	1,749	1,107
Great-West Life	ESpWL	2,927	323	1,470	1,133
Jefferson Standard	WL	3,137	316	1,771	1,050
Jefferson Standard	L90	2,907	315	1,814	778
Lincoln National	OL	3,246	317	1,746	1,183
Lincoln National	L95	2,875	320	1,616	939
Manufacturers Life	WL	2,855	324	1,433	1,098
National Life & Acc.	WL	3,182	315	1,867	1,000
National Life & Acc.	WLP	3,110	315	1,867	928
Occidental (Calif.)	C95	2,813	321	1,581	911
Provident Life & Acc.	WL	3,120	308	2,088	724
Republic National	L95	2,855	323	1,527	1,005
Southwestern Life	ES	2,850	312	1,974	565
Travelers	POL100	2,964	320	1,590	1,054
United Benefit	ExP	2,929	324	1,433	1,172

SUMMARY

Company Retention	Number of Policies
$ 500–$ 599	1
600– 699	0
700– 799	2
800– 899	2
900– 999	4
1,000– 1,099	9
1,100– 1,199	4
	22

Table D-9
Values for $25,000 nonparticipating straight life policies issued in 1970 to men aged 45

Company	Policy	Premiums	Protection Element	Savings Element	Company Retention
Aetna Life	WL	$5,972	$1,669	$2,955	$1,348
American National	EWL	6,248	1,627	3,210	1,410
Business Men's	PWL	6,369	1,658	2,996	1,715
Connecticut General	OL	6,369	1,677	2,931	1,761
Continental Assurance	WL	6,251	1,658	2,968	1,624
Crown Life	LL90	6,080	1,696	2,749	1,636
Crown Life	EWL	5,596	1,706	2,691	1,199
Franklin Life	PPWL	6,314	1,670	2,949	1,696
Great-West Life	ESpWL	5,993	1,699	2,733	1,561
Jefferson Standard	WL	6,407	1,648	3,038	1,721
Jefferson Standard	L90	6,116	1,637	3,118	1,361
Lincoln National	OL	6,425	1,657	2,985	1,783
Lincoln National	L95	5,988	1,672	2,895	1,421
Manufacturers Life	WL	5,863	1,710	2,666	1,486
National Life & Acc.	WL	6,383	1,645	3,095	1,643
National Life & Acc.	WLP	6,295	1,645	3,095	1,556
Occidental (Calif.)	C95	5,913	1,682	2,838	1,392
Provident Life & Acc.	WL	6,319	1,617	3,237	1,466
Republic National	L95	5,946	1,703	2,725	1,518
Southwestern Life	ES	5,792	1,627	3,192	973
Travelers	POL100	5,998	1,673	2,863	1,461
United Benefit	ExP	6,028	1,711	2,663	1,655

SUMMARY

Company Retention	Number of Policies
$ 900–$ 999	1
1,000– 1,099	0
1,100– 1,199	1
1,200– 1,299	0
1,300– 1,399	3
1,400– 1,499	5
1,500– 1,599	3
1,600– 1,699	5
1,700– 1,799	4
	22

Table D–10
Values for $10,000 nonparticipating straight life policies issued in 1970 to men aged 35

Company	Policy	Premiums	Protection Element	Savings Element	Company Retention
Aetna Life	WL	$1,824	$265	$ 946	$613
American National	WL	1,836	264	959	614
Business Men's	WL	1,848	267	903	677
Connecticut General	OL	1,818	267	938	614
Continental Assurance	WL	1,802	265	941	596
Crown Life	LL90	1,718	270	852	596
Franklin Life	PPWL	1,804	265	943	595
Great-West Life	ESpWL	1,706	272	839	595
Jefferson Standard	WL	1,830	263	962	605
Lincoln National	OL	1,870	265	946	660
Manufacturers Life	WL	1,669	273	818	578
National Life & Acc.	WL	1,837	262	995	580
Occidental (Calif.)	GWL	1,776	265	933	578
Provident Life & Acc.	L95	1,738	271	852	615
Republic National	OL	1,822	269	872	681
Southwestern Life	WL	1,820	260	1,028	532
Travelers	OL	1,837	266	913	658
United Benefit	SWL	1,781	269	871	641

SUMMARY

Company Retention	Number of Policies
$500–$539	1
540– 579	2
580– 619	10
620– 659	2
660– 699	3
	18

Table D–11
*Values for $100,000 nonparticipating straight life policies issued in 1970
to men aged 35*

Company	Policy	Premiums	Protection Element	Savings Element	Company Retention
Aetna Life	WL	$16,066	$2,653	$ 9,455	$3,957
American National	EWL	17,384	2,592	10,449	4,344
Business Men's	PWL	17,595	2,631	9,732	5,233
Connecticut General	OL	17,301	2,666	9,376	5,259
Continental Assurance	WL	16,958	2,646	9,409	4,902
Crown Life	LL90	16,301	2,704	8,517	5,080
Crown Life	EWL	14,929	2,721	8,278	3,930
Franklin Life	PPWL	16,282	2,655	9,431	4,196
Great-West Life	ESpWL	16,262	2,715	8,388	5,159
Jefferson Standard	WL	17,419	2,634	9,619	5,166
Jefferson Standard	L90	16,409	2,623	9,838	3,948
Lincoln National	OL	17,821	2,646	9,462	5,713
Lincoln National	L95	16,233	2,676	8,992	4,565
Manufacturers Life	WL	15,899	2,728	8,181	4,991
National Life & Acc.	WL	17,664	2,620	9,950	5,094
National Life & Acc.	WLP	17,350	2,620	9,950	4,780
Occidental (Calif.)	C95	15,890	2,690	8,796	4,403
Provident Life & Acc.	WL	17,213	2,568	10,638	4,007
Republic National	L95	16,056	2,713	8,478	4,865
Southwestern Life	ES	15,782	2,592	10,366	2,824
Travelers	PP	15,066	2,678	8,892	3,496
United Benefit	ExP	16,399	2,728	8,193	5,478

SUMMARY

Company Retention	Number of Policies
$2,800–$3,199	1
3,200– 3,599	1
3,600– 3,999	3
4,000– 4,399	3
4,400– 4,799	3
4,800– 5,199	7
5,200– 5,599	3
5,600– 5,999	1
	22

Table D–12

*Values for $25,000 five-year renewable term policies
issued in 1970 to men aged 25*

(For all policies in this table, the value of the protection
element is $353 and the value of the savings element is $0.)

Company	Premiums	Illustrated Dividends	Company Retention
Aetna Life	$1,288	$ 0	$ 934
American National	1,488	0	1,135
American United	1,229	157	719
Bankers Life (Iowa)	1,413	357	702
Business Men's	1,290	0	937
Canada Life	1,358	231	773
Confederation Life	1,091	5	733
Connecticut General	1,173	0	819
Connecticut Mutual	1,222	161	707
Continental Assurance	1,274	0	920
Continental Assurance[a]	1,187	0	834
Crown Life	1,074	0	721
Equitable (N.Y.)	1,251	252	646
Franklin Life[b]	—	—	—
Great-West Life	1,128	0	775
Guardian Life	1,274	206	715
Home Life (N.Y.)	1,251	314	584
Jefferson Standard	1,404	0	1,051
John Hancock	1,379	366	660
Lincoln National	1,109	0	756
Manufacturers Life	1,136	0	783
Massachusetts Mutual	1,299	310	635
Metropolitan Life	1,408	395	660
Mutual Benefit	1,269	240	675
Mutual of New York	1,340	364	623
National Life & Acc.	1,374	0	1,020
National Life (Vt.)	1,357	350	654
Nationwide Life	1,416	182	880
New England Life	1,217	255	609
New York Life	1,285	362	570
North American (Can.)[c]	—	—	—
Northwestern Mutual[b]	—	—	—
Occidental (Calif.)	1,134	0	781
Penn Mutual	1,264	264	647
Phoenix Mutual	1,161	92	716
Provident Life & Acc.	1,301	0	948

Table D–12 – Continued

Company	Premiums	Illustrated Dividends	Company Retention
Provident Mutual	1,209	178	678
Prudential	1,513	460	700
Republic National	1,206	0	852
Southwestern Life	1,184	0	831
State Farm Life	1,188	180	656
State Mutual	1,247	242	652
Sun Life (Can.)	1,039	0	685
Travelers	1,139	0	786
United Benefit	1,129	0	776
Western & Southern[d]	—	—	—

[a] Executerm 4/6 policy. First term is four years; subsequent terms are six years.

[b] Company does not issue a five-year renewable term policy.

[c] Premium for this policy is below company's minimum premium limit for five-year renewable term policies.

[d] Company's policy is not convertible until age 65.

SUMMARY

Company Retention	Number of Policies
$ 500–$ 599	2
600– 699	13
700– 799	15
800– 899	5
900– 999	4
1,000– 1,099	2
1,100– 1,199	1
	42

Table D–13
*Values for $25,000 five-year renewable term policies
issued in 1970 to men aged 45*

(For all policies in this table, the value of the protection
element is $2,131 and the value of the savings element
is $0.)

Company	Premiums	Illustrated Dividends	Company Retention
Aetna Life	$3,678	$ 0	$1,548
American National	3,733	0	1,602
American United	3,833	432	1,270
Bankers Life (Iowa)	3,695	707	858
Business Men's	3,527	0	1,396
Canada Life	3,734	550	1,054
Confederation Life	3,099	23	945
Connecticut General	3,464	0	1,333
Connecticut Mutual	3,664	390	1,144
Continental Assurance	3,614	0	1,484
Continental Assurance[a]	3,382	0	1,252
Crown Life	2,959	0	829
Equitable (N.Y.)	3,770	441	1,199
Franklin Life[b]	—	—	—
Great-West Life	3,206	0	1,076
Guardian Life	3,752	478	1,144
Home Life (N.Y.)	3,746	579	1,037
Jefferson Standard	3,809	0	1,679
John Hancock	3,886	838	917
Lincoln National	3,470	0	1,340
Manufacturers Life	3,134	0	1,003
Massachusetts Mutual	3,846	768	948
Metropolitan Life	3,742	672	940
Mutual Benefit	3,784	451	1,202
Mutual of New York	4,018	818	1,070
National Life & Acc.	3,565	0	1,434
National Life (Vt.)	4,077	1,044	903
Nationwide Life	3,942	572	1,239
New England Life	3,690	526	1,034
New York Life	3,927	888	909
North American (Can.)	2,937	0	806
Northwestern Mutual[b]	—	—	—
Occidental (Calif.)	3,195	0	1,065
Penn Mutual	3,699	508	1,060
Phoenix Mutual	3,613	446	1,036
Provident Life & Acc.	3,778	0	1,647

Table D-13—Continued

Company	Premiums	Illustrated Dividends	Company Retention
Provident Mutual	3,599	359	1,109
Prudential	4,249	968	1,151
Republic National	3,243	0	1,113
Southwestern Life	3,370	0	1,239
State Farm Life	3,441	405	906
State Mutual	3,696	321	1,244
Sun Life (Can.)	3,016	0	886
Travelers	3,698	0	1,567
United Benefit	3,249	0	1,119
Western & Southern[c]	—	—	—

[a] Executerm 4/6 policy. First term is four years; subsequent terms are six years.

[b] Company does not issue a five-year renewable term policy.

[c] Company's policy is not convertible until age 65.

SUMMARY

Company Retention	Number of Policies
$ 800–$ 899	4
900– 999	7
1,000– 1,099	9
1,100– 1,199	7
1,200– 1,299	6
1,300– 1,399	3
1,400– 1,499	2
1,500– 1,599	2
1,600– 1,699	3
	43

Table D–14
Values for $10,000 five-year renewable term policies issued in 1970 to men aged 35

(For all policies in this table, the value of the protection element is $322 and the value of the savings element is $0.)

Company	Premiums	Illustrated Dividends	Company Retention
Aetna Life	$820	$ 0	$497
American National	910	0	587
American United	840	108	410
Bankers Life (Iowa)	860	190	347
Business Men's	823	0	500
Canada Life	885	128	435
Confederation Life	734	4	407
Connecticut General	839	0	517
Connecticut Mutual	804	86	396
Continental Assurance	837	0	515
Crown Life	690	0	368
Equitable (N.Y.)	834	126	386
Franklin Life[a]	—	—	—
Great-West Life	774	0	451
Guardian Life	835	110	402
Home Life (N.Y.)	832	159	351
Jefferson Standard	875	0	552
John Hancock	915	198	394
Lincoln National	759	0	436
Manufacturers Life	750	0	427
Massachusetts Mutual	859	185	352
Metropolitan Life	965	201	442
Mutual Benefit	872	133	416
Mutual of New York	872	181	369
National Life & Acc.	835	0	513
National Life (Vt.)	882	222	337
Nationwide Life	912	143	447
New England Life	796	128	345
New York Life	862	211	328
North American (Can.)[b]	—	—	—
Northwestern Mutual[a]	—	—	—
Occidental (Calif.)[b]	—	—	—
Penn Mutual	830	141	366
Phoenix Mutual	770	78	369
Provident Life & Acc.	870	0	548

Table D-14—Continued

Company	Premiums	Illustrated Dividends	Company Retention
Provident Mutual	802	100	379
Prudential	988	219	447
Republic National	755	0	432
Southwestern Life	765	0	442
State Farm Life	737	93	322
State Mutual	820	112	385
Sun Life (Can.)	702	0	379
Travelers	807	0	484
United Benefit	729	0	406
Western & Southern[c]	—	—	—

[a] Company does not issue a five-year renewable term policy.
[b] Premium for this policy is below company's minimum premium limit for five-year renewable term policies.
[c] Company's policy is not convertible until age 65.

SUMMARY

Company Retention	Number of Policies
$300–$339	3
340– 379	10
380– 419	9
420– 459	9
460– 499	2
500– 539	4
540– 579	2
580– 619	1
	40

Table D–15
*Values for $100,000 five-year renewable term policies
issued in 1970 to men aged 35*
(For all policies in this table, the value of the protection
element is $3,225 and the value of the savings element
is $0.)

Company	Premiums	Illustrated Dividends	Company Retention
Aetna Life	$7,315	$ 0	$4,090
American National	7,996	0	4,771
American United	7,346	1,083	3,038
Bankers Life (Iowa)	7,894	1,904	2,766
Business Men's	7,344	0	4,119
Canada Life	7,523	1,275	3,023
Confederation Life	6,012	42	2,745
Connecticut General	6,630	0	3,405
Connecticut Mutual	7,382	862	3,294
Continental Assurance	7,313	0	4,088
Continental Assurance[a]	6,592	0	3,367
Crown Life	6,021	0	2,796
Equitable (N.Y.)	7,649	1,255	3,169
Franklin Life[b]	—	—	—
Great-West Life	6,147	0	2,922
Guardian Life	7,613	1,102	3,286
Home Life (N.Y.)	7,587	1,587	2,775
Jefferson Standard	7,867	0	4,642
John Hancock	7,828	1,983	2,620
Lincoln National	6,706	0	3,481
Manufacturers Life	6,176	0	2,951
Massachusetts Mutual	7,888	1,846	2,817
Metropolitan Life	8,155	2,011	2,919
Mutual Benefit	7,933	1,330	3,378
Mutual of New York	7,988	1,810	2,953
National Life & Acc.	7,645	0	4,420
National Life (Vt.)	8,162	2,221	2,716
Nationwide Life	8,415	1,426	3,764
New England Life	7,340	1,280	2,835
New York Life	7,935	2,114	2,597
North American (Can.)	5,146	0	1,921
Northwestern Mutual[b]	—	—	—
Occidental (Calif.)	6,277	0	3,052
Penn Mutual	7,808	1,413	3,170
Phoenix Mutual	6,990	783	2,982
Provident Life & Acc.	6,571	0	3,346

Table D–15—Continued

Company	Premiums	Illustrated Dividends	Company Retention
Provident Mutual	7,310	997	3,088
Prudential	8,999	2,191	3,583
Republic National	6,667	0	3,442
Republic National[c]	5,246	0	2,021
Southwestern Life	6,766	0	3,541
State Farm Life	6,483	925	2,333
State Mutual	7,464	1,125	3,114
Sun Life (Can.)	5,794	0	2,569
Travelers	6,828	0	3,603
United Benefit	6,403	0	3,178
Western & Southern[d]	—	—	—

[a] Executerm 4/6 policy. First term is four years; subsequent terms are six years.

[b] Company does not issue a five-year renewable term policy.

[c] Four-year renewable term policy.

[d] Company's policy is not convertible until age 65.

SUMMARY

Company Retention	Number of Policies
$1,600–$1,999	1
2,000– 2,399	2
2,400– 2,799	8
2,800– 3,199	15
3,200– 3,599	10
3,600– 3,999	2
4,000– 4,399	3
4,400– 4,799	3
	44

Appendix E
Values for Policies Issued by Non-Agency Organizations
(Figures correspond to those in the tables indicated)

Table	Policy	Premiums	Protection Element	Savings Element	Dividends	Company Retention
		Massachusetts Savings Bank Life Insurance				
4–1	OL	$4,835	$ 640	$2,671	$1,206	$319
4–3	5-YR RCT	1,676	806	0	622	247
D–1	OL	2,882	313	1,433	863	273
D–2	OL	1,368	186	779	248	155
D–3	OL	1,384	177	729	409	69
D–4	OL	3,496	308	2,023	856	309
D–5	OL	6,874	1,595	3,340	1,608	332
D–6	OL	1,934	256	1,068	482	127
D–12	5-YR RCT	1,075	353	0	429	293
D–13	5-YR RCT	3,275	2,131	0	938	207
D–14	5-YR RCT	670	322	0	249	99
		New York Savings Bank Life Insurance				
4–1	SL	$4,837	$ 650	$2,513	$1,084	$590
4–3	5-YR RCT	1,805	806	0	624	375
D–1	SL	2,956	313	1,433	762	449
D–2	SL	1,477	186	779	265	248
D–4	SL	3,555	312	1,852	849	542
D–5	SL	6,808	1,619	3,196	1,491	503
D–6	SL	1,935	260	1,005	434	236
D–12	5-YR RCT	1,236	353	0	507	375
D–13	5-YR RCT	3,322	2,131	0	983	209
D–14	5-YR RCT	722	322	0	249	150

Appendix E — Continued

Table	Policy	Premiums	Protection Element	Savings Element	Dividends	Company Retention
		Teachers Insurance and Annuity Assocation				
4–1	OL	$ 4,857	$ 644	$ 2,593	$1,572	$ 49
4–3	5-YR RCT	2,022	806	0	821	394
D–1	OL	2,671	313	1,429	712	217
D–2	OL	1,297	182	837	120	159
D–3	OL	1,153	177	729	160	87
D–4	OL	3,647	309	1,964	1,242	131
D–5	OL	6,648	1,610	3,232	1,972	−167
D–6	OL	1,943	257	1,037	573	75
D–7	OL	19,428	2,575	10,373	6,566	−85
D–12	5-YR RCT	1,308	353	0	629	326
D–13	5-YR RCT	3,678	2,131	0	1,167	380
D–14	5-YR RCT	809	322	0	272	214
D–15	5-YR RCT	8,086	3,225	0	3,564	1,297
		Ministers Life and Casualty Union				
4–1	WL	$ 4,553	$ 650	$ 2,506	$ 941	$ 457
D–1	E85	2,380	321	1,299	501	258
D–2	E85	1,270	187	752	205	126
D–3	E85	1,122	181	663	159	119
D–4	WL	3,273	312	1,851	642	467
D–5	WL	6,324	1,619	3,186	1,214	304
D–6	E85	1,908	262	968	439	238
D–7	WL	18,095	2,601	10,022	3,762	1,709

Appendix F
Addresses of Insurance Commissioners

Superintendent of Insurance
Alabama Insurance Department
Room 453
Administrative Building
Montgomery, Alabama 36104

Director of Insurance
Alaska Insurance Department
Room 410 Goldstein Building
Pouch "D"
Juneau, Alaska 99801

Director of Insurance
Arizona Department of Insurance
1601 West Jefferson
Phoenix, Arizona 85007

Commissioner of Insurance
Arkansas Insurance Department
400 University Tower Building
Little Rock, Arkansas 72204

Commissioner of Insurance
California Insurance Department
1407 Market Street
San Francisco, California 94103

Commissioner of Insurance
Colorado Insurance Department
106 State Office Building
Denver, Colorado 80203

Commissioner of Insurance
Connecticut Insurance Department
State Office Building
165 Capitol Avenue
Hartford, Connecticut 06115

Commissioner of Insurance
Delaware Insurance Department
21 The Green
Dover, Delaware 19901

Superintendent of Insurance
District of Columbia
Insurance Department
Room 512—614 "H" Street, N.W.
Washington, D. C. 20001

Commissioner of Insurance
Florida Insurance Department
The Capitol
Tallahassee, Florida 32304

Commissioner of Insurance
Georgia Insurance Department
State Capitol
Atlanta, Georgia 30334

Commissioner of Insurance
Hawaii Insurance Department
P. O. Box 3614
Honolulu, Hawaii 96811

Commissioner of Insurance
Idaho Insurance Department
206 State House
Boise, Idaho 83707

Director of Insurance
Illinois Insurance Department
525 West Jefferson Street
Springfield, Illinois 62706

Commissioner of Insurance
Indiana Insurance Department
509 State Office Building
Indianapolis, Indiana 46204

Commissioner of Insurance
Iowa Insurance Department
State Office Building
Des Moines, Iowa 50319

Commissioner of Insurance
Kansas Insurance Department
First Floor—Statehouse
Topeka, Kansas 66612

Commissioner of Insurance
Kentucky Insurance Department
Old Capitol Annex
Frankfort, Kentucky 40601

Commissioner of Insurance
Louisiana Insurance Department
Box 44214, Capitol Station
Baton Rouge, Louisiana 70804

Commissioner of Insurance
Maine Insurance Department
Capitol Shopping Center
Augusta, Maine 04330

Commissioner of Insurance
Maryland Insurance Department
1 South Calvert Street
Baltimore, Maryland 21202

Commissioner of Insurance
Massachusetts Division of Insurance
100 Cambridge Street
Boston, Massachusetts 02202

Commissioner of Insurance
Michigan Insurance Bureau
111 North Hosmer Street
Lansing, Michigan 48913

Commissioner of Insurance
Minnesota Insurance Department
210 State Office Building
St. Paul, Minnesota 55101

Commissioner of Insurance
Mississippi Insurance Department
910 Woolfolk Building
Post Office Box 79
Jackson, Mississippi 39205

Superintendent of Insurance
Missouri Division of Insurance
Department of Business and
  Administration
P. O. Box 690
Jefferson City, Missouri 65101

Commissioner of Insurance
Montana Insurance Department
Capitol Building
Helena, Montana 59601

Director of Insurance
Nebraska Insurance Department
1335 "L" Street
Lincoln, Nebraska 68509

Commissioner of Insurance
Nevada Insurance Division
Department of Commerce
Nye Building
Carson City, Nevada 89701

Commissioner of Insurance
New Hampshire Insurance
  Department
78 North Main Street
Concord, New Hampshire 03301

Commissioner of Insurance
Department of Banking and
  Insurance
201 East State Street
Trenton, New Jersey 08625

Superintendent of Insurance
New Mexico Insurance Department
P. O. Drawer 1269
Santa Fe, New Mexico 87501

Superintendent of Insurance
New York Insurance Department
123 William Street
New York, New York 10038

Commissioner of Insurance
North Carolina Insurance
  Department
P. O. Box 26387
Raleigh, North Carolina 27611

Commissioner of Insurance
North Dakota Insurance
  Department
State Capitol
Bismarck, North Dakota 58501

Director of Insurance
Ohio Insurance Department
115 East Rich Street
Columbus, Ohio 43215

Commissioner of Insurance
Oklahoma Insurance Department
Room 408 Will Rogers Memorial
  Office Building
Oklahoma City, Oklahoma 73105

Commissioner of Insurance
Insurance Division
Department of Commerce
158 12th Street, N.E.
Salem, Oregon 97310

Commissioner of Insurance
Pennsylvania Insurance
  Department
108 Finance Building
State Capitol
Harrisburg, Pennsylvania 17120

Commissioner of Insurance
Puerto Rico Insurance Department
P. O. Box 3508
Old San Juan Station
San Juan, Puerto Rico 00904

Commissioner of Insurance
Rhode Island Insurance
  Division
169 Weybosset Street
Providence, Rhode Island 02903

Commissioner of Insurance
South Carolina Insurance
  Department
Federal Land Bank Building
1401 Hampton Street
Columbia, South Carolina 29201

Commissioner of Insurance
South Dakota Department of
  Insurance
Insurance Building
Pierre, South Dakota 57501

Commissioner of Insurance
Tennessee Department of
  Insurance and Banking
114 State Office Building
Nashville, Tennessee 37219

Commissioner of Insurance
Texas Insurance Department
1110 San Jacinto Street
Austin, Texas 78701

Commissioner of Insurance
Utah Insurance Department
115 State Capitol
Salt Lake City, Utah 84114

Commissioner of Insurance
Vermont Insurance Department
State Office Building
Montpelier, Vermont 05602

Commissioner of Insurance
Virginia Insurance Department
700 Blanton Building
P. O. Box 1157
Richmond, Virginia 23209

Commissioner of Insurance
Washington Insurance Department
Insurance Building
Olympia, Washington 98501

Commissioner of Insurance
West Virginia Insurance
  Department
1800 East Washington Street
Charleston, West Virginia 25305

Commissioner of Insurance
Wisconsin Insurance Department
212 North Bassett Street
Madison, Wisconsin 53703

Commissioner of Insurance
Department of Insurance
State of Wyoming
500 Randall Blvd.
Cheyenne, Wyoming 82001

Appendix G
Computation of Price-of-Protection and Rate-of-Return Figures for One Policy Year

The purpose of this appendix is to show the formulas for the computation of the price of protection for one policy year (assuming a rate of return on the savings element) and the rate of return on the savings element for one policy year (assuming a price of protection).

The price of protection

The price per \$1,000 of protection for a given policy year may be calculated by the following formula:

$$YPT_t = \frac{(P_t + V_{t-1})(1 + i) - V_t - D_t}{(F_t - V_t)(.001)}$$

where

YPT_t = price per \$1,000 of protection in policy year t
P_t = annual premium for policy year t
V_t = cash value for policy year t
D_t = dividend for policy year t
F_t = face amount for policy year t
i = assumed rate of return on savings element, expressed as a decimal

The rate of return

The rate of return on the savings element in a given policy year may be calculated by the following formula:

$$i = \frac{V_t + D_t + (YPT_t)(F_t - V_t)(.001)}{P_t + V_{t-1}} - 1$$

where

i = rate of return on savings element, expressed as a decimal
P_t = annual premium for policy year t
V_t = cash value for policy year t
D_t = dividend for policy year t
F_t = face amount for policy year t
YPT_t = assumed price per \$1,000 of protection in policy year t

Source of the formulas

The formula for the price of protection is a slightly simplified version of the formula presented in my book, *The Retail Price Structure in American Life Insurance*. The formula for the rate of return is derived from the formula for the price of protection.

Appendix H
Computation of Values

The purpose of this appendix is to show the formulas for the computation of the twenty-year values of premiums, protection element, savings element, dividends, and company retention. These values are shown in Chapters 4 and 5, in Appendixes D and E, and in a few other places in the book. It is anticipated that the primary use of this appendix will be by the actuaries of companies whose figures are not included in the various tables and who may wish to make comparable figures available to their agents and prospective customers.

Explanation of symbols

$i =$ assumed interest rate, expressed as a decimal

$v = 1/(1 + i)$

$q_t =$ probability of death in policy year t

$w_t =$ probability of lapse in policy year t

$_mz_t =$ probability of surviving and persisting from beginning of policy year t until beginning of policy year $t + m$

$j =$ index of summation

$P_t =$ annual premium for policy year t

$V_t =$ cash value for policy year t (special case: when $t = 1$, $V_{t-1} = 0$)

$D_t =$ dividend for policy year t

$TD_t =$ terminal dividend for policy year t

$F_t =$ face amount for policy year t

$PREM =$ value of premiums for first 20 policy years

$PROT =$ value of protection element for first 20 policy years

$SAV =$ value of savings element for first 20 policy years

$DIV =$ value of dividends for first 20 policy years

$R =$ value of company retention for first 20 policy years

Formulas

$$PREM = \sum_{j=1}^{20} (P_j)(_{j-1}z_1)(v^{j-1})$$

$$PROT = \sum_{j=1}^{20} (F_j + TD_j - V_j)(q_j)(_{j-1}z_1)(v^j)$$

$$SAV = \sum_{j=1}^{20} [V_j - (1 + i)(V_{j-1})](_{j-1}z_1)(v^j)$$

$$DIV = \sum_{j=1}^{20} [D_j + (TD_j)(w_j)](_{j-1}z_1)(v^j)$$

$$R = PREM - PROT - SAV - DIV$$

A note on the assumptions

With regard to the values for policies issued in 1970, the interest rate used is 5 percent for each year. With regard to the values for policies issued in 1950, 1940, and 1930, several interest rates are used. They are based on the interest rates paid on savings accounts in the various years by the Bowery Savings Bank. The interest rates used in the calculations are shown in Table H–1.

The mortality rates used in all of the calculations are those in the 1957–60 ultimate basic mortality table for males. The mortality rates for ages 25 through 64 are shown in Table H–2.

The lapse rates used in all of the calculations are those in Moorhead's Table R, with a modification that was used by The National Underwriter Company in its first edition of *Cost Facts on Life Insurance.* The lapse rates used in the calculations are shown in Table H–3.

It is assumed that premiums are payable at the beginning of the various policy years and that any cash values, dividends, or face amounts are payable at the end of the various policy years. It is also assumed, in the formulas shown above, that terminal dividends are payable on death or on surrender. Finally, it is assumed that $_1z_t = 1 - q_t - w_t$.

Source of the formulas

The formulas in this appendix are those presented in my article, "The Relationship Between Benefits and Premiums in Life Insurance," which appeared in the March 1969 issue of *The Journal of Risk and Insurance.*

Table H-1
Interest rates used in calculations

Policy Year	1950 Issues	1940 Issues	1930 Issues
1	2.00%	2.00%	4.50%
2	2.00	2.00	3.50
3	2.50	2.00	3.50
4	2.50	1.50	3.00
5	2.75	1.50	2.50
6	2.75	1.50	2.00
7	3.00	1.50	2.00
8	3.25	1.50	2.00
9	3.25	1.50	2.00
10	3.50	2.00	2.00
11	3.50	2.00	2.00
12	3.50	2.00	2.00
13	3.75	2.50	2.00
14	4.00	2.50	1.50
15	4.25	2.75	1.50
16	4.25	2.75	1.50
17	5.00	3.00	1.50
18	5.00	3.25	1.50
19	5.00	3.25	1.50
20	5.00	3.50	2.00

Table H-2
Mortality rates used in calculations

Age	Rate per 1,000	Age	Rate per 1,000
25	1.25	45	3.96
26	1.22	46	4.51
27	1.19	47	5.09
28	1.17	48	5.71
29	1.13	49	6.34
30	1.15	50	6.94
31	1.22	51	7.56
32	1.28	52	8.32
33	1.32	53	9.20
34	1.34	54	10.09
35	1.40	55	11.00
36	1.49	56	12.06
37	1.60	57	13.26
38	1.75	58	14.60
39	1.91	59	16.06
40	2.12	60	17.69
41	2.36	61	19.55
42	2.66	62	21.61
43	3.02	63	23.75
44	3.45	64	25.83

Table H-3
Lapse rates used in calculations

Policy Year	Rate per 1,000
1	120.00
2	35.00
3	30.00
4	27.50
5	25.00
6	22.50
7	20.00
8	18.00
9	17.00
10	16.00
11	15.50
12	15.00
13	14.50
14	14.00
15	13.50
16	13.00
17	12.50
18	12.00
19	11.50
20	11.00

Notes

Chapter 2: How Much?

1. These figures are derived from accidental death claim rates and over-all death rates published by the Society of Actuaries. Although not strictly comparable, they illustrate general magnitudes. See *Transactions of the Society of Actuaries*, "1958 Reports of Mortality and Morbidity Experience," p. 50; and "1962 Reports of Mortality and Morbidity Experience," p. 48.

Chapter 3: What Kind?

1. For a discussion of disability income riders, see O. D. Dickerson, *Health Insurance* (3rd ed.; Homewood, Ill.: Richard D. Irwin, Inc., 1968), pp. 451–462.

2. For a comprehensive treatment of the subject, see Stuart Schwarzschild, *Rights of Creditors in Life Insurance Policies* (Homewood, Ill.: Richard D. Irwin, Inc., 1963).

Chapter 4: From Whom?

1. Among these sources were *Flitcraft Compend* (annual; Morristown, N. J.: Alfred M. Best Co., Inc.); and *The Diamond Life Bulletins*, Vols. 8–11 (current loose-leaf; Cincinnati, Ohio: National Underwriter Co.).

2. Joseph M. Belth, *The Retail Price Structure in American Life Insurance* (Bloomington, Ind.: Bureau of Business Research, Graduate School of Business, Indiana University, 1966), pp. 165–166.

3. Joseph M. Belth, *A Report on Life Insurance* (Bloomington, Ind.: Bureau of Business Research, Graduate School of Business, Indiana University, 1967), pp. 37–97.

4. *1971 Who Writes What?* (annual; Cincinnati, Ohio: National Underwriter Co.), p. 52.

5. *Cost Facts on Life Insurance: Interest-Adjusted Method* (Cincinnati, Ohio: National Underwriter Co., 1970).

Chapter 5: Other Sources and Forms

1. Belth, *A Report on Life Insurance*, pp. 78–85.

2. Donald R. Johnson, *Savings Bank Life Insurance* (Homewood, Ill.: Richard D. Irwin, Inc., 1963), p. 221.

3. Joseph M. Belth, "Savings Bank Life Insurance Prices and Market Shares," *Journal of Risk and Insurance*, Vol. XXXVIII, No. 2 (June 1971), p. 197.

4. For a discussion of group life insurance on a cash-value basis, see Dan M. McGill, *Life Insurance* (Rev. ed.; Homewood, Ill.: Richard D. Irwin, Inc., 1967), pp. 703–706.

5. For a brief discussion of this subject, see Robert I. Mehr, *Life Insurance: Theory and Practice* (4th ed.; Austin, Tex.: Business Publications, Inc., 1970), pp. 830–833. For a comprehensive discussion, see Richard deRaismes Kip, *Fraternal Life Insurance in America* (Philadelphia: College Offset Press, 1953).

6. Belth, *The Retail Price Structure in American Life Insurance*, pp. 87–100.

7. Belth, *A Report on Life Insurance*, p. 140.

8. Joseph M. Belth, "Dynamic Life Insurance Programming," *Journal of Risk and Insurance*, Vol. XXXI, No. 4 (December 1964), p. 549.

9. For a description of the anatomy of this policy, see Joseph M. Belth and W. David Maxwell, "The State of Competition in the Life Insurance Industry," *The Antitrust Bulletin*, Vol. XV (Summer 1970), pp. 238–240.

10. Spencer L. Kimball and Jon S. Hanson, "The Regulation of Specialty Policies in Life Insurance," *Michigan Law Review*, Vol. LXII (1963–64), pp. 255–256.

11. For a detailed price analysis of split life plans, see Joseph M. Belth, "A Note on the Price of Split Life Insurance," forthcoming in *Journal of Risk and Insurance*.

Chapter 6: The Agent

1. Ivan Robinson, "Insurance Opposition Vocal at Hearing on Bank Ceiling," *Hartford Times*, April 14, 1967.

2. *Life Insurance in Focus* (Hartford, Conn.: Life Insurance Agency Management Association, 1960), Vol. I, p. 82.

3. For the details of this and several other examples of deceptive sales practices in the life insurance business, see "Statement of Joseph M. Belth," in *Consumer Class Action* (Hearings on S.984, S.1222, and S.1378 before the Consumer Subcommittee of the Committee on Commerce, U.S. Senate, 92nd Cong., 1st sess.) (Washington: U.S. Government Printing Office, 1971), pp. 216–235.

Chapter 7: The Fine Print

1. Oscar R. Goodman, "Public Policy and the Age and Incontestable Clauses in Life Insurance Contracts," *Journal of Risk and Insurance*, Vol. XXXV, No. 4 (December 1968), pp. 515–535; and Oscar R. Goodman, "A Statement before the NAIC on Protection of the Public Interest and the Misstatement of Age Clause in Life Insurance Contracts," *Journal of Risk and Insurance*, Vol. XXXVIII, No. 1 (March 1971), pp. 147–152.

2. Belth, *The Retail Price Structure in American Life Insurance*, pp. 124–127.

3. *1971 Who Writes What?*, pp. 225–228.

Chapter 8: As and After You Buy

1. For a discussion of the MIB by its executive secretary, see J. C. Wilberding, "The Medical Information Bureau," *Journal of the American Society of Chartered Life Underwriters*, Vol. XX, No. 2 (Spring 1966), pp. 176–181. For a critical analysis of the MIB, see August Gribbin, "Insurance Firms Maintain Secret Data Repository: Unmarked Offices Contain All Kinds of Information About 11,000,000 People," *The National Observer*, Vol. 8, No. 44 (November 3, 1969), pp. 1, 4.

2. For a critical analysis of life insurance sales to college students, see "Caveat Emptor on Campus," *Consumer Reports*, Vol. 37, No. 1 (January 1972), pp. 50–51.

Chapter 10: Conclusion

1. Belth, *The Retail Price Structure in American Life Insurance*, p. 239.

2. Stanford Sesser, "Critics Say Practices of Industry Confuse Life Insurance Buyers," *The Wall Street Journal*, September 5, 1967, pp. 1, 22.

3. "Hart Warns of 'Truth in Life Insurance' Bill," *National Underwriter* (Life ed.), October 26, 1968, pp. 15, 20–21.

4. *Report of the Joint Special Committee on Life Insurance Costs* (New York: Institute of Life Insurance, 1970).

5. For a detailed description and illustration of such a system, see William Macfarlane, "Belth Introduces Broad Policy Information Disclosure System," *National Underwriter* (Life ed.), May 13, 1972, pp. 1, 4–6.

Index

Absolute assignment. *See* Assignment
Accidental death benefits, 13, 30–31
Accountants, 18
Accumulation dividend option, 127–28
Acquisition expenses, 160
Actuaries, 179–80
Advance premiums, 156
Adverse selection, 134
Aetna Life Insurance Company: price information on, 64, 67, 70, 202–26 *passim;* mentioned, 151, 194
Age at which to buy, 17
Age last birthday, 77, 139
Age misstatement, 125–26
Age nearest birthday, 139
Agents: statements by, 5, 9, 126–27; role of, 18, 107–11, 158, 162; training and selection of, 109–10, 112–14, 179, 181; commissions paid to, 109, 111, 157; cost of, 111–12; completion of non-medical applications by, 147–48; presentation of financed insurance by, 154, 156–57; relationship of, to companies, 172–73
Aid Association for Lutherans, 93
Air Line Pilots Association, 31
Air trip insurance, 30–31
Alexander Hamilton Life Insurance Company of America, 75
Alfred M. Best Company, 56–60, 185. *See also Best's Life Insurance Reports*
Alteration of policy, 126–27
American Bankers Association, 123
American College of Life Underwriters, 110
American National Insurance Company: price information on, 64, 67, 70, 202–26 *passim;* nonsmoker discounts of, 76; policy provisions of, 139, 140; mentioned, 169, 194
American Society of Chartered Life Underwriters, 110–11
American United Life Insurance Company: price information on, 64, 70, 202–26 *passim;* mentioned, 194

Annual percentage rates. *See* Interest rates
Annual premiums. *See* Premiums
Annual renewable term. *See* One-year renewable term
Annuities. *See* Life annuities
Annuity rates. *See* Settlement options
Antiselection. *See* Adverse selection
Antitrust and Monopoly Subcommittee, 87, 184
Apathy, 181–82
Application for life insurance, 146–51
Arizona, 56
Assignment, 122–23, 155
Association group life insurance, 13, 90–91
Attained age conversion, 141
Attorneys, 18, 179
Automatic premium loans, 124, 132–33, 137
Aviation insurance. *See* Air trip insurance
Aviation restrictions, 124

Bands of premiums, 149–50
Bankers Life Company: development of guaranteed insurability rider by, 31; price information on, 64, 70, 202–26 *passim;* adoption of interest adjusted method by, 185; mentioned, 166, 194
Bankers Life Insurance Company of Nebraska, 57
Bank loan plan. *See* Financed insurance
Beneficiary designations, 117–19, 122, 158–59, 162
Berkshire Life Insurance Company, 177
Best's Life Insurance Reports: on companies with strong recommendations, 61, 194–98; on non-agency organizations, 82; on savings bank life insurance, 82–83; on Ministers Life and Casualty Union, 85; on companies offering split life, 106; on Summit National Life Insurance Company, 151; in illustrative cases, 164–77 *passim. See also* Alfred M. Best Company

Bonds, 15, 33. *See also* Savings bonds
Bowery Savings Bank, 37, 237
Business interests, 15–16
Business Men's Assurance Company: price information on, 67, 70, 216–26 *passim;* policy provisions of, 139, 143; mentioned, 194

Campus solicitation, 157–58
Canada Life Assurance Company, The, 64, 70, 194, 202–26 *passim*
Canadian companies, 61
Carrying charges. *See* Fractional premiums
Cash dividend option, 127
Cash-value group life insurance, 89
Cash-value life insurance. *See* Straight life
Cash values, 21–22, 34, 122, 135. *See also* Savings element
Century Life Insurance Company, 42, 59–60
Change of plan, 137–38, 162, 170–71
Charitable organizations, 118
Chartered Life Underwriters, 110–11, 113–14, 179
Chase Manhattan Bank, 55
Chase National Insurance Company, 55
Chase National Investment Company, 55
Children's life insurance, 17
Children's Social Security benefit, 13
Claim procedure, 162
Clipping, 126
Collateral assignment. *See* Assignment
College Retirement Equities Fund, 84
College student solicitation, 157–58
Columbus Mutual Life Insurance Company, 55
Commissioners of insurance, 55–56, 162, 230–33
Commissions paid to agents. *See* Agents
Committee on the Judiciary, 87, 184
Common stock, 15, 33
Company retention, 49, 61–73 *passim,* 78, 84–85, 202–29
Competition in reverse, 90
Complaint procedure, 162
Complexity of life insurance, 34–35, 180–81
Compulsory savings, 43, 46
Conditionally renewable, 105
Confederation Life Insurance Company, 64, 70, 166, 194, 202–26 *passim*
Congress, 14, 87
Connecticut General Life Insurance Company: price information on, 64, 67, 70, 202–26 *passim;* mentioned, 143, 174–75, 194
Connecticut Mutual Life Insurance Company: straight life policy of, 24–25, 35–36, 48–52; five-year renewable term policy of, 26, 51–52; price information on, 64, 70, 202–26 *passim;* mentioned, 26, 27, 57, 116, 136–37, 177, 194
Connecticut Savings Bank Life Insurance, 84, 108–109
Consumer credit business, 92
Consumer exploitation, 182
Contestability. *See* Incontestability clause
Continental Assurance Company, 64, 67, 70, 194, 202–26 *passim*
Continuability. *See* Renewability
Contract provisions, 115–45
Contributory group life insurance, 88–89
Conversion privilege: defined, 26; in five-year renewable term, 69–72, 140–41, 145; for Vietnam veterans, 86–87; in group life insurance, 89; in decreasing term, 100
Credit life insurance, 89–90
Creditor rights, 44, 46
Credit unions, 33–42 *passim,* 89
Crown Life Insurance Company: price information on, 64, 67, 70, 202–26 *passim;* mentioned, 171, 194

Data sources, 61–62
Death benefits, 116–17. *See also* Face amount
Death causes, 13
Death certificate, 126
Death claim procedure, 162
Death expenses, 10
Death rates, 133–34. *See also* Mortality rates
Death taxes, 18
Deceptive sales practices, 34–37 *passim,* 110–11, 183–84
Decreasing term, 99–101
Defunct companies, 42
Delay clause, 130
Deposit option, 119–20
Description of policy, 116
Diabetes, 151, 172
Disability income, 29–30. *See also* Waiver of premium
Disclosure legislation, 160, 186–87
Disputes, 162
Dividend histories, 24, 63, 65, 201–207, 228–29

Dividend illustrations: defined, 24; price information based on, 201, 208–15, 220–29; mentioned, 48, 49, 62, 63
Dividend options, 127–29
Dividends, 23–24, 34, 122, 127
Divorce situations, 118
Double indemnity. *See* Accidental death benefits
Dun & Bradstreet, 59
Dunne's, 59
Duplicate policies, 159
Duration of policy, 20–27 *passim*, 93–99 *passim*

Effective date of policy, 148–49
Employer group life insurance, 88–89
Endowments, 95–96
Equitable Life Assurance Society of the United States, The, 64, 70, 143, 194, 202–26 *passim*
Equity investments, 33
Estate estimation, 10
Evidence of insurability, 25, 128, 136–44 *passim*
Examinations for agents, 179
Executive Life Insurance Company, 106
Extended term insurance, 119, 136–37

Face amount, 21–27 *passim*, 93–99 *passim*, 105
Factors for calculating yearly values, 50, 73–74
Family income benefit, 100–101
Family policy, 103–104
Federal Deposit Insurance Corporation, 42
Federal income taxation. *See* Income taxation
Federal Savings and Loan Insurance Corporation, 42
Fellows of Society of Actuaries, 179
Fifteen-payment life. *See* Limited-payment life
Fifteen-year term. *See* Level term
Final expenses, 10
Finance companies, 92
Financed insurance, 154–58
Financial requirements at death, 9, 10, 12
Financial resources at death, 9, 12, 16
Financial strength of companies, 55–60
First premium, 148–49
Five-year renewable term: use of, 19, 158; nature of, 25–28, 47; renewability of, 25–27; convertibility of, 26, 27; versus straight life, 46–52; price informa-

tion on, 69–72, 201, 220–29; mentioned, 51–52, 97–99
Fixed amount option, 120
Fixed dollar savings, 33, 47
Fixed period option, 120
Forced savings, 43, 46
Forfeiture. *See* Nonforfeiture options
Fractional premiums, 76, 152–54
Franklin Life Insurance Company: price information on, 64, 67, 70, 202–26 *passim;* mentioned, 102–103, 138, 195
Fraternal benefit societies, 92–93
Fraudulent statements in application, 124
Front-end load. *See* Acquisition expenses
Full term addition dividend option, 129

Government agencies providing life insurance, 85–88
Grace period, 123–24, 140, 145
Great Depression, The, 130
Great-West Life Assurance Company, The: price information on, 64, 67, 70, 202–26 *passim;* mentioned, 139, 143, 195
Group life insurance, 12–13, 88–91
Guaranteed cash values, 42. *See also* Savings element
Guaranteed insurability, 31–32, 164
Guaranty funds, 42
Guardian Life Insurance Company of America, The, 64, 70, 76, 195, 202–26 *passim*
Gulf Life Insurance Company, 57–58

Hart, Senator Philip A., 87, 184–85
Hartford Life Insurance Company, 106
Health impairments, 151
Heart problems, 151
Historical dividends. *See* Dividend histories
Home Life Insurance Company: price information on, 64, 70, 202–26 *passim;* nonsmoker discounts of, 76; mentioned, 129, 143, 174–75, 195

Ignorance, 178–80
Illustrated dividends. *See* Dividend illustrations
Income endowments, 96–97
Income needs, 10–12
Income taxation: of life insurance, 37–40, 46; of insurance companies, 68; of settlement options, 121–22; of dividends, 127–28
Incomplete comparisons, 160

Incontestability clause, 124, 141–42, 145, 161
Increasing term, 101–102
Independent Life and Accident Insurance Company, The, 92
Individual life insurance, 88, 91–106
Industrial life insurance, 92
Inflation, 11–12, 14, 33
Inheritances, 15
Initial premium. *See* First premium
Inside interest, 37–40, 46, 155–56
Inspection reports, 147
Installment amount option, 120
Installment time option, 120
Insurability problems, 150–51. *See also* Evidence of insurability
Insurance agents. *See* Agents
Insurance commissioners, 55–56, 162, 230–33
Insured, 20, 116
Insuring agreement, 116
Interest: importance of, 11, 38, 68, 134; in evaluation of income needs, 11; in evaluation of Social Security benefits, 14; in calculation of values, 48; from date of death, 116, 120, 127; from premium due date, 124; payable in advance, 131; income taxation of, 153, 155–57
Interest adjusted method, 77–78, 185
Interest option, 119–20
Interest rates, 120, 127–28, 130–31, 152–54
Internal Revenue Code, 127–28
Internal Revenue Service, 155–57
International Life Insurance Company, 55
Interns, 157–58
Investment officers, 179
Irrevocable beneficiary designations, 118–19

Jefferson Standard Life Insurance Company, 64, 67, 70, 195, 202–26 *passim*
John Hancock Mutual Life Insurance Company, 62–63, 64, 70, 195, 202–26 *passim*
Joint life insurance, 104
Jointly owned property, 10
Joint Special Committee on Life Insurance Costs, 77, 185
Judiciary Committee, 87, 184

Knauer, Virginia H., 185
Knights of Columbus, 93
Korean War life insurance, 86

Lapse rates, 48, 237–38
Levelling factors, 50, 73–74
Level premiums, 22, 134–35
Level term, 97–99. *See also* Five-year renewable term
Liens against policies, 60
Life annuities, 121–22. *See also* Settlement options
Life contingencies, 120–21
Life insurance agents. *See* Agents
Life Insurance Company of California, 106
Life Insurance Company of Kentucky, 102
Life insurance needs, 8, 9, 16, 99–100
Life insurance ownership, 8
Life insurance policy dividends. *See* Dividends
Life insurance protection. *See* Protection element
Life paid-up at a given age. *See* Limited-payment life
Life Underwriter Training Council, 110
Limited-payment life, 93–95, 156
Lincoln American Life Insurance Company, 54
Lincoln Annuity Life Insurance Company, 54
Lincoln Benefit Life Company, 54
Lincoln Continental Life Insurance Company, 54
Lincoln Income Life Insurance Company, 54
Lincoln Liberty Life Insurance Company, 54
Lincoln Life & Casualty Company, 55
Lincoln Mutual Life and Casualty Insurance Company, 55
Lincoln Mutual Life Insurance Company, 55
Lincoln National Life Insurance Company, The: price information on, 64, 67, 70, 202–26 *passim;* mentioned, 54–55, 129, 195
Liquidity of savings element, 40–42, 46
Loan clause, 129–31, 137
Loan value, 122
Louisiana and Southern Life Insurance Company, 106
Lutheran Brotherhood, 93

Mail solicitation, 82
Mammoth Life and Accident Insurance Company, 55
Manufacturers Life Insurance Company, The, 64, 67, 70, 195, 202–26 *passim*

Massachusetts Mutual Life Insurance Company: price information on, 64, 70, 202–26 *passim;* mentioned, 142, 174–75, 195
Massachusetts Savings Bank Life Insurance, 83, 228
Medical examination, 147
Medical Information Bureau, 147–48
Metropolitan Life Insurance Company, 64, 70, 195, 202–26 *passim*
Midwestern United Life Insurance Company, 57
Minimum deposit insurance, 154–57
Ministers Life and Casualty Union, 82, 85, 229
Minor beneficiaries, 119
Misleading sales practices. *See* Deceptive sales practices
Misrepresentations by agents, 160
Misstatement of age, 125–26
Misstatements in application, 124
Monthly premiums. *See* Fractional premiums
Moorhead Committee. *See* Joint Special Committee on Life Insurance Costs
Mortality rates, 4, 48, 133–34, 152
Mortgage insurance, 101
Mortgages, 10, 11, 33
Mother's Social Security benefit, 13
Murder, 124
Mutual Benefit Life Insurance Company, 64, 70, 196, 202–26 *passim*
Mutual companies, 4, 78–79
Mutual funds, 33
Mutual Life Insurance Company of New York, The, 64, 70, 196, 202–26 *passim*

Names of policies, 62, 102–103, 199–200
National Association of Insurance Commissioners, 186
National Association of Life Underwriters, 110
National Credit Union Administration, 42
National Life and Accident Insurance Company, The: price information on, 67, 70, 216–26 *passim;* mentioned, 54, 143, 196
National Life Insurance Company: price information on, 64, 70, 202–26 *passim;* mentioned, 54, 63, 143, 196
National Old Line Insurance Company, 60
National Service Life Insurance, 55, 86
National Underwriter Company, The, 77–78*n*, 185

Nationwide Life Insurance Company: price information on, 64, 70, 202–26 *passim;* mentioned, 142, 143, 164–65, 196
Negative enrollment, 86
Net cost method, 77, 185
Netherlands, 106
New England Mutual Life Insurance Company, 64, 70, 140, 196, 202–26 *passim*
Newspaper solicitation, 82
New York Insurance Law, 131
New York Life Insurance Company, 64, 70, 196, 202–26 *passim*
New York Savings Bank Life Insurance, 83–84, 171, 228
New York State, 56
Nixon, Richard M., 185
Non-agency organizations, 82–85
Noncontributory group life insurance, 88
Nonforfeiture options, 133–37
Nonmedical applications, 147
Nonparticipating policies, 66–69, 201, 216–27
Nonrenewable term, 98
Nonsmoker discounts, 76
North American Life Assurance Company, 64, 70, 175, 196, 202–26 *passim*
Northwestern Mutual Life Insurance Company, The: price information on, 64, 70, 202–26 *passim;* mentioned, 138, 177, 196

Occidental Life Insurance Company of California: price information on, 64, 67, 70, 203–26 *passim;* mentioned, 129, 196
Occupational hazards, 151
Old Heritage Life Insurance Company, 55
One-year renewable term, 25
Optional methods of settlement. *See* Settlement options
Ordinary life insurance, 61, 92. *See also* Straight life
Original age conversion, 141
Overweight, 151
Ownership rights, 118, 122–23

Paid-up additions dividend option, 128
Paid-up insurance, 135–36
Paid-up policy, 94
Participating policies, 23, 62–68, 127, 201–15, 220–29
Payable, 21

Penn Mutual Life Insurance Company, The, 64, 70, 143, 196, 203–26 *passim*
Pennsylvania insurance department, 186
Pension plans, 15
Permanent life insurance. *See* Straight life
Phoenix Mutual Life Insurance Company, 64, 70, 76, 196, 203–26 *passim*
Physicians, 157–58
Policy dividends, 23–24, 34, 122, 127
Policy fees, 150
Policyholder, 20, 123, 162
Policy loans, 129–31, 137
Policy names, 62, 102–103, 199–200
Policyowner. *See* Policyholder
Policy provisions, 115–45
Policy purchase option. *See* Guaranteed insurability
Policy reserves, 34
Pre-existing conditions, 143–44
Premium bands, 149–50
Premium loans, 124, 132–33, 137
Premium reduction dividend option, 127
Premiums: nature of, 21; payment of, 21, 152–58; for straight life, 21, 27–28; for five-year renewable term, 25–28, 139, 145; as element of price, 34; values of, 48, 49, 62, 202–29; components of, 48–52; in decision making, 48–52; for limited-payment life, 93–94; for endowments, 95; for retirement income contracts, 96; for level term, 98; for decreasing term, 99; for one-year renewable term, 134; paid in advance, 156
Present expected value. *See* Values
Present values, 191–93. *See also* Values
President's Plan, 102–103
Prices of protection: variation in, 4; elements of, 34; calculation of, 35–36, 234–37; defined, 49, 51, 61; information on, 64–65, 67, 70–71, 201–29
Privileges of withdrawal, 119–20, 122
Probabilites of death. *See* Mortality rates
Probabilities of discontinuation. *See* Lapse rates
Probabilities of payment, in calculation of values, 48
Proof of age, 126
Pro rata refund of premium, 79
Protection element: defined, 22–23; in straight life, 22–23, 28; in five-year renewable term, 25–26, 28; as part of package, 35; values of, 48, 49, 62, 64–65, 67, 70–71, 202–29; in limited-payment life, 93–94; in endowments, 95–96; in retirement income contracts,

97; in decreasing term, 99; in change of plan, 138
Protection from creditors, 44, 46
Provident Life and Accident Insurance Company, 67, 70, 197, 216–26 *passim*
Provident Mutual Life Insurance Company of Philadelphia, 64, 70, 171–72, 197, 203–27 *passim*
Prudential Insurance Company of America, The: price information on, 64, 70, 203–27 *passim;* mentioned, 86, 174–75, 197

Quantity discounts, 149–50
Quarterly premiums. *See* Fractional premiums
Questionable sales practices. *See* Deceptive sales practices

Rate of return on savings element, 33–37, 45, 234
Real estate, 15, 33
Reduced paid-up insurance, 135–36
Reduction of premium dividend option, 127
Refunds, 23–24. *See also* Dividends
Regulation of insurance, 4, 90
Reinstatement clause, 125
Renewability: defined, 25; in five-year renewable term, 25–27, 69–71, 138–39, 145; in level term, 97–98; nature of, 134. *See also* Five-year renewable term
Replacement, 159–62, 184
Republic National Life Insurance Company: price information on, 65, 67, 70, 203–27 *passim;* mentioned, 169, 197
Reserves, 34
Resident physicians, 157–58
Retail Credit Company, 147
Retention method, 78. *See also* Company retention
Retirement income contracts, 96–97
Return-of-cash-value benefit, 101–102
Return-of-premium benefit, 101
Reverse competition, 90
Review of insurance programs, 158
Revocable beneficiary designations, 118
Rights of ownership, 118, 122–23
Ritter, George, 109
Rounding errors, 80

Safe-deposit box, 159
Sales executives, 179
Sample policies, 149
Savings accounts, 15, 33, 39–42 *passim*

Savings and loan accounts, 15, 33, 39–42 *passim*

Savings bank life insurance, 82–84, 108–109, 228

Savings bonds: income taxation of, 39; liquidity of, 40; safety of, 42; mentioned, 15, 33, 123

Savings element: importance of, 20; defined, 21–22; in straight life, 21–23, 28; in five-year renewable term, 25, 26, 28; nature of, 32–46; rate of return on, 33–37, 45; as part of package, 35; income taxation of, 37–40, 46; liquidity of, 40–42, 46; availability of, 40; safety of, 42–43, 46; annual amounts going into, 47, 49–52; values of, 48–49, 62, 64–65, 67, 202–19, 228–29; in limited-payment life, 93–94; in endowments, 95–96; in retirement income contracts, 97; in change of plan, 138. *See also* Cash values

Securities and Exchange Commission, 106

Semi-annual premiums. *See* Fractional premiums

Semi-compulsory savings, 43, 46

Semi-endowment policy, 95

Servicemen's insurance, 55

Settlement dividends. *See* Terminal dividends

Settlement options, 44–45, 46, 119–22, 137, 162

"Shopper's Guide to Life Insurance, A," 186

Single premium life annuities, 121

Single premium life insurance, 156. *See also* Limited-payment life

Social Security, 13–15, 85, 165–76 *passim*

Society of Actuaries, 179

Southwestern Life Insurance Company: price information on, 67, 70, 216–27 *passim;* mentioned, 66, 143, 197

Special class insurance, 150–51

Specialty policies, 102–103, 180–81

Specimen policies, 149

Split life insurance, 104–106

Split term addition dividend option, 129, 154–55

Standard insurance, 150

State Automobile Mutual Insurance Company of Columbus, 55

State Farm Life Insurance Company, 65, 70, 197, 203–27 *passim*

State insurance commissioners, 55–56, 162, 230–33

State Life Fund, 87–88

State Mutual Life Assurance Company of America, 57, 65, 71, 76, 203–27 *passim*

Stock companies, 78–79

Stocks, 15, 33

Storage of policies, 159

Straight life: use of, 19; nature of, 20–25, 35, 48–51, 95, 98, 99; versus five-year renewable term, 46–52; premium components of, 48–52; price information on, 62–69, 201–19, 228–29

Students in college, 157–58

Subcommittee on Antitrust and Monopoly, 87, 184

Substandard insurance, 150–51

Suicide clause, 125, 141–43, 145, 161

Summit National Life Insurance Company, 151

Sun Life Assurance Company of Canada, 65, 71, 164–65, 197, 203–27 *passim*

Sunset Life Insurance Company of America, 57

Supplementary contracts, 162

Surrender dividends. *See* Terminal dividends

Taxation of insurance companies, 68. *See also* Income taxation

Teachers Insurance and Annuity Association of America, 82, 84–85, 169–70, 197, 229

Ten-payment life. *See* Limited-payment life

Ten-year decreasing term. *See* Decreasing term

Ten-year endowment. *See* Endowments

Ten-year nonrenewable term. *See* Level term

Ten-year renewable term, 25

Term additions dividend option, 129

Terminal dividends, 79–80

Term insurance. *See* Five-year renewable term

Term to a given age. *See* Level term

Texas Insurance Department, 60

Thirty-payment life. *See* Limited-payment life

Thirty-year decreasing term. *See* Decreasing term

Thirty-year endowment. *See* Endowments.

Total disability, 28–29

Traditional net cost method, 77, 185

Training of agents, 179

Transfer of ownership, 123

Travelers Insurance Company, The, 67, 71, 197, 216–27 *passim*

Trustee as beneficiary, 118, 122
Trust officers, 18
Truth in lending, 131, 152
Truth in life insurance, 184
Twenty-payment life. *See* Limited-payment life
Twenty-year decreasing term. *See* Decreasing term
Twenty-year endowment. *See* Endowments
Twenty-year term. *See* Level term
Twisting, 160

Unearned premium, 116–17, 124
Union Mutual Life Insurance Company, 57
Union National Life Insurance Company, 57
United Benefit Life Insurance Company, 67, 71, 197, 216–27 *passim*
United Kingdom, 106
United States government "E" bonds. *See* Savings bonds
United States Government Life Insurance, 55, 86
United States Life Insurance Company in the City of New York, The, 55

Values: defined, 48; computation of, 236–37; mentioned, 72–76 *passim*
Variable life insurance, 106
Veterans Administration, 85–87
Veterans' life insurance, 55
Vietnam War life insurance, 86–87

Waiver of premium, 28–30, 77, 143–45
Wall Street Journal, The, 184
Washington, State of, 184
Western and Southern Life Insurance Company, The: price information on, 65, 71, 203–27 *passim;* mentioned, 138, 141, 164–65, 198
Whole life. *See* Straight life
Widow, 9, 11
Wife's life insurance, 17
Wisconsin insurance department, 186
Wisconsin State Life Fund, 87–88
Withdrawal privileges, 119–20, 122
World War I life insurance, 86
World War II life insurance, 86

Yield on savings element. *See* Rate of return on savings element

LIFEINSURANCELIFEINSURANCELIFEINSURANCE

The Author

Joseph M. Belth is professor of insurance in the Graduate School of Business at Indiana University. He is also president-elect of the American Risk and Insurance Association (an organization of insurance professors and others interested in insurance education), and has served on the editorial staff of the Association's quarterly *Journal of Risk and Insurance* since 1964.

Professor Belth was born and raised in Syracuse, New York. He holds an associate degree from Auburn Community College (Auburn, New York), a bachelor's degree summa cum laude from Syracuse University, and a Ph.D. degree from the University of Pennsylvania. He also holds the CLU (Chartered Life Underwriter) and CPCU (Chartered Property and Casualty Underwriter) designations. He sold life insurance in Syracuse for five years before beginning his graduate work. Following completion of his graduate study, he served for one year as a staff member of the American Society of Chartered Life Underwriters and the American College of Life Underwriters. He has been a member of the Indiana University faculty since 1962, and served for five years as chairman of the University's Committee on Insurance and Retirement Systems.

This is Professor Belth's fourth book. For one of his earlier books, *Participating Life Insurance Sold by Stock Companies*, he received the 1966 Elizur Wright Award of the American Risk and Insurance Association for "outstanding original contribution to the literature of insurance." He also has written more than twenty-five major articles on various aspects of life insurance, and has received five awards for articles published in the *Journal of Risk and Insurance*.